Solve for X

Solve for X

Essays

Arthur Saltzman

The University of South Carolina Press

© 2007 University of South Carolina

Published by the University of South Carolina Press
Columbia, South Carolina 29208

www.sc.edu/uscpress

Manufactured in the United States of America

16 15 14 13 12 11 10 09 08 07   10 9 8 7 6 5 4 3 2 1

Library of Congress Cataloging-in-Publication Data

Saltzman, Arthur M. (Arthur Michael), 1953–
  Solve for X : essays / Arthur Saltzman.
      p. cm.
  ISBN-13: 978-1-57003-707-8 (cloth : alk. paper)
  ISBN-10: 1-57003-707-8 (cloth : alk. paper)
  I. Title.
  AC8.S223 2007
  081—dc22   2007010802

This book was printed on Glatfelter Natures,
a recycled paper with 50 percent postconsumer waste content.

For EMS and WHG, who make me celebrate July 30, and for Jøy, who altogether graces the calendar

He means, I think, there's an out,

built of these fistfuls of yellows.
Means, I think, there's a door,

in this passionate and hard-won
approximation, in this rough push

and lemon smear, this difficulty,

there's—what?

Mark Doty, "Door to the River"

Contents

Acknowledgments *xi*

The Doctrine of Signatures *1*
Real Mature *10*
Duck-Rabbit Variations *17*
Getting Even with Dante *26*
Wunderkindergarten *38*
Because I Said So *48*
King Philip, Come Out, For God's Sake *56*
Something to Shoot For *63*
Turns for the Worse *75*
Solve for X *80*
Destiny as a Sentence by Henry James *96*
Staying Away *104*
Clothes and the Man *111*
Busy Signals *119*
Goodness Knows *130*
Let's Be Realistic *139*
Driving Concerns *145*
Only Just *154*
Afraid So *164*
Captivities *174*

Spitting Images   *182*
Why I Don't Write Best Sellers   *188*
Which Reminds Me   *201*
That Subtle Knot   *211*
In Praise of Pointlessness   *220*

About the Author   *228*

Acknowledgments

I gratefully acknowledge the following publications, in which some of the essays contained in this book originally appeared: *Ascent, Baltimore Review, Drunken Boat, Gulf Coast, King's English, Lilies and Cannonballs Review, Means, Out of Line, River City, Square Table, Summerset Review,* and *Tampa Review.*

With sensitivity, friendship, and unfailing expertise, Linda Haines Fogle and Barry Blose of the University of South Carolina Press have helped to see this and other projects of mine through to fruition. I am indebted to them for their long-standing and enthusiastic support of my work.

The Doctrine of Signatures

The biographer almost occupationally views his subject as living under the aspect of a singular destiny, with everything around him contributing to press his experience into its intended shape. Which of us feel some comparable sense of destination about our premillennial lives?

Sven Birkerts, review of *Safe Conduct*, by Boris Pasternak

At nine years old, Jeremy is anxious about wasting any more time than he already has.

"What kind of Ferrari do you like best?" he asks me from the back seat, flattering me, frankly, with the assumption that I could pick a specific model out of the herd.

"I don't know. Red, maybe?"

"Come *on!*"

"What makes you ask?"

"Well, I was wondering what kind I should get." He pauses to dig two parallel trenches out of a Nilla Wafer with his upper incisors, both of which are loose, both of which he's constantly worrying with his fingers or urging to fall out by eating apples and taffy, the better to get his permanent set under way. "But I'm thinking, you know, that since I'm going to be a professional soccer player, I'm probably going to be in limousines a lot, so it might not be worth it to get a really *good* Ferrari. What do you think?"

Jeremy is not usually given to speculation, that expenditure of time and effort typically being reserved for political commentators, radio psychologists, and ancient Greeks who each went by one unpronounceable name. Because this is a critical decision, one that he seemingly needs to make before his first decade on earth is out, Jeremy is making a temporary exception here.

The remarkable thing is that he is still in third grade, yet when it comes to his future, he is already down to a few niggling details. In this regard, Jeremy is in step with the majority of current college freshmen, or so the latest statistics garnered by the *Chronicle of Higher Education* would have us believe. Every ten years or so, the *Chronicle* sponsors a nationwide survey of undergraduates to discover their goals and concerns, resulting in enough statistical information to gladden the hearts and occupy the master's theses of a thousand rising pedagogues. The particular finding I'm referring to is the precipitous drop since my own generation was surveyed in the percentage of freshmen who have not already declared a major. Whereas it was once relatively common to enter college in order to explore interests and options, it is now rather unusual to do so.

The poet Theodore Roethke neatly summarized the discrepancy in one of his teasingly ambiguous lines: "I learn by going where I have to go." For me and many of my equally aimless peers, the pause would have fallen right after "going," which is to say that we didn't know where we were headed in advance; instead, if I might nod in the direction of another notoriously confused college student, by indirection we found direction out. Conscientiousness could turn options into emphases, novelties into necessities, but it was mostly flailing about by another name, as if we were novices at pinball trying to figure out the rules by lucking into points through constant flipping. Perhaps more accurately, we felt like the balls themselves being sent into the fray, swatted, banked, and expelled. Recent trends, however, largely oppose this sort of career-by-induction: freshmen now place Roethke's pause right after "learn" and simply go where they *already know* they have to go.

And it's only a brief pause at that, as brief as the curriculum will allow. Only grudgingly do students defer to the words of the dead poets who plague them in mandatory humanities courses and, like beggars ringing the ballpark or potholes in the road, retard their preconceived progress. Mention the values of well-roundedness to them, and they'll tell you that arrows are anything but; if they were round, they'd never fly so fast or so true. Round like a well? That's a static hole, whose water grows more fetid every stagnant year. After retirement, maybe, they'll bend over the edge and reflect.

Jeremy himself is still another nine exasperatingly long years from college—assuming, that is, that he can be persuaded to put up with yet one more postponement of his inexorable drive toward soccer prominence, which waits before his mind's eye like an open net. But if he does succumb to higher education, I confidently predict that he will fall in step with the dominant opinion now found in the *Chronicle*. I can imagine him ticking off his course requirements like a countdown at Houston Control or a prisoner's restless etchings on the walls of his cell. He will sign up for the maximum allowable credit hours every semester, petition to take his finals early, and introduce his essays with "In conclusion," the better to cut to the chase whose destination he will have already known for better than half the time he's been alive.

I'm charmed by his faith in his own fate. As one who even in his sixth decade cannot clearly discern the horizon, which to me has always seemed ladled over with gray, I am also more than a little awed by anyone who believes it's legible, who so unwaveringly takes its measure and, most wonderful of all, verifies that it is precisely the size of his conviction.

We pass a sign:

No

No Cruising

Ends

The opening of a haiku or a koan unto itself: I would pause to ponder it further were it not for the fact that I'm in the left lane and the traffic mandates that I maintain my speed. And pulling over is out of the question as well since Jeremy is already late for practice. (My fault: I put us behind because I didn't realize that by "next left" he meant the one after this instead of the next one we come to.) At the soccer field, before I've completely stopped the car, he is out the door and sprinting toward the coach, who, like a seasoned grammarian, is neatly parsing his team into sweepers and keepers, wings and backs. After soccer practice, there will be dinner, then homework, a ten-minute phone call to his father, TV and popcorn, then bed. All of Jeremy's avenues are carefully laid and prominently marked, and he sees at a flash, as fast as he can spot his favorite team logo or sports car, what pertains.

How enviable, to be able to rely so absolutely upon a preconceived system, and how rare. Or perhaps not so rare after all, not if one considers the perfect, discernible logic revealed by Nicholas Culpeper in *Astrological Judgement of Diseases*. Published in 1651, Culpeper's book was a physical dictionary of the symbiotic essence of the natural world. More explicitly, it was a systematic confirmation of the natural world's deference to us, as though God himself had autographed the entire ecosystem on our behalf. Following the lead of Paracelsus, the sixteenth-century father of modern chemistry and his predecessor in popularizing "the doctrine of signatures," Culpeper proposed that for every human lack, appetite, or malady there existed a specific natural substance ready to solve it. Moreover, Creation clued us in to the appropriate cure by imposing a physical resemblance to the afflicted body part upon the item suited to its needs. Accordingly, as part of a universally recognized set of arranged marriages between pharmacology and etymology, the liverwort would ease the woes of the liver it called to mind, the red sap of the bloodroot would dissolve blood disorders, and the fused leaves of boneset would heal fractures. Deep wounds surrendered to the sanguinary oils of Saint-John's-wort, while the viper's bugloss, with its brown stem pustules recalling snakeskin and its seed shaped like a viper's head, was nature's unmistakable remedy for snakebite. For brain malfunctions, Culpeper prescribed walnuts, whose shape and corrugations recalled miniature brains; in terms of resemblance, cauliflower came in a close second and, therefore, could serve as a generic alternative to the name-brand medication.

What a paean to convenience and common sense was Culpeper's dictionary, especially to those agnostics who'd sooner ingest a root than get religion. It was enough to know that a purposeful spirit permeated all metaphysics and all matter, constituting the lot with congruence and kinship richer than any king's genealogy. The right mushroom lay right under the swollen nose whose pocks and gnarls it imitated; a second sang to the aching ear whose contours it copied and whose aches it soothed. If one awakened daily with an atonal fanfare of farts, groans, blats, and snorts, sounding like nothing so much as a calliope being beaten to pieces under a tarp, there was vegetation ripe for him, a different fruit or herb to insert in every errant orifice. If one went to bed each night on a pain no masseuse could counter or pill overcome, Culpeper knew where to reach and where to stoop, what to unearth and what to pluck. Whatever the patient's complaint, so long as he chewed the proper piece of scenery, he was promised improvement.

As above, so below; as within, so without. That was the doctrine's mantra, which suggested tighter familial connections than the Cosa Nostra. And if you're given to wince at this, I'll bet Culpeper could have prescribed a wayside salve to smear upon the creases in your cheeks or a stem for you to suck. Still cynical? Swallow the scat of the moles that, like you, bash their wedgy heads against the wall instead of seeing what's in front of them. Suck bitters. Roll around awhile on thorns.

Modern science seems to me made of less estimable stuff than this. Centuries ago facts were hard and vertical. A collection of facts stood forth like solid columns. The aisles of the library's reference section put one in mind of a grove engineered by a civic group. By contrast, today's facts seem formed of relatively perishable material, puddling under our feet and destined to evaporate like rainwater or, again like rainwater, to sink into oblivion and the earth. It is hard to imagine a modern physicist leaping out of bed in the morning eager to greet the day when it is characterized by black holes, moody quanta, and the uncertainty principle. Given so tenuous a bequest, it takes a leap of faith to imagine him getting out of bed at all. Saddled with the conditional tense and shot through with disclaimer, contemporary scientific findings are mostly low-lying, ramshackle structures on the order of chicken coops, profligate and cowering as the researchers who constructed them. Theorems quiver as the wind blows through the cracks.

Is there a single scientist today who doesn't long for the pillared certainty of the past? Is there a doctor who wouldn't wish that the world's unassembled anodynes and antidotes, its veiled rain forests and impenetrable jungles were docketed and organized like labs with guaranteed funding? What a boon to be able to prescribe a slice of landscape for whatever ails you. The dream survives among herbalists and the incurably nostalgic: that there is a saving correspondence between what we encounter and what we crave, which is intimate down to the warts and rashes we conceal, accurate down to the grafts and extracts that cure them. Ideally there's not a stem that but bends under the specific weight of its obligation; there's not an undesignated acorn or a single mineral that can hide from its demiurge, not a duct undeduced or gland the goes begging, not a pelt, carapace, or unguent anywhere that's unattuned to the duty it's meant for. This is the earth as service economy, eternally blessed with full employment. From each element according to its abilities, to each sufferer or supplicant according to his needs.

My girlfriend is a birder. Because love occasionally demands that one show his fealty even when he does not share his lover's fascination—maybe especially then—I sometimes accompany her. My goal is to see what she's pointing to and to develop some appreciation of why that particular specimen merits the attention. Her son's goal—Jeremy is a budding birder himself—is to eclipse his mother's record for life birds. At present she leads by nearly four hundred birds, a list she's managed to enhance over the past twenty years with trips to India and Russia, but this superiority over her son, who up until now has been confined stateside, has not diminished his competitive edge in the slightest. To be sure, had he not been able to discover a way of turning birding into a competition, Jeremy would never have absorbed Joy's avocation. However, now that he has found a way to make it interesting, he is just as likely as she is to suggest a nature outing to improve his tally.

This afternoon we have chosen to enter a wooded area about fifteen miles outside of town. The way is pathless, and I lag behind a bit, spending as much time watching my feet to make sure that I don't misstep as I do on the lookout for worthy birds. Meanwhile, Jeremy is a good fifty yards ahead of his mother, scouting the upper branches, eager to score. "You go somewhere else!" he calls back to Joy. He doesn't want her cramping his style or horning in on the discoveries he's sure he's about to make. I imagine him employing his lessons in mathematics: *Let's see. Mom is thirty-five years older than I am, so if I am going to have more birds in thirty-five years than she has now, how many birds will I have to see every year. . . .* "Mom? How many times does thirty-five go into how many more birds you have than I do?" It is gratifying to find a practical side to what school foists upon us.

In secret, in order to decrease the advantages my companions have on me in terms of alertness and experience, I have been boning up on birds. For a couple of weeks now I've had a Peterson Field Guide under my side of the bed the way furtive lovers hide sex manuals, which I'd consult while Joy was busy in the bathroom or getting Jeremy to sleep. I am waiting for the right moment to impress Joy with my knowledge of the eight main visual categories—swimmers, aerialists, long-legged waders, smaller waders, fowl-like birds, birds of prey, nonpasserine land birds (which do not perch), and passerine birds (which do)—which I mean to insert into our conversation should I ever manage to nudge it near the subject. Out of love, I am learning the topography of birds. My plan is to master all of the cryptics from crowns to coverts, the better to find favor, the better to keep up. I am practicing the positions of their superciliaries, their scapulars, and their secondaries. The arcana of their abdomens and axillars and, in short, all that begs witness beneath the median line, in memory of my commitment to her, I am committing to memory.

Also I have been cribbing indicators to direct me to the quicker identification. A prospect wanders into my field of vision. How big is it? If I were to hypothesize a sparrow, would it exceed the boundaries of its outline? Is it big enough to burst a robin's red breast were I to superimpose one? Then there's the shape to consider: plump or slender; its wings rounded or pointed; its bill designed to crack seeds, pierce bark, or hook flesh. Perhaps I can catch sight of the tail, for which Peterson provides five distinctions obvious as a barber's chart: forked, squared, notched, rounded, or pointed.

Then there is that whole panoply of behaviors to sort out and select from. Does it wag its tail, hold it down, or cock it like someone sticking a finger in the air to check the weather? How long does it maintain its position, and when it leaves, does it return to the same position? If it climbs, how does it do so, spiraling or jerking, bracing itself with its tail, rappelling head up or plunging head down? What is its glide path when it flies—how straight, how sporadic, how high? If it's a swimmer, how deeply in the water does it sit, and does it cruise smoothly or dabble about? If it's a wader, does it tend to teeter, or does it bob like a shopper at the market? And the insignia! Field marks, tail patterns, rump patches, eye stripes, eye rings, wing bars, wing patterns: for scope and variety, the whole history of the armed forces has nothing on them. To say nothing of the semaphore feathers they signal with and whose messages only the most dedicated and discerning might intercept. To say nothing of the encyclopedia of trills, coos, squawks, burbles, and complex measures ranging from the delicate to the dread—the massive vocabulary and family songbook from which each given bird performs.

Yet all of it does me little good. Even with all of these features assiduously arranged and at my disposal, I am proving to be a bust at birding.

I stare and I stare, and I cannot tell lesser from greater, black-backed from ring-billed, royal from common. I cannot pluck one species of gull from its hundred subtly distinguishable cousins. A hundred barely disparate warblers blur. I could spend an eternity sorting out sparrows, trying to separate Lincoln's from Henslow's from Le Conte's from Nelson's from Bachman's from Baird's into their respective slots, to no avail. The pipits and thrashers, they task me; by waders and plovers, I'm soon enough undone. While my fellow detectives almost immediately clue into the shape, stature, and coloration from which they can induce the culprit that suddenly lands on a nearby branch and just as suddenly departs, I cannot even steady my gaze long enough to start the process of categorization. In the few seconds I have before it disappears into the foliage or, like a fighter pilot under attack, takes me up into the sun to wreck my focus, I have gotten no further than to register "bird!" And immediately I can't recall a single additional detail—hardly enough to limit the options to the right section of the guide, much less to the proper page.

To be honest you could stretch the thing dead in my hands, and I would probably still be unsure about its identity. You could let me rummage through my notes for an hour per bird while it waited as though it were standing for a portrait, and I'd be none the wiser about what model I'd been watching. You could take it apart from beak to claw, eye by eye and feature by feature and feather by feather, and lay out each discriminate bit like a gem on a velvet cloth before me, and I couldn't appraise it for you. Handicap Joy and Jeremy, restrict them to the briefest glances, while letting me live intimately with birds, scrupulously attended like St. Francis or Snow White, and I could not name my acquaintance, much less offer meaningful companionship or competition. As far as my psyche is concerned, every bird is a mockingbird, every elusive, insulting one of them.

At the end of the day, mother and son had each docketed a couple of life birds, which they would for several weeks giddily reminisce about like teenagers who'd gotten rock guitarists to autograph their books as they left the stage. As for me, because I couldn't in good conscience decide whether it was the red-shafted flicker or the yellow I'd surprised—unless it was really a red-bellied woodpecker, or possibly a hairy ("It all happened so fast, Officer!")—I opted for the integrity of irresolution and left my notebook as blank as the day I'd bought it.

It was already late when we got back to the house, and Jeremy still had to shower. I stopped to check the mail and clean out the back seat of the car, and by the time I came inside, there was a trail of Jeremy's clothes, like castings or shed skins, leading to the bathroom. A Cardinals cap, a splay of shirt, a coil of underwear caught in a puddle of pants. Some metamorphosis was taking place, apparently, and it was easy to imagine the striptease continuing, so that I could envision a severer progress further down the hall: a dump of muscle, a scabbard of skin, various emissions flowing in a little stream by the baseboard. A more pessimistic interpretation would have made him the meal of a beast that had divided him into courses, but I knew that Jeremy was built of sterner stuff than that and was meant to end more nobly.

Some species stay together for no more than a season of breeding; others mate for life. Absent plumage or an inflatable throat to show off, I depend on other means of making myself indispensable for the long haul. With this in mind, I decided to help Joy speed the process of getting her boy to bed. I began gathering his dirty clothes together, including his gym shoes, each of which Jeremy had signed along the outside edge— along the site of the primaries, if they were birds, if that helps you with location. This was customary: all of his gym shoes were signed like that. "Footnoted," I suggested, a joke that fell as flat as I knew it would before a tired nine-year-old and a harried mom. It wasn't that Jeremy was planning to take them to overnight camp or that he feared he might lose them in a scrum of shoes removed at a school sock hop. (He would always be able to identify his own equipment without having to resort to reading, no doubt.) No, he just wanted to get a leg up on posterity. A posterity that was owed to him, mind you. A posterity as definite as the contours of any of the species in Peterson or any Ferrari preening on the lot or the inimitable and ultimately coveted signature he'd been practicing for months. That way, when the inevitable contracts come, he'll already have it down.

Real Mature

Steve and Chris and Al and Ricky and Epstein. This was SCARE, a squad of neighborhood boys who in the mid-1960s patrolled the suburban turf around Oakview Junior High (whose sanctioned team, a swarm of Hornets, they did not join or jeopardize), cruising on Sting-Rays for the illusion of the impact they created.

Let's be clear: SCARE didn't scare anyone. They did not threaten elementary school children who wandered home solo. They did not set off M-80s in the alley or tie firecrackers to the tails of unattended dogs. They did not torment unwitting trespassers into their territory, boost stereo components, or even steal from the dime store; they never ransomed anybody's kid sister or vandalized a single car. Even the petty crimes that earned after-school detention, even the small-time insurgencies of authentic protocons and hoodlums-in-embryo, such as the defacement of stop signs or the ruination of rose beds with their bikes, was beyond them. They may have been responsible for the random juvenile prank or crank call, but SCARE was barely a sty in society's eye—at worst, a scythe of eyelash that briefly found its irksome way in. The local police might have occasionally confused Steve, Chris, Al, Ricky, and Epstein with other punks but never with real perps, and the squad cars rolled obliviously by. In sum, SCARE was not a club that pummeled, ever.

Their acronym was never intended to compete with Crips or to cause Bloods born to less prosperous city blocks to boil. The SCARE tag was restricted to sewer covers and the sides of curbs, and the chalk washed off in the rain. SCARE wore no gang colors, unless the motley assortment their mothers laid out for them each morning, which once in a while included Levi jeans for all five boys at once (a commonplace in every '60s ensemble, anyway) counted as such. They followed no formal manifesto; pretty much innocuous, they incurred no particular injunction, either. They advanced no politics, philosophy, portfolio, or program, operated sans charter or code. They had no SCARE protocol or constitution, no SCARE tactics to speak of at all. On the contrary, SCARE moved about beneath the radar of official notice altogether, so that they enjoyed, or endured, the impunity of the puny. The little ids of these little kids, whose waywardness came with implicit permission from the people in charge, may have urged them to practice cursing and to pitch quarters on the sidewalk, but they usually cursed out of adult earshot and crossed from one sidewalk to another at the corners. In short, SCARE never distracted anybody from genuine felons and bigger game.

The primary attraction of SCARE lay in the sheer fact of the organization. For Steve, Chris, Al, Ricky, and Epstein, it was enough that they maintained a composite alter ego. SCARE served solely as an organizing principle, which represented an end in itself. Having just breached his teens, each component kid could hardly muster an identity on his own or, at any rate, sufficient wherewithal ever to alert the media about. But as a constituent initial in SCARE, even though the five of them initiated nothing much, every boy believed he had a brotherhood; at least in theory, every boy had the back of a boy who had his back.

Not that this was ever tested. Unlike the Boy Scouts, they proved no special merit or mettle nor ever sought a badge to commemorate such an achievement. Unlike teams that tore about the ball fields or that radiation engendered in Marvel Comics, they neither stood for justice nor exacted any exotic revenge. It would be an exaggeration to deem them the unsung legislators of Lawndale Avenue. Apart from their private understanding, they moved about unexceptionally—undetected, unmarked, untattooed. They were not redoubtable by any stretch of the imagination, not even their own. Nevertheless SCARE did imply slightly greater prominence, boosting its affiliates just a bit, like lifts in shoes. If the whiff of aggrandizement was detectable to no one else but this fivesome, that was enough to make a difference. Hence Epstein, who'd have rather been "Robbie" to the rest of SCARE as he was to his mom, his teachers, and the rest of the uninitiated world, acceded to "Epstein" for the sake of the requisite spelling. He would not risk the possibility that SCARE would seek out an inherently obliging Elliott or Eddie in lieu of him to complete them. In contrast to the prospect of being negligible, the sacrifice of his given name was endurable, something on the order of a batter's "taking one for the team" by allowing himself to be struck by an inside pitch. So Epstein, as "Epstein," deferred, settling for the subtle but indispensable role of silent *e*.

For it was a tragedy at thirteen to be yourself only and alone, unattended by others equally unacknowledged apart from the main. Steve. Chris. Al. Ricky. Epstein. In isolation, unprepossessing nouns, every one of them. But taken together, like fingers balling into a fist in a pocket, they believed that they possessed a sense of potential they never broadcast or validated. SCARE finessed the middle term, so to speak, by buttressing the boys without their having to resort to rampages. The tacit establishment of the title itself was its own entitlement, certifying their greater weight in combination and, as they self-consciously commanded the middle of a side street on their way home from school, their broader swath.

It wasn't until recently that I was let in on the secret SCARE compact. Adulthood is centrifugal: many of the kids I went through school with have since been scattered all over the map, myself included. SCARE did not escape dispersal either, and by the time we had reached our mid-twenties, the original corporation had essentially vanished, with at least three of its erstwhile members resituated in noncontiguous states. During a visit to see family one summer, I happened to run into Steve, and in the course of our reminiscences he betrayed the confidence to me. He didn't act as if he were letting out a breath he'd been holding for thirty years. Actually he was now as cavalier about SCARE as he was about the crush he'd had on Debbie Kalnitz three decades and three daughters ago. And, indeed, he was right not to worry that CARE had had to carry on without him, bereft of the unique contribution of his that prevented them from devolving from a formidable concern into a sentimental, philanthropic one. On the contrary, SCARE was just one more passion that from our current vantage point seemed childish, one more thing on the order of Pixy Stix, acid rock, and afternoon masturbation that he'd relinquished over time. "Hey," he said, lowering his voice with melodramatic significance and seizing my wrist for emphasis, "maybe I . . . matured!"

I still remember when "mature" was used exclusively for mockery, as in "That's *real* mature!" Yes, it meant congratulations when a parent employed it—say, to honor a son who could properly knot a necktie on his own or whose self-reliance made it unnecessary to impose a curfew. But that only went to prove the point that maturity offered meager pickings. Maturity was still a distant rumor, in other words, a charmless condition that had something to do with recriminations, tax consultants, and aftershave. "Grown" echoed "groan" for a reason. It was the province of the weenified and the whipped.

"Any guy who matures past the age of fourteen is a wimp!" Greg Bain announced one day in social studies class. What he meant, of course, was that the rewards of rectitude, as advertised by adults (who had no choice in the matter), were not half so seductive as the returns on delinquency. Who didn't know that Peter Pan made the only choice any self-respecting kid *could* make when he refused inclusion in a permanently grounded society of clocks and encumbrances? Who apart from inveterate hall monitors would settle for gravity and good manners? Praise the on-the-looseness of unproctored kids! Take as big a bite as you can out of life because life won't hesitate to sink its teeth into you. An exasperated Tom Sawyer announced as much when he explained why he invented all of the needless schemes and machinations that protracted *Adventures of Huckleberry Finn* a good ten chapters past what the novel needed to complete its basic plot. "Well, that *is* a question, I must say; and *just* like women! Why, I wanted the *adventure* of it; and I'd a waded neck-deep in blood to—goodness alive, Aunt Polly!" You'd have to be a girl not to get it.

Or you would have to be under the spell of one to act otherwise. Should you see someone *deliberately* give up his gumption, trust the song's instruction: "Call it sad, call it funny / But it's better than even money / That the guy's only doin' it for some doll." True enough, no man can unman you the way a woman can, and for many boys the transformation into maturity was and always will be mostly a hormonal issue, against which Saturday night poker is powerless and baseball cards are reduced to cardboard and consigned to the dresser drawer.

In my own case, however, I suspect that it was the job I held during the summer of 1968 that marked the advent of my maturity. What was fashionably referred to as the "Summer of Love" was for me the summer of my first full-time work. I had had short stints doing after-school jobs —sweeping the aisles in a grocery store, busing tables, and undertaking other forms of teenage employment that could not honestly be called gainful. On weekends I had sometimes accompanied my father downtown to address envelopes and file papers in return for irregular, unpredictable cash rewards. But until the summer of 1968, when I spent nine forty-hour weeks knuckling down under the stolid glare of Joe Santos, the parts and packaging foreman at Industrial Audio-Visual, I had never experienced the consumptive quality of real work. I had been tired before —football practice took more out of me than I would ever have to be taken out of me again—but I had never been tired in *that* way. Worn-down tired. Wasted tired. Used up. I had never counted the minutes as I did that summer; certainly I had never before wished for a summer to end and had never before felt it slog by so slowly. That is, I had never *worked* for a living, nor prayed so hard that I'd never have to again, not for survival instead of for spending money, at any rate, and not like this.

I can recall the very moment maturity, which had been stalking me all season, finally ambushed me. I had just come home for supper, and I was ravenous the way only men who work for a living can be. Cued by the slam of my bedroom door and my grudging grunt in response to her routine "Is that you?," Mom returned to the kitchen while I flopped down, hoping for the first time in nine hours not to be bothered. Only when I felt capable of holding up my end of a civil conversation did I make my way to the table.

But I was not about to begin talking. I concentrated on devouring my roast beef, smacking and masticating with the legitimacy of the justly exhausted. For a minute or more there was no sound but the clatter of utensil and Coke can, the rudiments of tooth and claw.

"Art, did you hear that the Cubs won today?" my mother asked, eager to connect with her gruff teenage son. "Five to two. Ernie Banks hit a home run."

And it was just then that I realized that I had gone the entire day without knowing how the Cubs had done. I had not even wondered, not once, not at all. I, who had always considered myself to be pious about nothing *but* the Chicago teams, who was positively exegetical about poring over the sports pages every morning to see what I might have missed, who had always made a point of finding out how many points my favorite players had scored, and who withstood the Cubs' regular September descent in the standings—that other fall they call the Fall—like a penitent, simply had not cared all day and did not care now. I was hungry and tired, and food and sleep meant more to me—amazing to acknowledge this—than any major league.

What is more, I realized that I would rather have had a thirty-cent-an-hour raise at Industrial Audio-Visual or, better still, have twenty minutes shaved off the end of each shift than be guaranteed a Chicago pennant.

For the world was now too exacting and too serious for the World Series to enter into the equation of what now counted. And the teams I had screamed for, cajoled on television as if they could hear or would take my counsel anyway, and prayed for as they prayed for themselves before stepping into the batter's box or up to the line of scrimmage had never screamed for, cajoled, or prayed for me. Had not and never would. They did not hold *their* collective breath when my algebra test was returned, although I'd hung on every referee's decision and umpire's call on their behalf. They did not worry and gossip over the bunch of us as we took the bus to school as the busload of us almost daily did over them or give each other high fives when one of us succeeded even though we did when they came through for what we managed to imagine was for us. They did not crave our jerseys and hats, sport our signatures on their folders, buy our paraphernalia, or pretend to be us under any circumstances as we craved, sported, bought, and pretended in their direction. They had kept their welfare aloof from ours, about which they suspected nothing. No, they did not reciprocate or love us much at all.

And, definitely, no Chicago Cub or Bear ever aspired to SCARE. Discovering that Steve, Chris, Al, Ricky, and/or Epstein would have deserted SCARE for the longest shot at joining *their* ranks would not have impressed any professional player. Billy Williams never pretended to be Steve, Chris, Al, Ricky, and/or Epstein as he rounded the bases after launching a game-winning blast onto Sheffield Avenue. Gale Sayers never ran to daylight accompanied by internal commentary like "And there goes Steve, Chris, Al, Ricky, and/or Epstein cutting to the outside. . . ." Not once. Not at all. Any member of SCARE would have sold out his companions for the estimable company of Cubs or Bears, would have gladly run off unlettered for a shot at that, and would have been understood and forgiven by the other four. Meanwhile, no Cub or Bear, each relegated to his den to prepare to take the field or to lick his postgame wounds, knew, wanted to know, or cared. And the very same professional indifference applied to me.

Evolutionists will tell you that every adaptation is a liability at the same time. We eventually depend on the context we change to accommodate. As I say, SCARE ultimately spun out into five separate entities finding five separate adult orbits. Although I haven't investigated, I have no doubt that Chris, Al, Ricky, and Epstein, have, like Steve, long since moved on to live past the acronym that once contained them. Like Steve—like me, in fact—they have all astonishingly, unaccountably entered their fifties, and they have promises to keep aside from their adolescent pact even though their unspoken oath must have included not growing up and growing apart. I have little doubt that had their respective novels extended into their futures, Peter Pan would have lost track of the Lost Boys, while Tom Sawyer, Huck Finn, and the other gang members would have lit out for disparate territories, too.

Not that I could have extrapolated all this from the supper table at the time. I had just suffered the blow, remember, and hardly had the energy to wonder what Mom might have made for dessert. Suffice to say that after yet another long day's sullen industry at Industrial Audio-Video—shipping and receiving, we lay waste our powers—I sensed that my priorities had shifted radically and, as I would later learn, permanently. Batting averages? Touchdown totals? I just wasn't in the mood. I never would be again.

Epiphany is too strong a word for grasping what had always been there for the taking, not to mention what all men eventually have to learn to take. According to the kitchen clock, it was already after seven: just over twelve hours before I'd have to get up and go to work all over again. No one had to tell me that it was time to put away childish things. There's maturity for you, barging its way onto your block, leaving its unmistakable tag. (Mothers, do you know where your children are?) Whether it enters the scene like a sullen, unregenerate, undeterrable juvenile delinquent, sinister and aloof, or comes on like gangbusters, maturity is the scourge that claims every turf. The alley is narrow and blind, so you cannot steer clear. It ignores your intentions, your innocuousness, your transparent attempts to intimidate. And you cannot rely on the reputation of the pack you travel in. Do what you will, it just does not scare.

Duck-Rabbit Variations

Among his many talents, Charlie Chaplin was a gifted mimic. At Hollywood parties he was often implored to entertain the guests with celebrity impersonations. On one occasion he performed an astounding Enrico Caruso, demonstrating vocal range and purity no one suspected the silent film star possessed. "I never knew you could sing like that, Charlie," someone said. "I can't," he replied, "I was imitating Caruso."

That's the story anyway, and frankly I find it too appealing to jeopardize by trying to verify it. Assume a virtue, if you have it not, I figure. That went for Chaplin, too, who in his movies always seemed to find a way to turn his stumbles into demonstrations of grace. Impoverished in every other fashion (fashion included), the Little Tramp somehow managed never to run out of aplomb.

Drivers refer to this reflex as turning into the skid. It takes time to retrain your instincts, but eventually you'll get to the point that, having lost traction on the ice, you don't automatically jam on the brakes. Instead you release the accelerator and ease into the loop destiny has temporarily thrown you for.

"We are what we pretend to be, so we must be careful about what we pretend to be." So Kurt Vonnegut begins his novel *Mother Night.* The moral he means has to do with the danger of not being able to distinguish the man from the mask, until the mask is all of him we have. The condition imperils not only the wearer, who finds himself skidding off in the direction of his idiosyncrasies, but also the population at large, which has the misfortune to be in the way at the time.

A subtler but no less significant threat, however, is not that we succumb to the pretense but that we cannot sustain it. I think of friends of

mine whom destiny has dropped, snared, or seduced into avenues of employment they'd never wished for or imagined, and I wonder how they
accommodate themselves to conditions so disparate from their talents,
personalities, and expectations. Not all of the boys I played ball with
could realistically have expected to continue to play ball professionally—
all right, none of them could—and while it could be argued that realism
was hardly the point during childhood, it inexorably, inescapably became
the point as we grew up. "The fancy cannot cheat so well / As she is famed
to do," Keats complained. He was referring to flying after a nightingale
rather than to manning center field for the Sox, but the premise is the
same. As adults, we ache in permanent ways and in Latinate places that
previously never pronounced themselves at all. We grunt our way up
from the bench and all the way back down, as at the end of the inning we
ease our sore and sorry asses onto the pine. We cannot recapture our dash
in any direction for more than two steps at a time, and whatever spring
we once depended on for rebounding now belongs to a season that will
never return. We schedule workouts when once we simply, spontaneously
played. "Was it a vision, or a waking dream?" we wonder, slumped in the
sauna or rubbing liniment into our ankles and the seized-up smalls of
our backs. As Vonnegut puts it in another novel, "Maturity is a bitter
disappointment for which no remedy exists."

And what do we get in exchange for maturity and the relinquishment
of obsolete dreams? Portfolios. Gas grills. Desk caddies. Promotion. The
compensations of lives that are merely real and only what they are. "True
terror is to wake up one morning and discover that your high school class
is running the country." That's Vonnegut again, who lived long enough to
see not only his peers but also their progeny's progeny employed. Believe
me, it's a safe bet that the same fear as Vonnegut's goes for the rest of the
seniors in the yearbook, who never expected to fill the conventional work-
force either and are no less afraid.

Aristotle said that happiness is doing the right work—Aristotle or Alan
Greenspan said so—but identifying what's right for you is the rub. The
problem with most professions—or more precisely the problem I have
entertaining most professions—is that I can see myself performing only
some of their functions, and those only temporarily. I should explain that
this is what passes for career counseling in my self-analysis. It is not a

matter of potential income or aptitude or even desire, but a matter of whether or not I can recognize myself in that particular career. It's basically a vision issue. Here I am phoning prospects about term insurance. Here I am encouraging a buyer to consider adding the underbody rust protection, which comes with a life-of-the-car warranty, to the option package on his Pontiac Grand Prix. Here I am balancing my lunchbox on the girder beside me. Nope. Can't picture it.

Meanwhile, the careers I can see myself doing I can't see myself doing entirely. I have no problem envisioning myself trying to persuade a jury while I'm fortified by ethical passion and a double-breasted suit the color of the interior of a sea cave, but not totaling up billable hours or planning strategies for clients who deserve nothing but the competent defense I'm reluctant to provide. That's me all right, or it could believably be me, consoling a bereaved family after Dad failed to pull through, saying we did all we could (as a full-fledged member of that medical "we") but the damage was just too severe. But when I survey the operating room where all we could do was done, I can't find any sign of myself. I simply cannot see that kind of expertise coming out of me. Again, not opportunity but ophthalmology does me in.

Talent, surely, is a factor, but it is more fundamentally an issue of temperament, which is but one more way in which I will never be mistaken for Charlie Chaplin. Forget whether or not I can carry a tune, much less rival Caruso. Away from the front seat of my Honda Civic, I never sing at all.

Experts tell us that 50 percent of the jobs that people hold nowadays didn't even exist a generation ago, including not only those jobs held by everyone employed by NASA or stationed in cyberspace but also the job of determining that provocative statistic. It is reasonable to guess that a generation hence another 50 percent will turn over, as it will the generation after that, as part of an infinite series of Zeno-like halvings of familiar job territory, until only farmers and prostitutes will be recognizable to the elderly. Personally I'm already astounded by all the options that exceed the choices a child might think of: once I get past teachers, nurses, astronauts, baseball players, and firemen, I'm pretty much flummoxed. Pick your college major according to what's current, career counselors say, and go with the flow. Nice advice if you're a fish in a river, which doesn't have to guess the direction it's heading just to stay afloat, but a different matter for the contemporary job seeker. I mean, who among my friends ever dreamed of becoming a human resource manager, including the one who became one? Who ever dreamed of dreaming it? Vocation is as venturesome as any free verse and as impossible to predict. Consider the esoterica of systems analysts, the mysteries of mutual funds managers, the arcana of image consultants: unprecedented realms of endeavor, impenetrable and sublime. Friends who function in such climes make me want to flag down a trucker, hug a waitress, or call a cop.

Strangely the odder occupations retain their currency. One can still train for the Empire State Building stair-climbing relays or the strongman train-dragging competition televised annually on ESPN. One can study to be someone who calculates feng shui for federal prisons or master making novelties such as rubber vomit for the mail-order trade. One can aspire to replace the curator of the Plastics Museum in Pont Canavese, Italy, or groom oneself to undertake the online supervision of the American Package Museum when its webmaster takes a well-deserved retirement. One can devote himself to perfecting his aim and become the circus marksman who shoots a cigarette alight while it's in his assistant's mouth, then removes the offending cigarette with a second shot; or one can comb out her nerves and become the assistant who stands for that.

Say you are drawn to taxidermy. As a little boy, you were a prodigy of concentration who hovered over roadkill even as oncoming traffic scattered your companions with its horns. Eager to cut your teeth on the neighbors' cat when it succumbed, you urged the Millstein kids to smuggle the corpse to your basement rather than send it to the incinerator or bury it in a box in their backyard. (You didn't get your hands on Tuffy after all, but the intimations of your future calling were clear.) And now nothing so inspires you as the thought of having your hands deep in expired meat. While you drive your taxi or tend your desk, do you still dream of delving into the dead, of divesting them of vitals, of scouring their carcasses in a back room the way chefs strip, hollow, and core all day long in their kitchens? Does the prospect of being surrounded by skinned coyotes and imploded raccoons, of fingering clods of erstwhile gerbil and terrier remains fill your fantasies? Does the sight of a freshly extracted golden retriever's heart warm your own? Maybe the hope of bolstering the ruins of family pets with wadding and wire and erecting monuments out of freshly slain game to preside over hunters' dens delights you. Maybe

ives them toward our relatively unthreatening digs. English is not
they've intended at the end of their journey so much as the branch
grabbed as they skidded toward the cliff.
nd it a practical strategy and at least a momentary stay against
ssion not to pursue this idea to its conclusion, especially when I
lasses to gear up for. The English department's unwritten policy is
at these retreats as examples of newly discovered integrity, and we
ully enroll all comers regardless of the conditions they came from.
ou withdraw from your initial interest because you were baffled by
netism, German, or the tax code? Did phys ed or music leave you
ed? Did you feel nauseous when faced with the inner workings of
gy or innumerate in the netherworld of math? Did the hard sciences
you too sternly or the soft sciences turn to quicksand beneath your
These are some of the warning signs that you may be coming down
English. Statistically speaking, the symptoms are as reliable as an
moderate love of sentences or a metaphor fetish. Welcome to our cozy
e quarantine, where we try not to be right but compelling, where
biguities deepen rather than dissolve, and where by our peculiar lights
warm ourselves and shape our discontents.

en one has trouble focusing on even one pursuit, it is impossible not to
nire people who deftly handle two. When I teach American literature,
gularly make a point of honoring William Carlos Williams for being
octor by day and a writer by night without slighting the requirements
either. The Batman / Bruce Wayne duality is no more impressive to me
in this amphibious capability of breathing in two such disparate atmos-
eres as those. Wallace Stevens, too, was fluent—was *prolific*—in two
ofessions, poetry and insurance. The self-styled "connoisseur of chaos"
as a connoisseur of cost-effective term life as well. That poetry and
surance are not necessarily mutually exclusive ways of contending with
ernity does not minimize his accomplishment. Thus doubly busy and
oubly imbued, Williams and Stevens stand out in my course as exam-
les for students who have trouble juggling homework and child care or
orty hours a week on night shifts and final exams.
Williams and Stevens were duck-rabbits of the first order, their
essences unrestricted by the pinch of either-or. But we do not have to
explore the literary canon to find these kinds of hybrids, who have
evolved out of split love or necessity. I suppose that somewhere there

images of long tables strewn with hollowed fo
vade your day and beggar any other occupation
ing the bright tools of resurrection—the stainles
of chemicals recalling tales of Poe, the sly knives
broader and deeper than anything you saw at y
Day. Or maybe you simply believe that Norman B
the creatures that adorned the sets in *Psycho* was
insanity but the one activity that kept him from tu
more often than he did. Well, if so, there are places
Yellow Pages, peruse the classified ads, and be
schools to train and license you and working taxi
on apprentices. Call now. Operators are standing b

Assume a virtue, if you have it not, maintained
gle with vocation led to eviscerations that any taxi
Had he recognized and immediately embraced the t
for, the critical consensus says, he might have rulec
mark, not to mention a briefer play.

Look carefully. Is it a vase or two people kissing? Is it an
profile or a pretty young woman in a pinafore? Is it a
The image strobes, no matter how hard you try to focus
the harder you try. Both possibilities are plausible, b
exclusively convincing. Sometimes I wonder: do we res
the mirror?

I have never investigated the numbers on this, but my
a sizable percentage of English majors are English maj
have toiled in their company, as either college student or
for more than thirty years now, and according to my ex
as many come to this discipline by backing away from oth
by specifically seeking English out, eyes open and eyes fr
relationships can originate this way—the romantic in m
the chances are nearly as good that one can bump into his
the subway from behind as he can through a deliberate fro
but it does give me pause to think that for an undisclosed n
majors, English is not necessarily the most desirable but th
tionable, or last available, option. It may not be a love of
much as a loathing of biology, mathematical incapacity, or te

are butchers who wash off the blood to trade bonds and mechanics who degrease to sing opera. Somewhere there are gynecologists who put up drywall, arms dealers who run day-care centers, and halfback pastors. The shuttle driver who drops you at the airport may then hurry off to style hair, while the fellow who takes your order at the Burger King window may be making documentary films later that day. After work is more and other work. I defy anyone to come up with a convergence of the seemingly twain that hasn't somewhere, in the vast laboratory of the job market, been achieved.

Which leaves those of us unitarians who hunker down with one function on their résumés feeling a little underdeveloped. It's not as if Steven Hawking would ever have been asked, "Physics is fine, as far as it goes, but what's your fallback?" and no doubt Picasso never had to answer what else apart from painting he was prepared to do. Nevertheless, when advising, we tend to suggest to even our most gifted English majors that they pick up a business course or dip into computer programming, just in case.

Not that I ever did. Nor did many of my colleagues. In his memoir, *The Gatekeeper,* Terry Eagleton describes academe as a repository of "people who were there largely because they could not conceivably be anywhere else, as some people can only be in top-security psychiatric institutions or houses with views of the English Channel." Although he was recalling Oxbridge, less elite institutions may also serve as permanent hostels for those who, despite the fact that they make their living by their imaginations, cannot imagine living elsewhere or being otherwise engaged. Let me place myself, along with my closest faculty friends, into evidence: we may not live up to the register and regalia of eminent British dons, but we join them in recoil. Being ill equipped for alternative employment is as common where my colleagues and I gather in our usual corner of the cafeteria as it is at the High Table that Eagleton remembers. It is a privileged captivity, but captivity nonetheless. Eventually, perhaps a few years after tenure sets in, one cannot picture a world elsewhere, much less expect to flourish there.

For richly dimensioned dementia, nothing surpasses multiple personality disorder. The term has been widely and loosely applied, so much so that it is less dependable as a reference to a precise condition than as an implication of the acuteness of whichever of a range of related symptoms one happens to be suffering from. They say that the difference between per-versity and eccentricity is largely a matter of how much money buffers a given practitioner from public outrage or legal consequence. Similarly the diagnosis of multiple personality disorder is often determined by just how much disorder enters into the proceedings—by just how successfully or not one conceals, regulates, or bears up under his or her particular abnormality. In more ways than one, therefore, MPD is a matter of pub-lic relations.

MPD is undoubtedly the most infamous of the dissociative disorders; certainly it is the one that has spawned the greatest number of magazine articles and Oscar-nominated performances. Its definition remains hazy. Depending on whose expertise you trust, the predicament ranges from commonplace and typically innocuous lapses (including simple day-dreaming, woolgathering, or highway hypnosis) to contrapuntal Jekyll and Hyde or Abbott and Costello built-in buddy-system struggles for ascendancy to full-blown fugal states, featuring what might be called inner fission. The first-person plural preferred by editors and popes becomes in such cases a sort of internal terrorism, as the afflicted fear being sub-sumed by a slur of resident selves. According to analysts, the MPD census frequently features a depressed, exhausted host; a strong, angry protector; a scared, hurt child; a helper figure; and an internal prosecutor, who cas-tigates the other personalities for the abuse they've endured or are now causing. Not surprisingly analysts also report a high incidence of anxiety, depression, and suicidal tendencies among these patients. What must it be like being forever closeted with an entourage, with no true privacy to withdraw into? Imagine living every waking hour en masse.

And yet the outlook is not completely negative. There are some peo-ple with MPD who manage not merely to endure but to prosper. Meet Judy Castelli, or maybe we should say, meet Judy Castellis, given the forty-four "alters" she says dwell inside her. A *New York Times* profile describes her as an "artist, sculptor, singer, songwriter, author, musician, mental-health advocate, inventor, entrepreneur, teacher." Hers is a dizzying exam-ple of recombinant expertise, more various and irrepressible than da Vinci and enough to put simple binary operators like William Carlos Williams and Wallace Stevens to shame, even without taking into consid-eration the talents and tendencies of the forty-three other Judys scrum-ming behind the Judy who was interviewed. (They include Little Judy Girl, Gravelly Voice, Squeaky, and the One Who Walks in Darkness: a real Ego Descending a Staircase, as it were, or as they are—the stuff publishable studies are made on.) But Ms. Castelli is not daunted by the dire-sounding diagnosis of "chronic undifferentiated schizophrenia." Nor does she dream of being released or dispossessed, or of having her alters compost down one day and reconciled into a single occupant. On the contrary, she declares, "I can be anything I dream I can be." Based on the breadth of her vita, she always already is.

Psychiatrists will focus on different aspects of her different aspects, but the lesson for the rest of us might be that we deny our inherent retinue at our peril. The notion that souls are sole may hold sway in church, but in confinement the congregation gathers force, through many voices rising. While there may be some occasional confusion as to which persona gets to the telephone first, living exponentially can afford us the luxury of spending ourselves more indulgently and in several directions. On this point, Judy is unanimous. Instead of shrinking with the specialist, hedged and pruned back from waywardness or variation, we may assume as many virtues as our play will accommodate and our imaginations allow.

In this way are personalities established and motives made. Let us sally loosely and essay, by skidding find assignments out. We might begin like Williams to handle the scalpel and the stanza; like Stevens, we might figure in two disciplines at once. As to whether the duck is being shadowed by a rabbit or the rabbit is being supplanted by a duck, leave it to lonesome souls to determine which is the established path and which the sideline, which is the person and which the impersonation. Meanwhile let the intrepid abjure the confinement of the cloister, the constant character, the tenured occupation. Let us celebrate our compoundings and hazard the manifold.

"I resist anything better than my own diversity," proclaims Walt Whitman, that brave and pioneering MPD, who will not unify his yearning, who will not be resigned. "Do I contradict myself? / Very well, then . . . . I contradict myself; / I am large . . . . I contain multitudes." Like every poet worth his paradoxes, like a sensible career counselor, and like Charlie Chaplin, too, he represents the necessity of improvisation. He shows us how to populate a silence, and he urges us, even if at first glance it looks not to be in our natures, to sing.

Getting Even with Dante

[H]e is more out of place than ever. But then, so are other of his colleagues from the old days, burdened with upbringings inappropriate to the tasks they are set to perform; clerks in a post-religious age.

J. M. Coetzee, *Disgrace*

Writers will have their revenges. Beyond embarrassing, scarifying, or undermining characters they have created and come to despise, besides piling on dysfunctions or plain bad luck, writers will waylay on the page acquaintances that crossed them in real life. To right the ship of personal misgiving and to undo wrongs done to them, they will lay out the poisons, break out the hatchets, mete out the fatalities, explosions, and pains. They will entice their enemies into their stories, then strap them down and sentence them to the penalties life unaccountably spared them.

It doesn't take authors long to figure out the advantage holding the pen provides them, either. Asked to compose stories for school, half of the students in a typical junior high school class will take the opportunity to pay back bullies who abused them in gym class, turn the tables on members of the popular crowd who cut them down in public, or teach their parents the cost of neglecting them. Forget nobler aspirations. From the novice to the MFA-programmed writer and beyond, revenge is as dependable a motivation as you'll find in any fiction.

One of the most infamous examples of this practice comes from James Joyce, who is said to have thinly disguised those who'd earned his animosity—for instance, people who gainsaid his stature or begrudged him a loan—and humiliated them indelibly in *Ulysses*. And who can guess just how many poets have retaliated against loathsome relations, ghoulish ex-husbands, or an ambiguous God in fugitive magazines? If their reprisals proved less memorable than Joyce's, the principle of a literary eye for a literal eye was the same.

But of all that chose a literary genre instead of a law firm to represent them as they sued for damages, Dante strikes me as the most perilous person on record to have crossed, that is, if you go by the ghastly geographies that make up his *Inferno*. What all of that remorseless, devouring seethe comes down to—the scathing fates that encircle his miscreants upon their descent—is the poet's elaborate, variegated payback. With apologies to Hobbit followers, Dante was the original Lord of the Rings, in whose epic vengeance the punishments are apt, exacting, and tenured for all eternity. Long after the author himself passed into the empyrean, his judgments have remained lodged in the curriculum and hold fast, merciless unto the last persecutable dreg of every soul enclosed there. Indeed it is the uncompromising torments and not the names of the tormented we best remember, as if people become nothing other than the abuses they earn over and over again. Even as they congeal in the reader's mind, each tenant of hell persists in his own awful, final privacy.

The savaged membership of Dante's *Inferno* reifies the pun of phantom pain. That studied carnage, that calculated terror, has continued for centuries after its victims died and the Renaissance subsided; it will continue unremittingly long after the last whisper of Dante's frightful design leaves the last classroom and, along with everything else in the surface world, the Western canon winks out. For souls survive in Dante, but they cannot outlast the inexhaustible equity of their sins. They are dissected, mangled, and mutilated—no one else but God and Dante have such a massive vocabulary of reckoning—but never exterminated. Dante saw to it that his enemies, whether private or political, would not be let off the hook, and as anyone who's risked the wicked interior of his *Inferno* will attest, hooks are hardly the worst of it down there. Basically no one has ever given a damn like Dante.

Dante's triumph is that the Western civilization consents to the terms of extermination he has set for us. And yet precious little of all of that lurid consequence touched me in 1977, when I was introduced to Dante. This was not because I believed myself untainted by sin—although pretty much misdemeanors, my sins were still certifiable and worthy of a reservation in one of the earlier circles—but because it was my misfortune to latch on to Virgil's guided tour during what was one of the most idyllic summers ever recorded in central Illinois.

I call it "my misfortune," of course, only as the term applies to constraints upon my absorbing the keenest implications of the text; in every other way, that time seemed sublime. I'd grown up in Chicago, and my having been transplanted to college downstate was as near to the primeval as I'd ever ventured. Yet to even so inured an urbanite as I, the gentle respiration of the oaks and elms was infectious. Afternoons I'd laze beneath one of the immense trees that had been sunk a century earlier on the quad to accommodate my languor, its trunk about the circumference of a sofa bed. I had the accusatory paperback at the ready, but Dante could not sustain his rendition of the dangers of squandered grace against the melty contentment of mid-June. The full brunt of summer was still six or eight weeks away, and we could still exit an air-conditioned building without feeling as though we'd been thrust into a moldy garment bag. We were all of us embowered in a feeling of merciful, incorruptible release, a feeling of tranquility that seemed a continuous atonement all its own. The earth urged us to drowse and seemed intent on keeping every artificial tribulation—debt and traffic and family obligation and the daily news and, yes, Dante, too—safely out of range of every lusciously buffered sense.

Literary criticism may be seen as one pitfall after another of overdetermination; however, one factor I believe that the critics have underestimated is the effect of climate on the reader's reception. In that outdoor orgy of indifferent gorgeousness, Dante's vexations felt no more intense than the starlings' officious gibber or the boat-tailed grackles' keening over some loss that in the unblemished face of this afternoon I could barely imagine. Basted in easy sentiment and blissful, unsymbolic sunshine, I could not keep my mind or my mood on burning worse the way that Dante warned that the unsaved surely would. Forced to tour that tour de force of vindictive horror, where every malevolence, smolder, and chill was rigorously classified and lingeringly detailed and every deviation known to man was standard, I could not withstand the natural distractions. It was a time and place more conducive to rhapsodists of the Grange or Lake District or to the prime minister of Walden Pond than to any of the denizens of Dante's underworld, and I could absorb no more than one or two lurid stanzas at a time before nodding off. Generally speaking, just as you can't authentically relish the Romantics in a climate-controlled building whose windows won't unseal, you can't succumb to the judgments of the *Inferno* in the placid lap of June.

If the most insidious effect a writer might have is to coerce us into seeing the world in terms of him, irrelevance is the worst reversal he might endure. Basking on campus in the summer of 1977, succored by the same sun that tended the Frisbee players and the frisking dogs, I could not see Emerson's notorious forest of symbols for the messageless semaphore of the trees. Above me a million leaves convulsed in spangles that dropped no responsibility upon me whatsoever. The point is that sometimes the immanence of the given world resists the ulterior. And it needn't be mattress-grabbing rapture or the shock of God parting the skull that beggars our best literary inventions. It is enough at certain moments, such as when one feels temperate and immune to allusion under a lulling, seductive sun, that nothing but the beatified matter at hand much matters. Mindlessly I laid down my Dante and did not mind.

Any overdrawn wife would know enough not to lay the bank statement before her husband before he himself has been laid out in his recliner, composedly digesting his dinner. Just so, it would hardly be advisable to inflict Rilke upon him between halves of the conference football championship or to replace dessert with Henry James. As for Shakespeare, other appetites must serve his esteemed purposes or subside, seeing that "All impediments in fancy's course / Are motives of more fancy." The tenacity and treachery of great literature is that it discomposes the focus it demands. Common sense forbids us from taking required reading to the hair salon or the tanning booth, particularly since the object in those settings is to keep up appearances.

In short, doing justice to Dante's rough justice required danker confines than the dappled shade of the club oak on the quad that contained me. To parallel Virgil's ushering of the poet into the pit, a professor needs to lead his charges not into nature or into an air-conditioned classroom but into a badly lit basement. "Cathedrals are not built beside the sea," Wallace Stevens reminds us, the reason being that the text for the day cannot compete with the sounds and scenery pressing in at the windows. (Stevens's own poems should likewise be examined in isolation, befitting the weird bacterial strains specialists in Stevens expose themselves to.) If one means to be immured in Milton, he'll need a windowless office where

the dying bulbs sputter and the rusting radiators wheeze; to be mewed up
in Proust mandates a hospital bed. When the literary circumstances seem
most merciless or inert, the library is better kept indoors. You can't ask a
reader to grieve over *Medea* on a beach. Club Med is the anodyne for the
most calamitous description that Milton can dish out. Barely a minute of
all of Sophocles can withstand Hawaii, while Hamlet, Macbeth, and King
Lear unkink inside a spa, where hour-long massages smooth out their
soliloquies into wordless sighs. Thus with the *Inferno* decanted, canto by
excoriating canto, into that edenic day, Dante, too, was subdued.

Still, if my summer of 1977 disqualified drearier literature, it did not necessarily certify a more pacific syllabus, either. I especially remember Dan,
one of those career graduate students who preceded and would succeed
my own stay, gruffly reacting to the homilies of Professor Milo Kauff-
mann, who was leading our summer class through the delicious thickets
of the English metaphysical poets. Of all the teachers I'd ever had, Milo
indisputably seemed the best equipped to channel the supernatural. (It
was Milo who pressed Dante upon me as indispensable background
reading to help me effectively digest the test-eligible material.) There was
always a look of bemusement shading into delectation on his face, a look
that I'd ordinarily associate with one's having just obtained a fat refund
check from the federal government were I to see anyone else wearing it.
But because Milo idled at sublime, there was no message to read into his
expression but grace. Had I the chance to address those friends of mine
who depended on drugs to defuse their agitations, I'd have recommended
an hour's worth of unmitigated Milo as a less reckless alternative.

   Not that he didn't prove addictive to several students, who registered
for every course he offered as if determined to major in the man. Rumor
had it that Milo had the music of the spheres on cassette, so evidently
clued into transcendent satisfactions did he always seem to be. He always
had a slender volume of poetry with him, and he blithely advised us to
follow his example.

   "Ladies and gentlemen," he said, "because you never know when circumstances will land you with an extra ten or twenty minutes to yourself,
why not have poetry on hand to better occupy the time? I like to eat my
breakfast Danish at a corner table with Herbert, which makes Hardee's
more than bearable. It's not so bad having to wait in your car for a train

to pass when you wait with Traherne. Who better to finish your coffee with than John Donne? You see, you can fill in the gaps with poems."

It was no small task to rouse Dan from his regular lethargy at the back of the class. Rough hewn and rough spoken, Dan had made his way to graduate school from New Hampshire as the most recent in a series of diverse endeavors, which included lobsterman, air-conditioner repairman, paralegal, army corporal, telemarketer, and Peace Corps volunteer. Now he combined his literary studies with thirty hours per week working on a construction crew. Whether it was skepticism or disdain, philosophical ennui or plain old exhaustion that kept him slumped and noncommittal, no one had a better claim to immunity from Milo's barrage of sweetness and light than Dan.

But what a semester's worth of seventeenth-century poetry itself could not achieve, on this day Milo's urging that we plug every absent moment with verse did, inspiring Dan to comment. "Professor," he began, his voice sounding forced like a clot brought up from his chest, "I work construction. I carry sacks of cement. I cut sheet rock. It takes me the whole drive home just to get the noise out of my head and the shapes of my tools out of my hands. Whenever I have a chance, I collapse. At the end of a shift, I'm not hungry for Marvell or Donne. I'm just hungry. Poetry is the last thing I'm looking for. I want a cold beer, my music, and my bed. I want to get stupid or get laid. This pinkies-out shit about redeeming the scenery and your psyche by reading poetry, okay, you might believe in it, but you can *afford* to when the heaviest thing you lift all day is a Norton Anthology. No offense, I respond to literature as deeply as the next guy —more than the next guy, when it's a guy on site with me—but it doesn't make the job more than it is or other than it is. So, what were you saying?"

Dan was far too infrequent a speaker to be tapped as a spokesman for any cause. Nevertheless, now that it's my name on the syllabus some thirty years after that episode, I think that Dan spoke for all of those students of mine who come dragging into class from the tasks that they had to take care of before submitting themselves to the day's readings or who come dressed for the jobs they have to get to next. However eagerly I encourage them to do so, they haven't the luxury to trace and savor allusions, not with the kids and the dry cleaning still to be picked up. More often than not, my dilations over literary references and resonances face the same fate as dreams do in Gwendolyn Brooks's kitchenette building, where "rent," "feeding a wife," and "satisfying a man" land more substantially on the residents than any literary frippery might, even if it could survive the stench of "yesterday's garbage ripening in the hall." The metaphysical will have to wait, Milo, until the physical is dispensed with. That is where gravity is centered, which drags us down, which pulls us in.

School may not be hell, but, as some waggish students would have it, you can see it from there. And the consensus is that among the despairing vistas formal education provides, the view from school is, from almost any available angle, unobstructed.

Dante was beyond the ken and the curriculum of my high school. But the numbed and numbing regularity of Niles East High School suited several of the specs of his netherworld rather admirably. Unless the surveys lie, we mostly came out unwittingly looking like the creatures we were assumed and tutored to be—in Dante's words, "advancing tow'rds the middle / Where everything of weight unites together." As Samuel Beckett put it, "So all things limp together for the only possible." There is no need to complete the sentence we'd all been assigned. Anyway, that was my high school and, most likely, yours, since they all more or less abide by the same calendar, enforce the same drills, assume the same gestalt.

High school was anathema to almost any fantasy we might have had other than our getting through it, graduation serving as all the salvation high school ever promised. "No fame of them the world permits to be." No, Dante's *Inferno* was not part of our curriculum, but, as the saying goes, you could see it from there. "Let us not speak of them, but look and pass."

Nowadays, thirty-five years outside of my ex–high school's orbit, I don't have very much to do with Dante, either. As an Americanist specializing in more recent literature, I most often wrestle with texts published nearer to the hour and closer to home. On the other hand, Bill, my colleague down the hall, teaches Dante regularly, or let's say he does his damnedest to. He is convinced that inside every student, his or her reluctance to the contrary, there is a Dante-shaped hole that only excerpts from the *Inferno* can fill. (He usually makes do with the excerpts in the rental anthology, but privately he contends that a full dose of Dante is really what's needed.)

Nevertheless his reports from the front are no more optimistic than they were when I was an embattled graduate student, which is to say that his students are as averse to Dante's disciplinary procedures as I was when I first encountered them. Coerced into his *Inferno,* the students still cry, "Relevant" and "Practical," as if those two dactyls circling the classroom were the worst of all the scourges in the room.

Tedium isn't the only objection they have to spending two weeks in hell. Some are simply repelled by the bloodier cuts laid out before them in World Literature; apparently the sensibilities of students raised on gory video games become suddenly delicate when they have to deal with assigned readings. For they may be familiar with the thousand shocks the flesh is heir to, the whole encyclopedia of demise whose first volume alone runs from AIDS to Alzheimer's, but what really bothers them about Dante is his contention that what they dread is what they deserve. Others are offended by the penal system Dante presides over, finding his hierarchy of crimes as inconsistent or arbitrary as that of any god they might have grown up with.

Therefore, Bill has them construct alternative infernos—"designer hells," if you will—to edit Dante's anguishes and update his comeuppances. The revisions they submit range from the facetious to the terrifying. Their chief unifying feature is just how enthusiastically their inventors vent at the expense of the departed. Some avenge individual grudges against divorce attorneys or especially hostile representatives of the DMV. (These evildoers are frequently singled out by name just to make sure that God doesn't inadvertently omit them from the infernal roster. While sentencing them to death does gratify, assigning them horrid posthumous repercussions is apparently the crucial therapeutic gesture.) A few students focus on the quality of the tortures themselves, proposing more apt agonies and more gruesome retributions than Dante's howling winds, crushing weights, and ambient mire, so as to make their instructor suspect that they are in more immediate need of counseling than of a literature requirement. A few are happy to comply with Dante's identification of the vilest offenders, but they opt to reshuffle the *Inferno*'s organization of the gluttonous, the lustful, and the violent. They might insist that the heretics and blasphemers bunk together or that sowers of scandal and schism be sent to different corners of perdition the way fractious kids are separated in a grade school class. All elect a set of contemporary malefactors as substitutes for Judas, Brutus, and Cassius to be gnawed unendingly by Lucifer himself, with Hitler showing up as a staple on almost every menu.

These are the most heated arguments inspired by their reading. What sorts of transgressors should be condemned together? Who among the low down deserve to be interred lower down than whom? As you might expect, some are harshest on those who've transgressed against the Ten Commandments, thereby complying with the Judeo-Christian party line. Given the part of the country where we ply our trade, it is not surprising that several students relegate doctors who have performed abortions to an eternity one floor beneath the cellar where those who've had them performed are buried. (As an aside, these same students go on to mourn the acres of the unborn that populate the limbo they envision.) Many ensure that liberal Democrats have a miserable pit of terza rima reserved for their arrival. Dante himself shows up in a couple of hells as well, variously stationed along the devil's shaggy inseam. And while Bill has not specifically been forced to join him for having had the indecency to include Dante in the course—if the *Inferno* is merciless, what better could be said of the man who afflicts them with it?—the occasional implication is that they want to be sure that their professor can at least see the flames from wherever he ends up.

But never has any criminal borrowed from or added to Dante's faithless pantheon been remanded to an eternal Bermuda. No sinner, no matter how "sin" is defined or which sophomore has done the defining, is made to withstand the accommodations of a five-star hotel forever. When it comes to Dante, an appropriately appalling locale is everything. To do the dastards aptly in, you have to go to extremes or, in their absence, concoct them. You have to gird yourself against mercy and pray all the harder against those who've preyed upon you. If the heat is summery instead of scorching, if the setting is temperate rather than ravaging, if the denizens end up rested when roasted is what's called for, the lesson will be lost, and the class will have none of it.

There are times in the middle of my own teaching when the muddle drives me to what for a college professor passes for extreme behavior. Well, at worst, teachers get about as wanton as wind-up toys—their fits still fit their classrooms and offices and seldom threaten anything past a lesson plan—but rebellion is relative. A desperate animation overcomes me as I try to compensate for the settled rest of the room. You might find me capering about like the plate spinner on the old *Ed Sullivan Show*. Faster and faster he hustled and fretted about his airy construction lest the whole contraption crash to the floor. All the while the audience held its seats and its breath.

When it suddenly seems to me that the passion I'm manufacturing is a performance as odd and ill mannered as a tantrum in a temple, and a solo performance at that, I wonder what dear old Dan from grad school is doing. I wonder what transient compulsion he's up to. I will stop trying to pick the lock on the class's resolve not to care too openly or too much, realizing that it is probably not controversy but apathy that ultimately undoes Dante, finishes Donne, and disqualifies me. Then, when the class is drained of affect, willfully silent as arrested mobsters refusing to testify, I'll begin to announce golf, imitating the significant whisper that announcers effect on TV. "Tiger Woods looks over his putt. He's about fifteen, sixteen feet away. He's slightly uphill, and this one should break just slightly to his left. Now he stands over it. This is for birdie. Ah, he just pulled it, and it slid by about half a foot. A good effort from there. No one has made one from that side of the green all afternoon. He'll tap in for his par and stay at four under, two strokes off the lead." My students look at me as if I've lost it, which is not all that different from the way they regard me when I go on about some subtle, supple passage in our reading, which, in their estimation, is no more visible than the golf tournament I pretend to commentate on.

"It might help you to think of literature as a game, too, with rules and moves and tools to help you play it and terminology to help you talk about it properly. Like golf, it's tough fun. Rigorous the way golf is, too, and only slightly less ruthless and more perverse. Anyway, this is the course you're stuck playing, and you're expected to carry your own clubs." At which point the metaphor and their faith in its saving grace founders, as is metaphor's custom, and faith's.

Concentration is a kind of prayer, I tell them. But all things considered, they'd rather be happy.

And if they're right about literary fascination being an affliction, in which case readers deserves a circle to themselves, we had better quarantine people the moment they show signs of being intrigued. It was Sophocles who wrote, "Nothing vast enters the life of mortals without a curse." If that axiom betrays his own plays, just imagine the kind of execration epic-length obligations cause. So instead of trying to cultivate susceptibility and to breed reaction among the indifferent, maybe teachers need to turn their attention to the attentive minority and find a suitable remove for them. Let us deliver avid readers to labs or coop the clinical up in zoos along with the rest of the rabid and the mad.

Perhaps we can exempt those who confine themselves to nonfiction, readers whose nightstands hold no book but the telephone directory. That way those who've eliminated novels from their nightstands the way they rid their homes of mice or silverfish may go about their business uninterrupted. Following Plato's disdain for falsehood and the artfully rendered double cross, they exclude all printed matter but computer manuals and the odd mutual fund prospectus from the cave. I know of one local doctor who oscillates exclusively between medical journals and newsmagazines, and he recycles the latest digested lot every Saturday morning; he reserves his bookshelves for family photos and his imagination for trips to the Caribbean. He is on his way to the office or to see his tax attorney. Stand aside. I recall how Kafka's Gregor Samsa filled his leisure time by poring over railway timetables. Although a metamorphosis as outrageous as any Dante dreamed up ultimately destroyed him, certainly no excess of amazement over anything ever interfered with his making his train. He, too, scuttles past, undeterred by curriculum.

William Carlos Williams declared that "men die miserably every day / for lack / of what is found" in the poetry they repudiate; Wallace Stevens heard their "voices crying without knowing for what." Suffering seems all the more poignant when the stricken cannot realize what essential news they are missing or figure out a form of reprieve. Don't the inhabitants of hell's first circle face a similar predicament? It is there, on the outskirts of damnation, that Dante the Pilgrim encounters a group of suspended souls, whose only defect in life was that they lived before the blessing of Christ became available. Accomplished yet unredeemable, they abide in limbo, without torment, without hope. (They enter their respective hells at different depths, the poets and the roaches, I suppose.) Overwhelmed with pity, Dante petitions Virgil, his "teacher": "Came any one by his own merit hence, / Or by another's, who was blessed thereafter?" It's a common injustice to lay travail at the teacher's feet, particularly with bliss seemingly so far down the list of the day's itinerary. That eloquent witness is the most he can reliably bear out of the pit with him is a pretty mortifying confession for any teacher to have to make. Then again,

> If I believed that my reply were made
> To one who to the world would e'er return,
> This flame without more flickering would stand still;
> But inasmuch as never from this depth
> Did any one return, if I hear true,
> Without fear of infamy I answer.

Students of Dante do finally escape, blinking into bright day, his arduous images for the time being safely beyond reach. They spill out onto a quad where the new science building is under construction. Over and over, a hammer strikes a stone, and both hammer and stone insistently ripple and ring. It is only a carcass so far, a work-in-progress whose gaps and faults in this condition are more evident than the purported whole. The wind searches through what there is of it, and when the wind is right, the thing whistles and howls like a titanic aeolian harp, or so it could seem to an audience inclined to music. To others, maybe those who've had their noses too deep into Dante, it probably sounds like something stricken.

Look. The sun is still fixed in the sky, where it gazes down without indictment. Earth, fire, ice, and every other element, no matter how the poet of the *Inferno* employs them, are only that, mute and in themselves unforbidding. But imagine that on the drive home one erstwhile reader detects an omen in the stalled traffic. Another senses an edict in the static on his cell phone. Just as Dante does not completely cast off hell the moment he climbs out of the *Inferno*'s last canto, each reader inevitably retains some taint of the text. Who knows what announcement is about to shape the evening for him or whether a tolling bell will overtake the air?

The paradox of the *Inferno* is that so much of human undertaking is submerged there, yet every botched and blessed structure sings. In this way, revenge is relative, and so is relief. The onset of the world is at once the poem's condition and its contradiction. And the poets marooned on the verge of salvation know this most intensely. Their illumination lies inside a legacy of shades. Their journey leaves off just out of touch with loveliness and just before the ascension of stars.

Wunderkindergarten

It could begin with an eruption of wit, a sudden pun he puts together out of casual comments at the dinner table. Listen: between morsels of Gerber's, he is conjugating irregular verbs. Soon he is doubling and tripling up on entendres while his peers are still trying to chant the alphabet.

Or say his doodles do more than merely endear him to those who would love him regardless. His pals play with finger paints just for the fun of gooshing; meanwhile, without prompting, he's producing post-Impressionist knockoffs. While Nicky and Bobby are using their Tinker Toys to gouge the carpet or harry the cat, he is giving Louis Sullivan a run for his money. Out of the mundane timber of Lincoln Logs, he has a miniature Parthenon under way.

Perhaps the first sign of his election comes in day care. When the other infants squinch their faces, it just means they are filling their diapers, but he is preparing to squeeze his first insight out. He picks up chess the way the rest of them picked up colds. The teachers and aides at La Petite Academy quickly single him out, or rather they can't help but notice how he separates himself from the sticky pack. "He'll be a grand master before he's ten," says Miss Ashley. "He'll give a concert at Carnegie Hall before any of the rest of them can play a measure," says Miss Julia. "It'll be close whether he'll get his Ph.D. in physics or reach puberty first," says Miss Karinne. These women always idle at "nice," but for once they are not just being nice. "They'll have to hoist him onto the stage to accept his diploma," they agree.

Prodigies come to a rolling boil in their cribs. As young as age three, they are urged to perform in front of company. Because they startle even their own doting parents, their fathers set them out with the hors d'oeuvres to astound the company. Their mothers beg them to wait until the video recorders are ready. Just listen to them read! Only three, and they handle complex sentences as readily most kids their age do Legos. Or have them do math. They can add any pair of double digits in their heads, and they can already multiply through the nines. Or how about capitals? They don't miss one in fifty. They don't confuse North and South Dakota or mix the Virginias, ever. They've memorized all the songs from *Oliver!* and sing all the parts, with all of the proper histrionics and the accents intact. They spell like champs, and I don't mean "dog" and "cat," either. I'm talking "ancient." I'm talking "celery." I'm talking "carburetor" and "ridiculous." Go ahead, honeys. We're all waiting.

And every prematurely endowed one of them toddles up and does so, smoothly and dutifully, pitch perfect and error free, solves the equations, recites Shakespeare, impersonates Jimmy Stewart, stretches the species. Urging does not trouble him. A crowd does not. He is destined to star at academic contests after all. His bedroom bulletin board will soon be strewn with ribbons from science fairs; his bureau will be covered with trophies from assorted mental Olympics.

In elementary school, although the day's allotment of nasal drip frosts his upper lip, he ticks off the periodic table of the elements. He cracks crossword puzzles before he's cut a third of his adult teeth. He wades into set theory while the rest of his age group is still stuck on Dr. Seuss. With pudgy fingers he beetles flawlessly over the piano keys—he also plays a mean miniature viola and a tiny violin—and in doing so proves that Mozart is a child's game after all. Whatever his specialty, he always awes the guests, in spite of the fact that when he goes to sleep he still wants the light on and wets the bed. (Imagine a brain instantly able to unearth square roots or to dismantle Latin but unequipped to command the bladder.) But it is his capacities and not his lapses that define him, that set him apart and compel us.

"He was a sage baby," his dumbfounded folks tell CNN. "Only a few birthdays in, he was already figuring the family taxes!" It is a joke, but just barely. And it is a nervous humor they turn to, knowing the statistics regarding the prolonged childhood of prodigies. Dad may have to dress his boy until he is old enough to vote. Mom may be cutting up his meat at his wedding rehearsal. Just like parents who have children with disabilities, they have familiarized themselves with the oddities and the odds. They are already girding themselves for the prospect of long-standing dependency and deferral of their plans to retire to Boca Raton. The way that their friends have studied the hottest stocks, the prodigy's parents have studied the vicissitudes of human potential. At dinner parties their friends show off their fluency in foreign films or the National Football League; the prodigy's parents can tick off textbook cases by name.

And so the quizzed kid continues, flashing bits of aptitude that supersede anything that might have been bequeathed through the genes, given the average status of Dad, the mediocrity of Mom. And the reaction to him has always been unanimous and not merely polite. For other friends' children—for their own nonprodigies as well—there is always a warm enough reception, for whom it is sufficient to win applause that they not spill their tippy cups or probe their noses. But *this* child was never meant for the sweet but limited achievements appropriate to his age. He so obviously and early on flew past sufficiency that he earns a place in their conversation even after he's been excused to return to his room.

Remarkable, that boy, and frankly rather unsettling too, like something embryonic in a jar, which is where Harvard would house him if they had their druthers. Maybe more off-putting than enviable when you get right down to it, on the order of a potato shaped like the head of a president or a two-headed calf. The kid's too young for copyright law, and a circus, though appropriate, would be cruel. If he continues to blossom at this rate, his head will have to hatch, that is, if he doesn't blow his bright little wad before puberty. (Not all prodigies swell to grown-up prominence as reliably as they plumped inside their mothers shortly before.) And can you imagine the tribulations that await him at recess? Every generation finds playgrounds soaked with the blood of Poindexters, who scrabbled blindly about after their routine beatings to recover their snapped protractors and spilled calculus notes. (Admittedly there is the occasional exception of an Alexander, who graduated to "the Great" while the rest of his class was still years away from serious career planning. Even the most brazen bullies didn't risk tripping him.) It can't be easy to lead an untimely life like that. They will suffer for being so special.

Historically speaking prodigies were as likely to be treated as demons as they were to be honored as prophets. We prize excellence to be sure, but deviance to this degree is always at least a little disagreeable whatever direction it takes. As David Henry Feldman, a professor of developmental psychology, writes in *Nature's Gambit*, the prodigy phenomenon seems "to violate the natural order of things," and Feldman takes pains to point out that the etymology of "prodigy" includes connotations of monstrosity. We may not banish or abominate prodigies nowadays, but we haven't exactly taken the targets off their backs, either. Soloists remain fair game for clean shots; a more comfortable fate can be had in the middle of the choir. An elevated I.Q., like an elevated white count, will upset the classroom and freak out the parents—the stricken kid needs constant watching.

Remembering the eight-hour-a-day practice sessions mandated by the early evidence of her remarkable musical abilities, violinist Yeou-Cheng Ma confesses, "I traded my childhood for my good left hand." Ravenous for the violin before the age of three, Nils Kirkendahl was already straining the expertise of teachers in several conservatories in the Boston area by the time he was eight years old. Watching the boy flog his talents forward, his composition teacher reports that Nils is not only "fantastic" but "too good to be true. He has no faults and that's terrible, it's frightening —marvelous, but frightening because you just can't believe that this is all going to happen." That level of brilliance and overdrive is quite a plight to wish on a kid, we tell ourselves, more than a little relieved to see the occasional mistake on our own children's homework, grateful that their intensities can wane sufficiently for them to get to sleep. Better to be my routine daughter, my unexceptional son, and be able to bank on ordinary chances for happiness.

Television has long been drawn to prodigies, but television usually portrays them as merely precocious. Frequently they are the youngest sons in sitcoms, whose elevated syntax, unflappable manners, and penchant for dressing like recently hired executives emphasize their distinction from mortal children, not to mention from their reliably flummoxed fathers. If they are daughters, they are pixie cute with needle-keen vocabularies and lethal wit, but once again it is at the expense of their flustered mothers or woebegone dads. These are transparent caricatures, of course, tailored to the constraints of the half-hour format. Rather than challenge the human perimeter in any profound or permanent way, they end up as snugly as the commonplace children in the cast. Whatever intellectual antics they demonstrate are designed to tweak a scene or two at most; they haven't the substance to carry a half hour's plot. Real life would obviously expose their flimsiness, and at any credible school they'd never last out a single day's abuse.

Occasionally television will feature real-life children, dangling their tiny shoes just over the lips of their chairs, showing off their lisps, cowlicks, and gums like high marks on their report cards. I especially remember how Art Linkletter's *Kids Say the Darndest Things!* enchanted viewers of all ages. Parents enjoyed their inadvertent insights and uncensored sense of things; the host's avuncular, sidelong smile put the kids at ease and reminded the adults in the audience that laughter, surprise, nostalgia, embarrassment, and love were all acceptable responses—the host was open to any combination. Housebound kids watched their televised counterparts as well, partly for the Tom Sawyer–like satisfaction of seeing a grown-up brought down, partly to guarantee their distance from their primped and mincing example. Who knows how many kids watched kids say the darndest things just so they could damn them? But aside from the odd Shirley Temple wannabe who actually had the goods, Linkletter's lot weren't prodigies per se, only extroverts. Their future was in class clowning and, later on, in sales.

When prodigies appear in fiction, they either tend to struggle with or just plain regret their own endowments, or they exasperate the rest of the family, who have to face the glare of incipient genius day after day. J. D. Salinger's Teddy, for example, is so gnomic a little boy, so imperturbable a picture of equanimity, that when he *does* make a mistake—on a family cruise, he refers to the porthole as a "window"—his father carries on with mock astonishment, gleeful as any junior high kid in detention who got to witness his teacher trip over the wastebasket. Indeed practically all of the Glass siblings in Salinger's stories descend from their eminence as radio stars into disappointment, dissolution, or some other ruin.

The hero of Percival Everett's *Glyph,* an astoundingly erudite baby imbued with language and literary theory, also consternates his father, a lesser poststructuralist, who has a flimsier grip on his wife's devotion than the baby has. Parents, psychiatrists, government agents, and would-be abductors are at once astonished, threatened, and consumed by him, "And it all sat on me like a weight, a kind of self-referential density," he reports. "I was like a loaded gun resting on a table in front of a bludgeon of convicts. And like that gun, the fear seemed present in all the faces near me that I might at any second go off, whatever *going off* might come to." Similarly, in Myla Goldberg's *Bee Season,* nine-year-old Eliza Naumann has lived as an indifferent student well beneath the radar and has never had to bear the burden of excellence her older brother does. But when she reveals a championship-caliber talent for spelling, giddiness is tempered by dread. Until now, mistakes were as normal and readily dismissed as grass stains on her skirt; as she moves to higher levels of competition, however, she feels defeat lurking in the auditorium, passing among the preadolescent contestants like the Angel of Death. Nor does practice ease the pressure of expectation upon her:

> She dreams a sky black with swarming letters. They fly with thick, stubby wings barely able to hold their fat bodies aloft. They brush against her skin, nest in her hair. They crawl up her nose, into her eyes. The ground is covered in torn and broken letters that crunch beneath her feet with every step. The sound of letters fills the air, making thought impossible. The letters squeeze themselves between her lips and flutter their terrible wings inside her mouth.

Rita Dove, whose father drilled her with flash cards to help her keep her top-of-the-class edge, would have understood Eliza's nightmare: "the faster / I answered, the faster they came," she recalls, as if the cards assaulted her like malevolent birds. Yes, Eliza Naumann and Rita Dove might have commiserated with one another, were it not that elevation is so isolating.

Then there is thirteen-year-old Briony Tallis, in Ian McEwan's *Atonement*, with her several idiosyncrasies: a gift for writing, a passion for plots and secrets, a compulsion to control the older folks in the vicinity. "Was everyone else really as alive as she was?" she wonders. "For example, did her sister really matter to herself, was she as valuable to herself as Briony was? Was being Cecilia just as vivid an affair as being Briony?" The prospect of being central and powerful, the fascination of real-life intrigue, and the opportunity to truly author the destinies of adults tempt her to arrogance, with tragic consequences for almost everyone else. "And though it horrified her, it was another entry, a moment of coming into being, another first: to be hated by an adult. . . . To be the object of adult hatred was an initiation into a solemn new world. It was promotion." Everything is magnified for the prodigy, disaster as well as opportunity, failure as well as acclaim. Her ascent is more dramatic than most; so will be her fall.

Most of us can barely conceive of the brains we're born with. If we think of what is doing our thinking at all, we might conjure something akin to those misbegotten embryos kept in jars for high school biology students to poke at and gag over. A vague concoction vaguely concocting, which does its mulling with a rubbery consistency that must give even seasoned neurologists pause. Something of a color between raw liver and bad cabbage. Something hunched in the skull like a hedgehog. I know that I am in the majority when I say that any viable metaphor for the physical brain, from runny sponge to blood pudding, puts me off my feed, as well as reminds me that I haven't the stomach for dissection. That it might be my own brain under inspection makes my gorge, not my curiosity, rise.

Doubtless it's more natural to remain oblivious to the brain even when one is using it to brood with. Honestly, who among us appreciates the huddled lobes, the occipital, parietal, frontal, and prefrontal portions drawn in like linemen protecting the pocket? Who has an inkling of the amygdala, wound like a friendship bracelet worn in secret, or the medulla, depending like a slice of inner Illinois? What of the cingulate gyrus, which sounds like an animal grazing on the Serengeti, or the mysterious activities of the wily hippocampus? Who else but a surgeon bothers to comprehend the contours of our knowing? The brain's greasy sluices and hidden switches, the pitch and yaw of thought, the sentience welling up, the humid mangle of it all. It's an unfathomable hemisphere altogether, when you come to think of it, and more than a little gruesome, too. Then there is aging to face, with the prospect of one cerebral neighborhood after another surrendering to blight until the whole head's disintegrated and uninhabitably dim. The strange relays growing annually stranger, the precious current leaking, the axons atrophying and dendrites drying out. Synapses once easily leaped yawning wider and wider. Once-limpid thoughts limping dully along. Awful to contemplate while one still *can* contemplate, futile to try to do so once the circuitry fries. No, basically, the general population does not keep the mind in mind.

However, in the same way that no one anatomized hitting so meticulously as Ted Williams did, prodigies probably visit above-average interest upon their above-average mentalities. Surely they are aware that certain times and places have proved especially conducive to their kind. They know about a clot of juvenile classical pianists performing in and around Prague, about a cache of chess masters who disdained the playgrounds of St. Petersburg to work on their boards, about a bumper crop of Berlin-area mathematicians who proved ripe for renown while their playmates were still raw youths. Don't they suspect that these and not their run-of-the-mill siblings are their true kin?

Likewise, just as the bodybuilder flexes intently in the mirror, admiring the muscles that separate him from those who sweat to far less benefit at the gym, so might the prodigy linger on the gray matter in which his distinction is pitched. Surely it isn't much of a stretch to suppose him alone in the lab or sandbox colluding with his own cranium, considering his intelligence brewing the way a witch in a fable oversees the magic in her pot. All of us have muscles, but most don't merit reflection; by the same reasoning, all of us have brains, but given the opportunity, it's the prodigy's brain you'd pick. For the prodigy himself must be awed by his own accelerated metabolics, must in the midst of all he ponders ponder how and why his mind is able to fix and tighten around a problem when the minds of most kids, confronting difficulty, merely mush and puddle. The ordinary child's brain must be at best a frail government of a developing nation; it comes awake fitfully, sluggishly, like a low-level employee on a Monday morning or one of the fluorescent bulbs he'll spend the day under. But the brain of a prodigy, with the next fresh understanding forever leaning on its doorbell, well, that bears watching. See the prodigy iris in, hone his focus, lock down on his task like a raptor sizing up its prey. Doctors, take out your notepads.

What analogy can accommodate a prodigy's thought processes? The prodigy himself might picture a derrick under construction, manned by an ideal team of riggers. He might think of ideas erected out of stainless girders, whose bolts hit their holes exactly. Its corrugations are tailored to every specification; its components are solidly machined. By contrast, my own preschool thoughts never came close to the tolerances "ideas" require to deserve the term; "notions" was more like it, the sorts of things a boy might pick dripping out of the marsh and not be allowed to bring into the house. While the prodigy can apprehend a concept like a culprit, systematically stalking it, cornering it, and dragging it cuffed into the light, when I was a child, I spake as a child and surmised as one as well. My interior life was probably as sloppy as the room I slept in, and so was pretty much every other kid's. But a prodigy's mental landscape, tilled and fertile, its broad fields crosshatched with corollaries, promises a ripe future and a regular return.

And yet, not long after puberty, the erstwhile prodigies may very well stop producing. Experts report that, more often than not, prodigies fail to remake their disciplines in their own initial images. Ninety-nine out of a hundred prodigies do not sustain their climb into the true artistry of the adult master, says Yuli Turovsky, who conducts I Musici of Montreal and who has seen many young musicians break down or burn out. "It can be devastating to realize that you've done everything as a child and there are no more challenges for you as an adult." Indeed, there are fewer stories of their unchecked ascent than there are of whiz kids wearing out: the human computer's stunts stunted, the child composer's creativity decomposed, the minilinguist's perceptivity dispelled. Some former prodigies handle the decline into normality well enough; others are traumatized. They let their chemicals evaporate, their rough drafts and canvases yellow, or their calculations stall in the basements that had been remodeled to accommodate their respective gifts. They abandon their chess sets to the spiders and dust. They dash their treacherous instruments against the wall.

The descent of a prodigy into the typical is as unpredictable as his creation was and potentially as troubling in its repercussions. In the realm of sensational mental events, he had always been a prince; we should not be surprised if he takes his exile hard. For the first time he must envision a relentlessly credible future, with his uniqueness tamped down into mere adequacy. He will have to suffer the insult of finitude like the rest of us. Sensing his diminishment, the prodigy might grow erratic, clinging desperately to the vestiges of his distinction. Asked to organize his sock drawer, he might hypothesize the structure of a new subatomic particle. Urged to finish his vegetables, he might scratch out a sonata on his napkin. On his birthday, told by his mother that she loves him, he might escape her squeeze to sketch out a map of Africa; while she is finishing the decorations on his cake before the party starts, he is anxiously dotting on the capitals and detailing the crimps and fissures in the coasts.

In the end, the arc of the prodigy's career is inexplicable. Therefore we should not wonder at the prodigy's own tendency to fix on the mystical to explain himself to himself. He is certainly no less likely than the relatives, professors, and audiences he amazes to suspect that his gifts are not accidental, that he has been chosen. Not only is the prodigy not immune to claims of reincarnation, astrology, and other otherworldly realms, he might actually be more acutely attuned to them. And why shouldn't the prodigy be given pause by his own implausibility? Why shouldn't he be puzzled by the puzzle he poses? As Professor Feldman writes, "History and evolution seem to have given the prodigy privileged access to some of our more demanding symbol systems and allowed them to master some of our most complex domains. Is it not possible that other extraordinary capabilities and sensibilities might be part of the package as well?" Thus we may have to alter the manner of our marveling at him. Maybe when Adam thrashes in his bath because of *Kristallnacht* he is remembering not a conversation between his grandparents in the kitchen but the actual smashing of the glass. Perhaps when Randy awakens from his nap and starts spouting spiritual aphorisms, he is not inventing a testament but channeling the dead.

One day the prodigies will receive invitations to an international conference devoted to assessing the destinies of the innately favored. Ex-prodigies will gather to share drinks and compare accomplishments. One-time owners of photographic memories will stand cheek by jowl with bygone microbiologists and spent cellists. Some will have continued to gain altitude from the promontories they were born upon; others will have subsided into the same standard fates as everyone else whom PBS never bothered to feature in any special. They will be gainfully if not garishly employed. They will learn what has always been common knowledge among the commoners, which is that even among the excessively blessed, things get more ambiguous the older you get.

Let us not forget that child prodigies are children no matter how prodigious they seem. They need bucking up and looking after. We are duty bound to tell them to practice, certainly, but it is also up to us to tell them to finish their cereal, use the potty, go out and play.

Have fun! we cry as they take off for who knows where. But don't go too far.

Because I Said So

Talk not to me of blasphemy, man; I'd strike the sun if it insulted me.

Herman Melville, *Moby-Dick*

Arrogance. The word contains a weapon: an arrow, followed by a gust, the fatal forward thrust. If Nabokov's Humbert Humbert believed that his beloved displayed her delectation in her very name—"Lo-lee-ta: the tip of the tongue taking a trip of three steps down the palate to tap, at three, on the teeth"—the name of "arrogance" implies its expulsion of others and immitigable aim. Do not confuse arrogance with stubbornness, which, while it may occasionally masquerade as arrogance, is at least a couple of classes lower born. Stubbornness may sneer, but its assaults do not wither its victims from well above them; on the contrary, it reveals the wearer's inner disappointment instead of any genuine, outbound disdain. When stubbornness spurns, it mainly kicks at the curb; it steeps at street level. One can be stubborn as a bucket of tar gone cold, but to be truly arrogant demands an altitude that the merely stubborn among us— recalcitrant kids, grumbling plebes—cannot rise to. Stubbornness now and then gets employed as an understudy to arrogance, but when stubbornness takes the stage, the diminishment is clear: the nose is held too low; instead of grandly dismissive, the mouth settles for grim; and the sneer it take years of self-assurance to hone is altogether absent or a transparent sham.

Ambition also falls short of the mark. Granted, ambition is a perfectly earnest noun, but it lives forever in the shadow of arrogance and, frankly, eats its dust. Arrogance has feasted in advance—the main course has already been cleared by the time ambition arrives on the scene. While ambition girds itself for action, arrogance has already selected its medals; in fact, arrogance comes self-anointed, preadorned. At best, ambition plays Ralph Bellamy to arrogance's Cary Grant. Brazen and raving, Grant gets the girl; humble and pie faced, Bellamy gets the gate.

'Twas ever thus. Kindergarten preaches kindness as vigorously as it does keeping your elbows off the table and your hands to yourself, when in the long run it may pay off to start kids off with sass and shape it into a full-blown attitude as they grow up. Everything from solicitous aunts to *Sesame Street* would have us all sparkle as assiduously as a children's photographer at the mall. But the preadolescent lesson that reaches deepest comes from *The Wizard of Oz*, which is that the only thing standing between the Cowardly Lion and his rightful kingship is his lack of nerve. His companions alternately cajole and chide him, and Dorothy caresses him to soothe his misgivings, but a healthy helping of hauteur would render all of that attention unnecessary. From arrogance, all other trappings of majesty derive. Mastering that, the lion could make the forest quake and its creatures kowtow. For if the squeaky wheel gets the grease, imagine what reward awaits the roaring lord. Because an undeflectable distemper is the real core of kingliness. The sovereign who is shot through with prerogative the way a liver brims with bile or a tick fills with blood is the one who truly rules.

"There is no sophistry in my body," declares the hawk in Ted Hughes's poem. "My manners are tearing off heads." More often than in human communities, in the animal kingdom we discover ascendancy, without question. So pronounces the high priest of advantage:

> It took the whole of Creation
> To produce my foot, my each feather:
> Now I hold Creation in my foot.

Of course not every example of arrogance is so regal. Consider the flatulent fellow who, unfortunately and nonetheless, gives in to his penchants for cabbage, raisins, and cheese—all notoriously catalytic when it comes to the noxious end of digestion. You might think he'd avoid cubicles and elevators, not only to spare the other inhabitants who happen to be confined with him, but also to dilute his odor for his own sake. (Standing in his own proximity without relief, as he has to, must be like living

downwind of a hog farm.) You might think he would distribute air fresh-
ener throughout his office and his home to ensure that he is never more
than a few feet away from cleansing the atmosphere of his signature
smells. You might think he would be constantly, religiously apologetic,
excusing himself from the room when he could sense the coming burst
in time, excusing himself even more acutely when he could not. You
might think he would take note of the movie cliché of the soldier who
falls on the live grenade to save his fellows. You might think that he'd be
relegated, like the smoker who cannot stop, to practicing his foul habits
shamefacedly and on the sly. But the arrogant farter is unregenerate.
Offending without inhibition, he freely exercises his nature and implies
that sneaking is for the defeated. (Nor can lesser men, even if they successfully disavow their discharge or manage to get away with their vul-
garity undetected, escape their essential stink, which sticks to them like
sin.) The arrogant man passes gas coarsely and with conviction. Instead
of slinking off to a corner for secret release, he remains fixed in place, his
posture so rigid he could be auditioning for a monument in a public
park; it's a wonder pigeons don't shit on him, so rigid, so redolent is his
example.

Yeah, that was me. That was mine. What's *your* problem? What's your
point?

Say that you are contemplating a marriage proposal. Congratulations.
Do you worry that your darling is too disdainful for your taste? Do you
first want to test her propensity for arrogance the way the state will make
you test her blood? You might begin by investigating her relationship
with James Joyce. How she handles him speaks volumes about your
prospects together. Before you commit, before you boast that your love
is as absolute and inevitable as a fable, insert Joyce into a conversation.
Make it casual but unavoidable, like a belch, so she'll have to react. "Imagine what James Joyce would have made of your cousin Eileen," say, or "His
reasoning makes James Joyce seem straightforward." She has to know
who Joyce is—that's a given. If she remembers a title or can sketch out an
episode from one of the novels, that's commendable. If she owns a copy
of *Ulysses*, so much the better; if it's marked by brackets and notations
she's made, that's better yet. But be on the alert lest it progress any further. If she knows there's no apostrophe in *Finnegans Wake*, beware. If
she is reading Joyce outside of a course requirement, perhaps that's for-
givable, but just barely. If she can remember portions of text verbatim, if

she in fact quotes Joyce while she's tearing squares of toweling to blot a spill or while she's pulling a week's bramble of hair out of the shower drain, that's regrettable and, according to several reputable analysts, outrageous, and you should tell her so. If she references a literary critic, run.

Or, depending on your predilections, rush out and buy the ring. Softhearted sorts, who puddle before puppies and Romantic poetry, who sigh when Humphrey Bogart sacrifices and weep when Ingrid Bergman weeps, might miss the virtues of arrogance. They equate it with brazenness or simple bad manners. Who wants to have anything in common with a crow on a carcass or a stray dog sauntering across a busy street? Horses whipped for spitting the bit, which stop not ten seconds later to spit the reinserted bit again, feel in every breeze the sear of scars that never heal. That's not eminence, just effrontery, they think. They see America's youth mimicking the struts and scorn of football heroes, they see them emulating the manner and message of rap stars, they see them practicing a hundred ways of getting *hard,* and these sentimentalists can only shake their heads over our country's future. They find no enchantment in a callus.

Their instinct is to blame popular culture and to prescribe spiritual teachings. Run the afflicted through a few cycles of church, whose special softeners and detergent action will make the children suitable to be seen in public once again. Yet it is just possible that religion helps to instill what it is ostensibly designed to eliminate. There is arrogance in the sense of election Sunday services provide. There is arrogance in prayer when it is inspired by petition and the pleader has no appointment. There is arrogance in the aspiration to sainthood and the expectation that sanctity or suffering puts one on the fast track to beatification. Behind the T-shirt I saw at the gym last week, which read "Liars Go to Hell," whether it was meant as a prediction or as a curse, there is arrogance, just as there is arrogance in the bumper sticker that boasts "I'm Not Perfect, Just Saved," as if that bit of hedging in the opening clause obscured the size of the brag.

The Bible itself is rife with examples of the exaltation of the arrogant. (If the meek will inherit the earth, scripture insists that it will be only after the arrogant have had their fill of it.) Take the story of Samson. His genius and his devotion were chiefly manifested in deeds; you might say that he was the original action hero of our heritage, the prototype of the halfback swaggering after the touchdown or the slam dunker who rushes back to the hotel to see his achievement replayed on ESPN. Samson wasn't much for words, in other words. "Get her for me, for she pleases me well." That's the style of a man whose method is ripping apart lions with his hands, that rare individual whose endowments rival those of Hughes's hawks. When Samson calls upon God, it is not for help in punishing the Philistines for their impieties against God but to settle a personal grudge. He prays for strength "that I may be avenged upon the Philistines for one of my two eyes." Again, this is only one of many egregious examples of human arrogance in the Old Testament, which range from Cain's infamous disclaimer in response to his Maker's asking after Abel, to Jacob's making a name for himself by grappling with an angel, to Moses's supposing he can bargain with the God that charged him.

There is a Yiddish word for this capacity—what *isn't* there a Yiddish word to cover?—which has proved so useful as to have entered the vocabulary of people who've been weaned on white bread and mayonnaise. In *The Joys of Yiddish,* Leo Rosten defines *chutzpa* as "that quality enshrined in a man who, having killed his mother and father, throws himself on the mercy of the court because he is an orphan." "Enshrined," precisely. "What *chutzpa!*" we cry, but not without admiration and, yes, a little envy. For *chutzpa* is the Gold Card of the soul, the version of divine right tailored for the marketplace. Do you know the one about the beggar who rewards his compassionate host by helping himself to the expensive *challah* instead of the regular bread, then assures him, when his host notes the price, "Believe me, it's worth it"? And how about the one about the writer who creates a fan page for himself on the Web, complete with prospective dust jacket photos (judiciously lit and artfully posed) even before he gets a book contract? Or the one about the hitchhiker who withholds his thumb until a car he'd deign to be seen in rolls up? Or the one about the aging pitcher who, although he's lost a good foot on his fastball, remains determined to try to pump strikes past the hitters? (He's kin to the intractable gunner in basketball, who launches three after three with impunity from far beyond the arc instead of involving the other guys on the squad. Throw the homily his way that "there's no *I* in *team*," and he'll swat it right back at you, saying, "Well, there's one right in the heart of *win*.") And do you know the million ones about the meager species that debates with, rages before, interrogates, scolds, and scoffs at the Lord for failing to explain, refusing to foster, or otherwise falling short? Admittedly there is no evidence that bravado gets anyone to heaven. That may make bravado all the braver.

The adage tells us that to forgive is divine, but going by the Old Testament in particular, godliness includes a heavy dose of arrogance. Don't be fooled by the tinge of "might" in "Almighty." There is neither maybe nor misdirection in his thunder. "Hear this, O Job; stop and consider the wondrous works of God." Whereupon the Lord ticks off some of the entries on his inimitable résumé, rendering his servant's replies irrelevant in advance. But what else might you expect from the one who with one whump could unmake us utterly? We live beneath his heavens, but not beneath his contempt. There is no more massive priority in the universe than that which the Lord of the Torah perpetually asserts. As to why he sometimes seems to see fit to harrow the pious and the perverted alike, our Heavenly Father, like any father whined at by his kids, occasionally resorts to "Because I said so!" writ large. Let Milton justify. Let congregations quibble and exegetes explain. I am that I AM. Everything in this house has my name on it. The bills all come to me. Make your own Creation, if you're able. Until then, make way.

On a more modest, human level, it pays to cultivate a small, private plot of arrogance to sustain you through periods of misunderstanding, neglect, and harsh weather. For every desktop Zen garden designed to quiet the heart, there should be a device to help exercise its insolence. Society tends to exaggerate the perils of arrogance when, actually, for every outlaw animated by it, a hundred inventors are born. Fortunately, to compensate for the pedants, politicians, or general pains in the ass that arrogance spawns, there is the possibility of the authentic paradigm shifter. Perhaps it pays to live, if only for a little while at a time, by a "not if, but when" aesthetic. For instruction, check out Oklahoma tornado chasers or golfers who in spite of the lightning are determined to finish their rounds before leaving the course. Every oceanographer who lets himself be dangled in a shark cage has it. So do the girls in John Updike's "A & P," who, blithely indifferent to protocol or dress code, stride through the grocery store in bikinis. For the men, there's Clint Eastwood, who in his westerns, no matter the number of gunmen who await him, affects an unshakable stance and an unalterable expression. For the women, there's Joan Crawford, a solid three-quarters of whose roles show her determined to crush out the least hint of susceptibility like a cigarette in an ashtray. Even small children are not too young to appreciate ways of making the world move aside for them, which explains the enduring popularity of Dennis the Menace and other prodigies of mischief and rascality. Then there's Linus from the *Peanuts* comic strip, who explains to the incurably self-conscious Charlie Brown that the reason he shines only the fronts of his shoes is that he does not care what people think of him when he leaves. Pretty impressive, I'd say, and germane to any age.

Still, even as I extol the arrogant, who appear never to parry but only to thrust, I should confess that my own blusters only occasionally escape the page. Like most people, I tend to succumb to the conditional tense, and I grumble about what I should have said or could have done under the conditions that have just passed. Oh, I can be commanding in my kitchen, an admiral during the drive home. But it is not only that I don't smoke that prevents me from being mistaken for the guy who lights up in the No Smoking section of a restaurant. While I do stand up for my rights when they're jeopardized and, more often than you might think an English professor would rise to it, I will stand up for yours when the situation calls for it, I'm nevertheless the type who cannot pass a police car without worrying that I'll set off his siren and spark pursuit. When his rollers fill my rearview mirror, I automatically begin rehearsing my apology even if I honestly cannot imagine what in the world I've done wrong. Do people really contend with the cops in real life the way some characters on television do? "What's *your* problem?" they say, whereas I start by assuming that whatever the problem is, it's mine.

By now the cop has blown past me on his way to worthier prey. I'm more than a little relieved and, when I think about it further, almost as much insulted.

A few miles further on, I come upon an unattended fire. It is no more than two hundred yards from the highway, and it is huge. I slow to appreciate it—the flames rise at least a hundred feet into the air and ripple like a massive flag heralding some insurgent nation. While I presume that the blaze is under control—*someone* must know what he's doing—I am a little concerned that the operation (the term implies another presumption on my part) has been abandoned. My first reflex is to suspect that there must be some kind of statute prohibiting this; my second is to suspect that, wearing a glare reflecting the fire's own, the man responsible would tell me that statutes are only paper, and paper burns. Sheriffs would cower and attorneys scare before this hypothetical culprit, who would not throttle back his incentive, halve his wrath, or withdraw even a foot from the flames he'd made. "I turn and burn. / Do not think I underestimate your great concern," declared Sylvia Plath, summoning more heat than is customary among people of poetic persuasion. Plath and Hughes: you'd be hard pressed to name a more incendiary combination of talents and personalities anywhere in the canon.

Yet at this scene there is no one to rebuke or decry. It is hard to know what to make of a fire in the middle of nowhere, making more nowhere, making its way in a way that asserts there is no other, and that is one reason why the sight is so intimidating. "I kill where I please because it is all mine," says the hawk, glowering. Nothing but wanton, grasping appetite to witness, a licking, snapping, demanding, stentorian, villainous fire, a monument and pompadour of blaze. Didn't Milton's Satan embody such an infernal, purging burn as this, carrying and emitting hell like the bad gas of himself wherever he went, making more nowhere, devouring all?

> We know no time when we were not as now;
> Know none before us, self-begot, self-raised
> By our own quickening power, when fatal course
> Had circled his full orb, the birth mature
> Of this our native heaven, ethereal sons,
> Our puissance is our own.

Smother *that*, if you're able, if you have the nerve.

I wonder if lightning might have started it—that would account for what strikes me as the arbitrary purpose and location of the fire—but I travel this highway regularly, and I know that there hasn't been a storm for at least a week. Anyway, I keep driving. I have no plans to call the authorities to register my worry or my complaint. Meanwhile, in the darkening distance, filling my mirror, the fire glows like an omen and, it must be said, gloriously.

King Philip, Come Out,
For God's Sake

*So we are stuck with a theory, and we do not know whether it is right
or wrong, but we do know that it is a little wrong, or at least incomplete.*

Richard Feynman, *Six Easy Pieces*

Think of the odds against us. There are experts—handicappers of the hard
sciences, if you will—who do just that. The odds they posit are positively
daunting, enough to make one lose one's faith or find it. Their figures
suggest that nothing else in the universe prepares us for us. As to whether
that means we are the goal of the system or the glitch in it, the jury is still
out.

That out of the original rabble of atoms instigated some fourteen billion years ago anything viable at all could have been constructed, much
less on human beings' suppositious behalf, is a bet no bookie would handle. Those were all the atoms that ever were or will be, mind you, and out
of that vast but stable economy something lobbied to shuffle the funds to
become us, something saw fit to scrape a vanquished star for our mak-
ings, the way the indigent salvage tobacco from an ashtray, perhaps, yet
not even that ignoble analogy kept us from eventuating. It takes only as
much science as a layman can take in to realize that if we were a bet, you
wouldn't take us.

In truth, science shows us that existence is essentially a numbers racket, and the numbers run against us all the way. Cosmologists, biologists,

physicists, paleontologists, and all other -ists worth their government-funded -ologies prove to be accountants at the core. Any one of them would wager on a string of hard eights harking all the way back to the Big Bang or risk drawing to a billion consecutive inside straights before he would venture on anything so outrageous as our arrival. Yet here we undeniably, odds defyingly are, which must compel specialists to want to weigh the dice and inspect the deck. For to have had any shot at all at the lottery of being, we would have had to purchase tickets by astronomical powers of ten.

Take the fact that we have apparently landed in the one minuscule district (galactically speaking) that would have us, in the one universe among all the equally possible outcomes of the Big Bang uniquely conducive to our idiosyncratic needs. It is so remarkable that out of the chiefly unyielding everywhere there arose an ergonomic sliver suitable for human use that "remarkable" doesn't come close to covering it. The earth is so anomalous, its populations so outré, that every animal should be walking, flying, swimming, inching, or slithering about in a constant state of astonishment over the fact that their respective welfares have been indulged. As Bill Bryson notes in *A Short History of the Universe,*

> If the universe had formed just a tiny bit differently—if gravity were fractionally stronger or weaker, if the expansion had proceeded just a little more slowly or swiftly—then there might never have been stable elements to make you and me and the ground we stand on. Had gravity been a trifle stronger, the universe itself might have collapsed like a badly erected tent, without precisely the right values to give it the right dimensions and density and component parts. Had it been weaker, however, nothing would have coalesced. The universe would have remained a dull, scattered void.

And obviously there'd have been no Bryson to complain about the absence of decent scenery. His book, like most scientific primers, is a paean to extremes—things extremely large, small, distant, and long ago—which is continually interrupted by exclamations about the improbability of the whole shebang culminating as it has. The earth would not have been habitable had its orbit been slotted a few percentage points closer to or further from an unusually hospitable sun. About as likely as a tumble of bricks down a hillside automatically constituting as a cathedral below is the deployment of the planets, let alone the special dispensations allotted ours. What is more, our species has poked through during a rare hiatus between epoch-long absolutes of fire and ice. Don't blame Bryson and his kind for implying that the fix is in.

Or let us return to the implausibility of our own bodies, which take maybe a hundred miracles apiece every moment to sustain. Consider that the molecular sequence of any one of the million or so types of protein in the human body requires that the regiment of hundreds of amino acids line up instantly and precisely whenever an engendering reveille occurs. For that matter, consider those gerrymandering atoms that somehow effected a consensus out of each one of us—a consensus that should be the envy of any congress. Who could have supposed that our species lay among the dumb sputters of stars freshly hatched and planets long dissolved, that the initial ohms and first ergs would germinate into our supposing so? Who could have conjectured that a ragtag dispersal of particles and processes would soldier on toward Homo sapiens, into each human body's individual coalition of cells? What were the chances? Not nil, admittedly, but very nearly.

As I say, one interpretation of the narrative of the universe deems our species the collective protagonist of Creation, whereby all of the physics and cataclysm that the universe has expended was done to invent us. From mankind's internal terra incognita, our intricate engineering and chemistry welter down to the fiat of DNA that trellises uniquely and repeatedly through every scintilla of us—remember its four chemical components, adenine, guanine, cytosine, and thymine, with the phrase All Geese Come Together—to the darker harmonies beyond our recording and our ken, there is reason to believe that some sort of oversoul underwrites us, urging us to count ourselves kings of infinite space. On the other hand, the very same data may be used to argue that there is nothing much ultimate about us after all. Homo sapiens would assert the legitimacy of our reign where our very relevance is in question. (Indeed, even on our earth, bacteria, termites, and frogs have greater provenance and a stronger argument than ours.) Perhaps we are not the inevitability but the "glorious accident" Stephen Jay Gould alludes to; perhaps there is less ingenuity than fluke to us. Unfortunately there is nothing and no one else in the vicinity to discuss this with. The preponderance of creatures are at best about as ambitious as lichen and thus cannot muster an opinion

—a situation that only adds to the suspicion that it is not logic but luck that governs.

Since for the foreseeable future we are evidently destined to contemplate the concept of a purposeful birth on our own, we may select test cases without fear of contradiction. Two especially consternating ones are conception and extinction.

Just imagine for a moment the moment of the procreation that enacted you. You derived from the most recent of a daisy chain of ejaculations, any one of which could have been targeted elsewhere or timed otherwise. The riot of unlikelihoods that produced you here and now— even leaving aside for now the ones that produced the here and now you happen to occupy—is startling, to say the least, even if you buy into a master plan that includes you. For every sperm that earns purchase, legions founder and fail. Even under the most auspicious, calculated circumstances, when the time of month is ideal and the incentive is love, sex is largely a botched invasion, in that in the wake of the foray only one finds the beach. The consolation Stephen Crane's official spokesman offered in "Do Not Weep, Maiden, for War Is Kind" that "little souls" were "born to drill and die" does not inspire much confidence in the overall campaign. Weep not over the squandered, he counsels, and we might extrapolate from this that there is precious little difference in the long run between the short run of the soldier who's cut down in the field and that of the ill-fated seeds no soldier ever sprung from.

In intercourse as in other assaults, the unfathomed masses win no eulogy and spawn no heir. Destiny looks indifferently down on these efforts like Tolstoy's Napoleon, contemptuous before the earnest, drowning troops that plunged ecstatically into the Viliya River to demonstrate their allegiance. Or we might view each sexual episode the way we do the toddler's messy attempt to pour his own milk: more spills on the table or splashes on the floor than touches the intended cup. Literally millions are wiped out with each wiping up. The pun must sober us: when we come, we mostly come to nothing.

As in the end, we will anyway, obsolescence being the default setting for every species. Make it through delivery intact, and elimination still looms. All begettings occur on the edge of apocalypse. Seeing as only about $\frac{1}{100}$ of 1 percent of all of the species that the planet has ever hosted has not disappeared entirely, we could say that all biology represents the earth's disposable income. Being is a bum's rush, and the rate of absence and the weight of evidence say that we'll soon enough be among the bums being rushed. The overwhelming majority of entities have been overwhelmed already; almost everyone that anted up over the course of the world's history is history, leaving us with a trash of also-rans so inclusive as to make one wonder whether or not he should commit himself to his obituary from the beginning.

When theologians try to pick the responsible deity out of a lineup, they might look twice before passing over a slapdash, prodigal god.

Of course there's no need to wait for the next version of the great Permian extinction before we're brought up short. (That was one of the five chief extinction episodes in the life span of our planet, by the way. They were, in chronological order, the Ordovician, Devonian, Permian, Triassic, and Cretaceous. Wholesale evacuations, which we can remember via the phrase Only Demented People Talk Crazy.) Leaving aside for the time being the increasingly real possibility that our abuses to the ecosystem will annihilate us before nature does us in—we don't need scientists to remind us that we tend to treat the planet like a rental property—the chances that a new human life will earn a permanent place on the record are about as slim as his or her inceptive cell itself. For every indexed eminent in the encyclopedia, there are numberless unremembered others. I speak here—fleetingly, faintly—of the surfeit of serfs throughout history that had to add anonymity to the curses they suffered. I speak of the hod carriers covered by the shades cast by the hods they carried and of every negligible *zek* that ended in eclipse. It is difficult to imagine them even temporarily in isolation; instead they flood the mind in force, or in what small force they ever mustered, much the way Lewis Thomas describes the seeming inseparability of ants from the colony. A director like DeMille would outfit peasants by the trainload to fill his epic scenes to the edges of the CinemaScopic frame, the better to surround his stars with contrasting mass. Digital imaging does the trick nowadays, replacing barely dimensioned extras with completely nondimensional ones without sacrifice to credibility. "Life's but a walking shadow," mourned Macbeth, who at least had notoriety to usher him to his demise. Wouldn't the doomed king have been amazed to see the paces we currently put shadows through. A slur of *pluribus,* they swarm, celebrate, or expire by the ton, and they are none the wiser for their brief, crowded hour upon the stage. It's what waits for most of our species, as well as for every other: not a king's remembrance but a candle's end.

We can debate whether it is the scientist's or the philosopher's responsibility to field the question: why is there something instead of nothing? The old saw still cuts. Just as significant a question, however, is why is that rare something rescinded?

As always, numbers may not solve the problem, but they do verify the predicament. As James Trefil writes in *101 Things You Don't Know about Science and No One Else Does Either,* fewer than 1 in 10,000 species have made it into the fossil record; according to the calculations of paleontologist Richard Leakey, the chances are worse—about 1 in 120,000. Rotten odds, but no one as yet has devised a superior means of permanently retaining our impressions. A susceptibility to depression has kept me from doing the math, but I'm guessing that one's shot of getting a tenured spot in the next edition of *Who's Who* isn't much more heartening.

So here we are—well, a paltry few of us, statistically speaking, are here, and only temporarily. And that may be why we're so determined to detect the presence of otherworldly life, to feel less lonely before we exit the census forever. Thus Lear longed for his fool, if only to play his speechifying off. Thus Odysseus, for want of more regal fellowship at epic's end, bedded down with a swineherd to exchange stories with. (In a pinch, he'd have settled for the swine, being so hungry for company.) Even a king longs to escape the boundaries of his kingdom, just to see. Give us an animate other or two to swap atoms with. Sentience would be a bonus, certainly, but we'd treat single-celled emissaries with pomp and circumstance. The least promising precincts on and under the earth—the tops of the highest, oxygen-depleted peaks, the scorching walls of ocean vents, the dismal interior of old ice—are residences for *some* doughty organisms. The odds should be decent at least that in all of outer space the specs are good enough to sustain a neighborhood.

And yet nothing that gravity's dragged in so far has altered our solitude. And every round of cosmic prospecting, too, has up till now come a cropper. So far as we know—and measuring by *Voyager 1* and *2,* which have been advancing the investigation outward at a rate of thirty-five thousand miles per hour since 1977, we know pretty far—the earth's been abandoned to its own devices. None of our technology has contradicted these findings—or rather, lack of findings—to date. Battalions of radio telescopes grope hopefully about without reply. Many of the probes we've launched don't even so much as report back on their new digs, as if in respectful observance of the protocol of extraterrestrial silence they get lost in. We could blame the instruments or conclude that we've been sweeping for lost keys in the wrong corners, but there we are. And where we are is a fine but private place.

Nevertheless science keeps trying to engage the universe through a Socratic method. Or we would be more likely to call it that if the universe were not so loath to answer back.

When my family moved to what for me was a strange part of the city, the first thing I did was to scope out the new block for potential playmates. A natural impulse: solitaire and pitching balls against your own building is only so entertaining. We want to test ourselves against an outer context.

As to what our data might look like from a distance, asking that is also in our nature, a common obsession of the species. Think of that other mnemonic we learned in college to help us recall the Linnaean taxonomy of kingdom, phylum, class, order, family, genus, species: King Philip, Come Out, For God's Sake! Which is the issue science is always pressing, isn't it? Come out, for God's sake, we say, scratching at cell doors, petitioning the skies. Come out and talk to us. Come out and play.

Something to Shoot For

The gun spit and jerked in his arms and the shot went wide, but Edsel was as thrilled as if he'd made the metal ring. He'd entered grown-up land where the power was. . . .

Stephen Wright, *M31: A Family Romance*

I went to one of the eleven gun shops in the area, to see what it was about guns.

Do not mistake me. I am not disdainful of people who collect guns. I don't think of men who spend hours lovingly disassembling and cleaning their rifles as insecure or as fearing they're insufficiently phallic when they are too long apart from their armories. I do not think that they are compensating for any thwarted prowess at work or in bed. While I am alert to the symbolism when Faye Dunaway's Bonnie Parker fondles the pistol by her pillow because Warren Beatty's Clyde Barrow leaves her frustrated, I am not convinced that it applies outside the theater. Yet although I don't equate rifles with erections, I do appreciate how a gun offers one more way to be reckoned with, and in a society in which people often feel invisible or at bay, I have some idea where the ferocity of the pro-gun bumper stickers comes from.

For my own part, though, aside from the toy guns I grew up with back when sociology saw fit to leave kids to their own demeanors and devices —hell, I had a toy chest chock full of plastic ordnance from Mattel—I was raised unarmed. My brother and I kept the requisite cowboy accoutrements in our basement as all boys and brothers undoubtedly did in theirs. We also had a tommy gun, which shot only sound, a Dopplering growl that was closer in quality to a complaining cat than to any firearm's report. Then there was our deadliest weapon: a Gatling gun, which fired plastic ammo, or at least it did in the infrequent event that the thing didn't jam. But our gunplay was always and only that, with the definite emphasis on "play." And limited play at that. I never practiced in the mirror a Maverick-slick draw, nor did I dream of shooting straight and true as Burt Lancaster or Kirk Douglas could in the double features my parents abandoned us to on summer Saturday afternoons. Had it been up to me, my ideal career would have been spent with the Cubs, not in the marshal's office or the FBI. And any prayers of mine to become lethal and fast had to do with pitching, not with picking outlaws off their horses or sniping enemy spies.

Let me testify, too, that not one of my toy guns inflicted any damage whatsoever, either physical or psychological, at either end of the barrel. Neither my brother nor I grew up to have a gun in the house, and neither of us has ever considered committing a violent crime or voting Republican. To my mind, that causal connection has always been a myth. To imagine that gangsters pass their gats on to their kids like some awful genetic legacy is the stuff of docudrama and too glib to believe in completely. To think that committed paintball players, with their twice-weekly amalgamations of Walter Mitty and Audie Murphy, are likelier than the general population to be institutionalized for destroying more than just the laundry does not hold up statistically. To argue that Bugsy Siegel was given a Beretta instead of a fountain pen as a bar mitzvah gift and that's what set him on his fatal course is pretty simplistic and just plain false. Our toy artillery notwithstanding, in my house there was nothing more substantial than my father's temper and an ambiguous belief in suburban election to stave off infiltration into our apartment building. You might have found dirty pictures tucked deep in a dresser drawer, but never a pistol. Nor did anyone I knew own a gun, most of my friends' fathers having surrendered their weapons the moment they'd come ashore after spending their rounds in Europe or Japan.

Face it: Morton Grove was a geographic refutation of the M-16, no Nazi threatened the equanimity of anyone ensconced in Skokie, and no one ever visited Old Orchard Mall for ammunition. Oh, a couple of buddies had BB guns they'd harass birds with. Mike Wasserman's older brother did manage to assassinate a sparrow or two in the maple in front of their apartment building, or so Mike reported. Keith Banazak used to set up empty bottles and jars in the alley before his one-man firing squad. He eventually graduated to his dad's Pabst cans—full ones, because of the luscious bursts they made when hit, followed by the dark, dramatic bleeding of beer. (Keith liked to pretend they were gut-shot Cong.) At least a few guys I knew must have assaulted windows of half-built housing projects at some point, entertainment always being an elusive commodity in those days. But by and large, Evanston, Skokie, Park Ridge, Wheeling—the entire north suburban area, in fact—constituted a DMZ for as long as I lived there.

In the so-called heart of the country, however, where more folks can recite the Second Amendment than can name a single poet, I've discovered that nearly everyone seems to be packing some sort of heat. Where I live now, men don't hand down shotguns to their children just for show; they don't plug their rifles just to be hung on the living room wall like antiques from Pier 1. We're talking about guns that are functional and at the ready. My neighbors assure me that there is a special bond between father and son that only gunning down game can forge. I do not doubt their civic-mindedness, mind you—these are my neighbors, remember, who leave their garbage each week at the end of the driveway and retrieve their mail the same time I do every day. Still, I can't help wondering whether they have a stronger affiliation with the guy who was just arrested south of town for having an ammo dump in his kitchen than they have with me. For theirs is the Other America, identified by NRA memberships, gun racks in truck cabs, and scraps of successfully downed animal adorning darkly paneled dens. They live in the Other America, where boys are more likely to have been introduced to hunting before junior high school than to have played in Little League. In this Other America, kids can distinguish a revolver's caliber and heft more readily than I could have figured out at their age which subway train took you to Wrigley Field. This is where it isn't unusual to see someone in the grocery line or at the gas pump who has a gun stuffed in his waistband or poking partway out of his pocket like an extra genital. To be sure, in this part of the Republic, more children have fired weapons than have *taken* trains. (Did I mention that my phone book lists eleven gun dealers in Joplin alone?) Depending on my audience, my confessing in this Other America to never having fired a gun in my life casts doubt upon my parentage, my patriotism, or my sperm count.

Or to be accurate, where I was raised was the Other America, if in definition the majority rules. Growing up in Chicago, the city that featured
the ascendancy of Al Capone, I should know as much. (When on vacation in Italy, Cubs legend Ernie Banks told a waiter he was from Chicago,
the man beamed with recognition: "Ah, Chicago! Bang, bang, eh?" Banks's
Hall of Fame credentials could not guarantee the renown that his tenuous connection with a killer did.) Here in southwest Missouri, I am far
enough from an urban center that the boundary between military and
paramilitary thins, and the term "background check" always inspires
someone within earshot to spit. I've learned that in the Show-Me State,
often as not, it's your artillery you'll be asked to display. Furthermore, a
half hour's drive south puts me in Arkansas, the Natural State, where,
notwithstanding Rousseau, the state of nature is an armed camp. You can
buy bullets in any grocery store. Don't be distracted by the cookware and
the clothing: for a sizable percentage of its clientele, Wal-Mart exists primarily for its munitions. A straw poll of my students reveals that a mili-
tia could be mustered in ten minutes flat because, by my count, pretty
much everybody can lay hands on at least one piece apiece.

In short a far greater percentage of the local citizenry prove their legitimacy by being able to dismantle and load firearms than by producing
their Phi Beta Kappa keys, which, to tell the truth, never opened any door
anyway. Unless the artist or philosopher I mean to extol had earned a
passing score on a target range or, better yet, shot his way through a
thicket on foreign soil, well, save it for the classroom, Professor. Truly I
have no answer to the contention that had Shakespeare the means to arm
his heroes properly, his tragedies might have come to better ends. Imagine how much faster—and, frankly, with no greater bloodshed—Hamlet
could have expedited his vengeance with a .44 Magnum than he managed
to do with all his brooding. "I have seen the day, with my good biting
falchion / I would have made them skip," claims Lear, who with a semi-
automatic weapon at the ready might have regained both his virility and
his throne.

Weaponry is so directed, so purposeful, in a way that poems, with
their vague aims and circumlocutions, never are or pretend to be. In *The
Shootist*, John Wayne, in the role of aged gunman John Bernard Books,
spells out the secret of his longevity: "I've found most people aren't willing. They bat an eye. They hesitate. I won't." Pausing and flinching, edg-
ing and inching—the Duke's disdained "other guy" sounds like everybody

I went to graduate school with. It also applies to the nature of the novels and poems we focused on. Surely there is no chance that my reference to Wallace Stevens a couple of sentences ago would have resonated with even one of the absolutely resolute characters John Wayne ever played.

However, even the so-called elevated literature I have always preferred, where most of the action is grammatical and takes place between the ears and whose movie versions would never tempt a Schwarzenegger or Stallone to sign on to the project, occasionally attests to the appeal of automatic weapons. In particular I think of a moment in Don DeLillo's novel *White Noise* when, at his father-in-law's insistence, a previously pretty feckless professor accepts the gift of a 25-caliber Zumwalt. As a result, he enjoys a visceral impact—a power surge—that no successful class or convention paper could conceivably match. "There was something unreal about the experience of holding a gun," he thinks, the paradox being that he confronts the life force more immediately than ever before by handling a deadly weapon. In contrast to the ambient static, in which meanings are illegible and sensations fleeting, the gun seems to root him to something solid and nonnegotiable. "How quickly it worked a change in me, numbing my hand even as I sat staring at the thing, not wishing to give it a name." That is the gun's secret genius; it travels through the hand, imparting consequence. Evidently there is something estimable about a gun, something inherently transitive in a way that no instrument teachers ever wield can be. It is an instrument of clarity that has nothing in common with the ambiguous means and materials a literature professor employs. Something there is about a gun, that wants it discharged. With this in mind, I decided to sneak out of the nook of liberal naivete, out of my cranny of tenured pacifism, and find out for myself.

As gun shops go, Brandon's Gun Trading Company is comparatively upscale. It appears to cater more to the weapons aficionado and the gun connoisseur than to thrill-seeking teens or vengeful relatives (not that the latter would be easily discerned or denied admittance). There are glossy magazines detailing the latest in high-performance firearms and featuring advice columns with titles like "Views from the Bunker," "The Shooting Gallery," or "Setting My Sights," in which readers endorse or dispute recent refinements made on their favorite guns. There are price guides and brochures, thicker and more explicit than anything you'd find at a car dealership. (I flipped through the *Ruger Catalogue of Fine Firearms,* whose lavish descriptions and close-up photography of this year's auto-loading rifles, rimfire pistols, and double-action revolvers recalled the quality and content of architectural digests, science journals, and top-shelf porn.) There are displays of cunning mounts and plush holsters for the discriminating shooter. There are a dozen or so gun cabinets, some of them polished steel, some hand-carved oak, richly inlaid, their glass fronts frosted and etched with wilderness scenery. There are long counters featuring intricate new ammunition, all "quality-cast," whose subtle advances you'd need a jeweler's loupe to do justice to. Brandon's is like a gun boutique, really, including lighter, especially fetching pieces for the ladies, as well as starter pistols for the kids. Racks of rifles to riffle through like designer dresses. Every stock gleaming in the fluorescent light. Every barrel oiled bright.

Nevertheless I couldn't help feeling intimidated by the artillery, as if I'd strayed into enemy territory and was unable to affect the foreign accent convincingly enough to pass, here where a wood-burned sign advised ALL VISITORS ENTER AT OWN RISK. I moved self-consciously among the Magnums, Lugers, and Glocks, muttering the guns' guttural names, thuggish things for all their precisely machined reputations, words loaded with grunts. Although I had no plans to fire a weapon that day, I found myself involuntarily bracing for recoil. At the register, the owner (Brandon himself, I presumed) carried on a chummy conversation with a couple of regulars (another presumption) about rumored changes in local permit laws and whether the stopping power of the slimmed-down Glock 36, which one of them was looking at for Father's Day, holds up. A spread of black ammo clips, designed to tantalize, spooked me; they made me think of the joints of some prehistoric predator. Tactical scopes and speed loaders positively seethed with danger. Bullets glinted wickedly on beds of felt.

I bumped into a stand of riot guns, alerting Brandon. Nothing discharged, which was a pleasant, if unreasonable, relief.

"Expecting trouble?" I said. My humor tends to grow more pointless and obscure the more nervous I become. Maybe a Glock would settle me down.

Brandon—"The Friendly Expert," as advertised—waved me over. It was stifling in there—no open window or air-conditioning, not even a fan to stir the air—and his golf shirt was black beneath the pits, where twin Ohios of sweat had already formed before noon. Next to the register was propped a photograph of the Brandon women, his wife and three daughters, smiling intensely and looking milk fed and secure, posed in crinoline and Christian commitment to one another's welfare. At least, that was the effect. It was easy to envision the Brandon clan sitting around the living room together swabbing out the family arsenal the way other families play Monopoly. The wall behind Brandon was plastered with photocopies of truculent antiliberal editorials from the *Globe,* at least one of which I could see he'd authored. Also patriotic cartoons and bumper stickers with sayings like SELF-CONTROL, NOT GUN CONTROL and THE SECOND AMENDMENT IS PART OF *MY* CONSTITUTION. Taped above the rest was a caricature of Hitler giving a Nazi salute, with the caption "All in favor of gun control, raise your right hand."

Brandon reserved his biggest grin for my concern that gun ownership might actually jeopardize personal safety instead of help to secure it.

"You teach out at Southern, don't you?" A tip to urbanites used to the impunity afforded by metropolitan living: apart from decent deli food and jazz, the hardest commodity to come by in the hinterlands is anonymity.

"Right. English."

"English. Uh-huh. I thought I recognized you. So, listen, do you have a wife? Kids?"

"I have a girlfriend. I have a daughter."

"So we're talking loved ones, right? Well, the next time you're out of town and someone decides to break into the house, you tell your girlfriend how much safer she should feel without the means to protect herself. Or when some pervert stalks your daughter on her way home from band practice, you tell her not to worry because Dad *doesn't* have the means to deal with it if the situation escalates."

"Obviously," I answer, risking a defense of my impractical lifestyle, "if you come home to find someone about to kill your family, emotion is going to take over. You're talking burglars and perverts, and in those cases, sure, whose first reaction *wouldn't* be to shoot? But I don't know that I want to establish policies based on that kind of extreme possibility. I don't know that I want to *live* that way, anticipating the worst. I just don't think that my case warrants owning a gun, is all."

"Uh-huh. Tell me something, Professor, do they get the newspaper in your part of town? Do we live in the same world, or what?"

This wasn't the first time by any means that someone had questioned my sense of reality and found it oblique at best. You spend twenty or thirty uninterrupted years in the classroom, you live your life in bookish isolation from the repercussive and the tangible, and condescension just goes with the territory. However I did take Brandon's meaning: if I truly wished to understand anything about guns, I would have to take my education beyond the hypothetical realm where I typically hid out.

Wyandotte, Oklahoma, is so nondescript that the odds are I'd have missed it without the help of the printout I'd made off of MapQuest. It's just one exit off of Highway 60, and taking the bend too fast after Seneca, I had to double back. So far as I know, Wyandotte's single claim to fame, even among the locals, is that it is the home of the Firing Line. Reportedly, marksmen come from miles around to compete in the regional tournaments the Firing Line sponsors, and indeed, I wonder if gunnery is the only reason to go to Wyandotte at all. I came on a Tuesday afternoon, when I hoped it would be relatively cleared out and quiet, figuring that there was no need to embarrass myself in front of more people than I could avoid doing.

The Firing Line looked like a converted warehouse—barely converted, at that. Most impressive was the sheer square footage of the place: a combination sales area, instructional center, and firing range, it stretched further back than the average bowling alley. I was also struck by how gloomy it was—not the drear of Poe or the precipitant dark of film noir so much as the greasy gray of an auto body shop. As opposed to Brandon's emporium, the Firing Line suggested the grimier end of the gun enterprise. The effect there was sparer and less wholesome and, with the exception of motivational paper targets sporting pictures of Osama bin Laden, Saddam Hussein, and Mu'ammar Gadhafi, less given to winsomeness. If Brandon's was designed to put the customer at ease, the Firing Line was designed to put him on guard. In this context even the warning sign on the soda machine telling the buyer to be careful when opening cans struck me as ominous.

The proprietor was chatting at the far end of the sales area with a couple of regulars. I started toward them, moving warily past bins of bullets and rifle arrays. I did not interrupt the men but waited quietly until there was a break in the conversation. This wasn't reverence on my part but tentativeness. Apart from scripted glibness on TV, I was a stranger to the proper argot and behavior of people who frequented places like the Firing Line, and I did not want to be obvious about it. There was no advantage in pretending to knowledge I didn't have, and I was worried about profaning the place the way American tourists, loaded down with flash cameras and their own cultural baggage, are wont to do in European cathedrals.

"What can I do for you today?"

"I've never fired a gun. I'd like to. Can you help me out?"

By the reaction of all three men, I could see that I had immediately shown myself to be one of a category of patrons, small but predictable, whom they'd sized up as fantasy campers. Some guys with enough disposable income reacted to their midlife crises by purchasing a workout with the Los Angeles Dodgers; others went skydiving. My bent was cops and robbers. Having no particular explanation for my interest, I let them assume. Frankly I couldn't have explained the day to my friends either. Years ago my divorce stunned many of them, yet I guarantee you that nothing extramarital I'd done would have struck them as being more out of character for me than my pilgrimage to Wyandotte to open fire.

For the next twenty minutes, while his pals drifted off to inspect some of the more advanced ordnance, Phil, the fellow in charge, instructed me on the capacities and perils of several different handguns. For my maiden shoot, we settled on a .22 and a twenty-five-dollar price for his time and a box of one hundred and twenty rounds.

A couple and their eleven-year-old son came in to buy, so Phil excused himself to run down the criteria they should consider. "Whether you're purchasing something for home defense or a carry gun," he began, "you want something that you're not gonna be more afraid of than the guy you're pointing it at, am I right? I tell all my customers, too, that if it's a gun you're gonna depend on to save your life, spend some money. The better weapons aren't cheap—the ones that guarantee that the guy you hit won't just get mad or suffer. The function of a gun is to protect your loved ones, isn't it? And when you're out of the house, Dad, they're gonna want something they can handle. I mean your boy, too. And whatever you end up getting, get familiar with your gun. I'd say once a week go out and empty a cylinder. Put a mag through it occasionally to keep it and you in tune. So look a few of these over, and I'll be right back with you."

While eavesdropping, I was practicing my lessons on preparing and dismantling my weapon. And how to be sure the safety's on, how to be sure the chamber's empty, how to rest your finger outside the trigger assembly before you're ready to fire, how to rest the gun on the counter after discharging it: I said these precautions under my breath as I did them, much as one murmured during a seder service. On the counter before me was the translucent box of ten dozen bullets, noses up. Expectant, it seemed to me.

"Ready to do some shooting?" Phil asked me. He gave me glasses and headphones. "The safety glasses are up to you, but you'll need the muffs, believe me." Unquestionably, I thought as we passed through the two sets of double doors to the firing range, I was moving into a new climate. It made sense that he had me dress for it.

He set me up at my booth and, flipping a toggle switch at my left, brought a backboard abruptly toward us on its pulley. He stapled a large paper sheet to it, then sent it back to a distance of about twenty-five feet. Once more he reviewed the process, making me copy each action to ensure that I was using the right fingers to accomplish it. Pianists begin like this, I thought. Surgeons, too.

"The middle finger presses the cartridge release, remember. The ammo box has a slide top, so you can spill out exactly ten bullets at a time into your right palm, and that's the hand that fills the magazine. Pinch the spring with your left index finger and thumb as you hold the magazine against the table, then force it down. Slot the bullets in back first, one at a time, like that, right hand, right. Once that's done, smack it back in the handle. Go ahead, harder, it can't go off, there's nothing to fire yet and no way for it to fire." And so on, methodically, trying to deliver the rhythm into my hands. "After half a box or so, you should have already developed some muscle memory. Eventually it'll all seem natural."

Lastly he closed his hands over mine and showed me how to place my left hand beneath my right to steady it. Even without firing I sensed a shudder: potential energy, perhaps, or the gun's own pulse.

"That way, when the gun jumps, it jumps up, not to the side. You know how they say, 'Don't jump the gun'? Well, in this case, the gun does the jumping. That's how you can remember it. All right? Keep the gun far from your body. Arms locked and out. The straighter you stand, the straighter you'll shoot. Safety off? Okay, whenever you're ready."

The gun barked and snapped in my hands, and it was as if both of us, gun and gunman, were startled by the eruption. I felt less like a soldier or a secret agent than like someone who'd accidentally stepped on a dog's tail.

"The faster you fire—pop, pop, pop—the tighter your spread will be," he called, having to penetrate the headphones. "Go ahead, squeeze 'em off."

And so I did. When Phil was satisfied that I wasn't going to kill anyone or ruin his insurance, he left me for the other customers, the family of three, who had ventured in with the .38 they'd selected. As he had them take turns practicing filling its cylinders—round rounds into round holes, a psychological test for toddlers—I blasted away, adding spent shells ten at a time to the huge pool of them like a crowded koi pond below me. Sometimes the shells bounced toward my cheek or trickled over and nibbled at my arms, but as I grew easier with the procedure (if not more expert), I was able to ignore them and the odor of burning that increased with each clip I emptied. And I could tell that I was starting to corral my scatter, shotwise, into a reasonable facsimile of aiming. I was, in the broadest sense of the term, homing in. But I never surrendered to adrenaline, at least not to the extent that I stopped repeating the stations of the gun as I performed them. I made sure I heard that last whispered click denoting a finished clip before relaxing my stance. I looked each time to make sure I'd covered the red patch with the safety before putting my weapon down, barrel pointed away.

Phil slipped in between fusillades. "I've been watching you. You've been tightening your radius all right. Let's have a look." He flipped the switch, and the target squealed close. "There. See? Here's where you were earlier," he said, indicating six or seven holes, "and here's the last couple of groupings. See your improvement?" He traced a more compact constellation. "Folks talk about 'gun control'? This is what 'gun control' *really* means. This is the control that *counts* for something. It'll come with practice. You get a discount for ten visits, you know."

Once I exhausted my allotted shots, I toggled the target over to detach it from the board. Only then did I realize that Phil had stapled it on backwards. The concealed front featured a human silhouette—clearly a broad-shouldered male and, despite its lack of features, rather menacing. Concentric rings rippled outward from the center of his chest. To my credit, I suppose, and certainly to my surprise, most of my shots had scored; a few had even struck the X'd heart.

I did not ask Phil why he'd reversed the target for me. Possibly it was common practice. Perhaps the contemporary atmosphere of political correctness was so pervasive as to have seeped even into Wyandotte's principal establishment, despite the fact that people were not perfecting their plots against other people but only shooting at paper. Or maybe Phil had marked me as a vacationing liberal who'd have been inhibited by the sight of a human figure and winced while firing, leading to more collateral than concentrated damage, plus an unimpressive point total. After all, the Firing Line wanted to give even novices like me the incentive to return.

Whatever the logic, I had the perforated figure of an imaginary intruder to take home as a reminder of what I was capable of, and woe to those who'd underestimate me. The sheet looked like an oversized roll for a player piano, and I considered tacking it to my front door: it would filter the breeze, filling the neighborhood with a song of my prowess and my expanded personality.

Undressing for bed, I wondered what the reaction of my beloved was going to be to this unprecedented aspect of me. Confusion? Amusement? Arousal? If I'm increasingly complex, she is equally so, so it was going to be difficult to predict. It was when I took off my shirt that I found a second souvenir: a shell casing, which must have leapt into my pocket in the midst of one of my barrages. I decided against offering it to her as something to remember me by. My thinking was that since it wasn't representative of the man she knew, it was unlikely that she *could* remember me by it. On the other hand, throwing it away was out of the question.

I ended up setting it on a bookshelf, in front of the Hemingway. For the time being, anyway, it seemed like a decent compromise.

Turns for the Worse

It is distressing to realize that a field has already grown up around the rubble of the World Trade Center. Experts say that our post-9/11 anxieties are only the most obvious symptom of a siege mentality that in recent years has locked down upon America like . . . well, like the nuclear winter we number among our fears. The millennial frets of the 1990s have not subsided so much as re-emerged in other areas and other editorials. The media imply that life is one awful slide straight down catastrophe's oily chute, and if it were to turn, it would only turn for the worse. Leaching toxins and global warming, viral outbreaks and bombs unaccounted for: the news should come with its own product warning, preferably with its own antidote.

In short, we are not safe. Exercise, financial portfolios, and tenure guarantee nothing. Even the venerable are vulnerable; even CEOs shiver in the wind. Check the skies for signs: our future is being concocted in all of the multisyllabic contaminants in our atmosphere, while the wheeling buzzards know something the rest of us just haven't figured out yet. We walk a narrow path between chasms, nagged by the possibility that it's fate's third rail we're treading. The consensus is that at our best we are all of us barely functional, and that only for the time being.

Thus the extraordinary success of *The Worst Case Scenario Handbook*. This is the inaugural volume in a series—yes, one book is insufficient to cover the spectrum of crises we might encounter nowadays—designed to simultaneously allay and validate our paranoia. (It was one of the ten most popular books of the Christmas season a couple of years ago. Give the gift of anxiety to the ones you love.) Feeling disturbed, vulnerable, or otherwise at bay, the reader can turn to these guides and discover how to survive a plummet in an elevator or a runaway train; he can learn how to escape from quicksand, a car sinking in water, or being tied up; he can master techniques for treating a bullet wound, landing a plane when the pilot has blacked out, or preserving a severed limb for future reattachment. Are you lost in the desert, buried under an avalanche, or locked by mobsters inside the trunk of your car? *Worst Case* has you covered. Or perhaps the animal kingdom has it in for you. Do alligators slaver and leeches convene to plot against you? Are you facing assaults by piranhas, scorpions, or venomous spiders? Never fear: each of these eventualities is indexed. Do you need to fend off the attack of a shark, the charge of a bull, or the inscrutable revenge of angry bees? Just consult chapter 6 in advance of the brunt or bite.

And should disaster move faster than you can digest under pressure the appropriate preventive method, *Worst Case* contains a multilingual collection of handy phrases: Please do not hurt me. Please call the police. Please take me to a clean hospital.

Frankly I don't know whether to feel fortified (I can handle even the most exotic calamity that might arise!) or frightened (even the most exotic calamity might arise!) by the step-by-step delineation of deterrence and dread. In all, there are over one hundred dangers that these books qualify us to manage or adapt to, over a hundred injuries, perils, and traps against which to grit our teeth and gird our loins. But while it is gratifying to know how to survive a gas fire or how to stave off rabid animals, it is unsettling to learn just how many people think they'll *need* to. Despite the smooth if-then assurances, my concern is that *Worst Case* will not stop our nightmares but broaden their range.

Moreover, in my case *Worst Case* is the least of my worries, for the scenarios that threaten, unman, or overwhelm me are mounted well beneath the series's radar. At present, anyway, my predicaments are too quotidian and my disasters too mundane to be cited in its pages. The trouble is that the wrong sort of trouble troubles me, or so these handbooks lead me to suppose. I can count on my fingers the number of times anyone I know has had to handle an undetonated grenade. That all of us have our original complement of fingers to do the counting on shows just how distant from detonations we live. Browsing these survival guides, I am relieved and, I must confess, a little ashamed to admit how uninspired my crises are. Yes, I now know how to cover my trail after a prison break by splashing my way through a creek that cannot carry my scent back to the dogs, assuming I'm ever imprisoned and break out and do so where a creek happens to be running. But I can't escape committee meetings or outstrip officious relatives or elude the jaws of the IRS. I can composedly contend with poisons and handle stabbings with aplomb, but cholesterol is an infestation that I cannot seem to stanch, and my pipes keep leaking at the joints. I have learned how to apply tourniquets to prevent people from bleeding out, but my own blood tests result in anomalous numbers that, however I alter my intakes and conduct, I cannot consistently keep inside the recommended guidelines.

I catch a whiff of gas in the kitchen. Secretly, savagely, the APR on my monthly Visa bill is climbing. Insistent and pained, my students surround me, crowd before my office, or lurk down the hall, readying the inquisition; meanwhile the dean is about to ambush me with a smile full of teeth. Unexceptional crises, absolutely, but they are *my* crises and, although they'll never make the papers, crises nevertheless.

For it is the milder, middle-class infarctions that beleaguer me and that are likelier than bullets or grizzly bears to bring me down. Most mornings the odds are that it will be a pothole instead of a stampede that thwarts me; if I miss an appointment, it's safer to assume that my carburetor fouled than that my parachute didn't open. There hasn't been a hostage taking in my neighborhood within memory, and for terrorist activity, the Friday night cruising of local teens will have to do. But there is still the dark at the top of the stairs and the dull and dulling routines at the bottom, looming, which might find me out if not completely do me in. The flesh is heir to a thousand shocks survival handbooks don't address. Any college-level course in tragedy, in fact, warrants an edition of *Worst Case Scenarios* all its own.

Remember the day outside of Wrigley Field when someone from the vague, voluble, shambling subclass targeted you as being well intentioned or a soft touch? His eyes swam with indictment and clumsy benediction at once. A hole opened up in your heart. Given the few tools at your disposal and your own tendency to fumble about anyway, how do you repair it? The world is rife with people rummaging through various funks and dumpsters. Not to mention tetanus in the alley, perverts in the park. There but for the grace of God (and perhaps only temporarily) go you. And, God forbid, your children risk the same streets you do. Are you prepared for whatever comeuppance, newsworthy or not, the next morning might come up with? As for the moment your little girl, her face already churning because of the death of the family pet, asks if you, too, are going to die, I haven't seen a manual yet that takes this scenario on. You'd expect to find guidance in the same chapter that explains how to break the news about hurricanes, the Holocaust, and a God inconsistent in everything but inscrutability, but that chapter has yet to be written.

The first step is to stay calm, I'd guess. It usually is. Of course, "stay calm" begs the question of one's level-headedness in the first place. I'm afraid that my own resting heart rate renders "resting heart rate," like "Social Security," a contradiction in terms. I suspect that CNN-addicts, conspiracy theorists, hypochondriacs, and those whose purchases of the *Worst Case Scenario* series made it a best seller also idle high. I don't deny that there are those whom no neurosis ever bothers, who rise each day like fresh bread for the sun to butter, then bask in the dapple of uninterruptible summer, but I haven't met them. Certainly there are not enough of them to make books about *best*-case scenarios sell as well as the volumes in the pessimistic series do.

If calm is beyond you, an alternative tactic could be to simply stay low. Be as typical as possible, and no extreme will root you out. Keep to the tall grass of the ordinary. Do not settle for putting emergency phone numbers on speed dial, memorizing the map of your floor in case of a hotel fire, and ensuring that you are always seated nearest the exit door of the restaurant. Never settle at all. Instead, cultivate statistical norms the way some people cultivate roses; strive to maintain the sort of résumé that no one thumbing the yearbook would ever light upon. Practice a few simple defenses against the sensational—don't slow for accidents, avoid enterprises that require immunization, stay out of the big pots—and rest assured that the authors of *Worst Case* will discover nothing about you to require a new edition.

Not that I've had to make any such conscious effort. Maybe my real grievance against the *Worst Case* books stems from the fact that they render my own grievances mediocre or moot. When Microsoft Word automatically judges my every linguistic ingenuity to be an error, I rail shamelessly at the cold and glaring screen; however, in light of what goes on in Africa, the abuse my sentences get hardly deserves a hearing. Each day's mail contains a plea from another worthy charity, and the effect is to disqualify the nature and size of anything I might have to overcome. What arrogance to believe my bills are a bother! What crust it takes to complain about my meager upsets when entire populations aren't eating! Leave fear and trembling to the profoundly impoverished and the war torn. With no earthquake within hundreds of miles, with no tiger within thousands, how dare I despair, I with my minor gripes and cheap whines, who mourns his scars that never, by any honest comparison, felt a wound.

Actually the worst-case scenario for most of the folks who buy, and buy into, *Worst Case Scenario* could be that the book encourages arrogance. Bravado is a greater danger than bad dreams. Armed with his handbook, a given reader might be convinced that daring, not discretion, is the better part of valor and seek out means of demonstrating his newly acquired mettle. "Where's the fire?" he might cry, in order to run toward it. To get my money's worth out of the chapter on how to perform an emergency tracheotomy, I need to try one.

But when it comes to promoting this level of confidence, no one outdoes our own government, which tells us to stockpile canned goods, duct tape, plastic sheeting, and gold to insulate ourselves from terrorist attacks. By being on the alert for the way strangers wear their clothes and betray their heritages, for how they pay for their plane tickets and carry their briefcases, we can, within reason, ensure our safety. With enough shovels, we're told, we can dig in against nuclear blasts—"limited nuclear war" is an especially lovely governmental construction—and dig our way out again, intact.

Be consoled: dependable methods for dealing with worst-case scenarios are available in paperback. Be wary: based on the proliferation of cautionary tales and consumer guides on worst-case scenarios, there is no longer any other kind.

Solve for X

I'm the sort of person who stops talking when the elevator gets under way. By way of showing respect to the physics we're privy to, I close my book during take-off. About a hundred inscrutable laws are at stake here, surrounding and sustaining my progress—a progress, mind you, I needn't understand to depend upon—and so out of reverence for the gravity of the activity and the gravity it defies, I go silent. Hoping that the counter-intuitive Bernoulli effect *remains* in effect to refute my intuition of doom, not to mention the dooms of my fellow passengers—though they may ostensibly be otherwise engaged, they surf the very same phenomena as I—I grip the arm rest a bit tighter than someone familiar with the sta-tistics showing that flying is far safer than driving across town in your Volvo ordinarily would.

That all of us and everything that's ever been swim incessantly in an ocean of physics has long been a source of anxiety for me. I own more than a half dozen books on the subject, all primers. (Like manuals for Latin, auto repair, computer programming, and postmodernism, books on physics are inevitably introductory and, for my money, still pitched too high.) They have titles like *Fear of Physics, A Beginner's Book of Since the Beginning, Physics for Poets, After the Big Bang: A First Book of the First Seconds and After, Of Black Holes and Other Dark Matters,* and *The Universe Shut Up in a Nutshell* (for I, too, am a beast that wants discourse of reason). These consoling, playful, punning titles are designed to coax the freaked, the shuddering, and the mind-fucked out of hiding. When the obsession gets the better of me, I'll open one to see how long I can sustain some semblance of coherence before I blear. I'm seldom more than ten minutes out of port before the fog sets in, but I've never gotten rid of any of these books; moreover, when the next layman's bible arrives at the local library, you'll find my name on the reserve list.

Perhaps it was my geometry teacher, Mr. Dvorak, who first encouraged this attitude. Something in the way he'd walk his oversized wooden compass across the blackboard like a stiff-legged crane patrolling a parabolic swamp suggested that there were hidden intricacies and pitfalls lurking in any surface one might traverse, any of which might be on the next test. Evidently, or at least evident to one so geometrically inclined as Mr. Dvorak, the very air was as subtly flounced and plaited as Debbie Seidman's hair—and just as captivating, begging measurement. To hear him tell it, we inhabit a universal terrain of graph paper misted with digits and covered with cross-hatched hills and plotted pastures, whose hypothetical points exceeded what in a billion lifetimes a billion Seurats could ever freckle their canvases with. As the astrophysicist Lawrence M. Krauss puts it, "The fate of the universe has become a matter of bookkeeping." Space is a spreadsheet scribbled with equations that buoy our boats and planes, wrap neatly about our windshields, and canopy our sleep. I find it astonishing how insistent an architecture the initiated can abstract from what looks like vacancy, much the way magicians pluck animals from empty hats. We are gulping functions wherever we go. Wouldn't you expect our breath to catch at least occasionally on the countless binomials we're breathing unseen?

Not that I'm anything close to the ideal one to run the numbers, what with my being more or less innumerate myself. With apologies to the battery of high school math teachers who passed me hurriedly up the line like a leaky bucket, not only do I not recall whether our distance from the moon is in the thousands or millions of miles—put me at the wheel of the bus, and I might miss our stop by several planets—but my estimate of the damage done by a representative hurricane may easily be off by a factor of ten. Whether the national debt has climbed into the billions or the trillions of dollars is immaterial to me, seeing as I'm equally unable to afford a four-star hotel either way. I realize that it's only a movie, but I might be convinced that *The Matrix* has it right: the savior of the race is the fellow who manages to penetrate the number-glutted atmosphere and sees how everything and all of us are commonly denominated by a steady, luminous rain of miniature integers.

The universe is a book "written in the language of mathematics," said Galileo, a founding exponent of the exponential and a man better able than most to get his hands on a clean first edition. "Its characters are triangles, circles, and other geometric figures without which it is humanly impossible to understand a single word of it; without these, one wanders about in a dark labyrinth." *With* these, I'd say, one wanders about in the same labyrinth, with only slightly better light to show where the walls are. He may be crazy with jungle fever, but I find reason in the raving of Colonel Kurtz's manic acolyte, the photojournalist played by Dennis Hopper in *Apocalypse Now:* "It's very simple dialectics. One through nine, no maybes, no supposes, no fractions—you can't travel in space, you can't go out into space, you know, without, like, you know, with fractions— what are you going to land on, one quarter, three-eighths?" In his book *Everything and More,* David Foster Wallace quotes G. K. Chesterton's conviction that "poets do not go mad; but chess players do. Mathematicians go mad, and cashiers; but creative artists very seldom." There may be small consolation for the literary among us in that formulation if we surmise that poets do not *go* mad because by choosing that career they've proved that they have already made the trip, troping where others dare not transgress. (Craziness is a crowded neighborhood in any modern literature syllabus.) My sense, however, is that if mathematicians are threatened mentally by their abstract obsessions, how much more vulnerable to insanity are those of us who are thrust into that rarefied atmosphere minus the apparatus and the training necessary to survive at all. In a discipline whose variables swamp constants and in which both are outnumbered by unknowns, I'm at a loss no matter what the balance sheet may show. Galileo's resolution notwithstanding, if God means for us to forego what Robert Frost disdainfully refers to as the "oh's and ah's" of "sunset raving" and to depend instead on calculation to appreciate what's here and hereafter, I will undoubtedly have to trust the expertise of others, signing blindly off on their findings just as I do the tax forms I pay an accountant to handle for me.

Meanwhile, in my mind Mr. Dvorak stalks an eternal blackboard in mostly private consultation, chalk dust gusting all about him as he paces before the problem he's laid out. Beneath his insouciant feet unimaginable microbes are massacred, their execution anonymous as their scant metabolism had been only seconds before. Light-years distant, photons are mounting perpetual insurrection against an autocracy of black. "Can anyone come to the board and solve this for us?" he asks. A single hand goes up: it belongs to the Chosen One, the messiah of middle school, who has tapped into something far more marvelous than the major league standings and whispers of secret recess liaisons the baffled rest of us settle for.

I once awoke in my own damp from a dream about the infiltration of English by numbers, which relentlessly led to a full-scale takeover. Conversations conventionally composed of words began to give way to numbers, until there was nothing in the unmattered world but math. "Can I see you later?" "I have to tell you something first." "You have to 49312?" "Don't 2226 unless you 93198." "291714483?" "5!" Dismissing it as a nightmare may have gotten me back to sleep, but that explanation couldn't account for the terror. Even now I'll feel a shiver go through me when I produce a typo that embeds a number inside a word; it stops me the way the flash of a piece of glass would were it lodged in an apple I was about to bite. A list of Social Security numbers on my class rosters may seem to me as invidious in its organization as any right-wing rally. Collecting ISBN numbers for next semester's book orders makes me imagine a rising white blood cell count, and I need to lie down. Give me a cold compress and a dose of alphabet, and I should pull through.

In face of the hard sciences—a tautology if ever there was one—nonchalance has never seemed to me to be a pinnacle of human achievement anyway. It strikes me rather as an enervation and a leveling off. Virginia Woolf's Mr. Ramsay, who sums up his scholarship as the study of subject, object, and the nature of reality with the matter-of-fact assurance of a man recounting the components of his breakfast, depicts his accomplishment as a scrubbed kitchen table, as if darkness could be as readily swept away as crumbs of toast. But I think it arrogant to assume that ambiguities will succumb to our aptitudes, to believe so unassailably that the scrubbed tables won't turn. Science and human existence itself share the same purpose, writes Richard Powers in *The Gold Bug Variations:* "not efficiency or mastery, but the revival of appropriate surprise." What sort of breakthrough is blasé, anyway? It's like bursting in on your wife while she's folding laundry on the bed instead of fondling her lover there or discovering oatmeal that's gone cold in the bowl. "Fuck you. Show some amazement!" someone chastises his complacent companion in Don DeLillo's *Underworld.* And while I may not rhapsodize every second about the science of the surroundings we're all indentured to, in my vague layman's way, I am surprised, I am amazed.

Even as a child I knew enough of how pitiful a hold I had on the oblique conditions that held me not to take the science I inhabited for granted. Nor did I have to grab after the biggest questions to feel the strain. Where are we going? How did we get where we're going from? Are we part of a planned excursion or a long con, and who's the agent we signed on with in either case? The ball I casually tossed as I sat in the front of the Number Nine bus on my way home from baseball practice fell back in my glove instead of landing in a back seat somewhere behind me, and it didn't take all that much Newton and Einstein to recognize that the two of them were riding implicitly beside me. (So as not to disrupt their subtle company, I kept quiet.) On my first visit to the top of the Empire State Building, where we were positively whipped by the physics we stood naked before, I saw men casually smoking at the reinforced railing. Women were driven hysterical, but it was only their inability to keep their skirts down against the updrafts that drove them so. Even other kids seemed to take the altitude in stride, darting about the exposed hundredth floor as heedlessly as they charged after grounders at ground level, as all the while the planet spun the entire team at about a thousand miles per hour. But as my own dad directed my attention to the swath of city we'd surmounted, his manner confident and proprietary as any urbanite who hurtled dozens of stories up elevator shafts as a matter of course, all I could think of was how unlikely it was that so tall a building still stood intact and, then, that it continued to stand under all of us, smokers and windswept women and heretical kids, now. Still, I said nothing—it would have been hard to hear me up there, anyway, where even screams got swallowed, and by the time we'd recovered the street the sensation had sufficiently dissipated to allow me to focus on the next problem, which was where in a city of seemingly infinite restaurants to opt among should we have our lunch.

Many grades later I would learn that a skyscraper, although it might seem to be a still point in the turning world, is actually built to bend in the wind. Neither tourist nor tenant detects it, but the Sears Tower perpetually shimmies a few inches east and west, redistributing its weight like a tackler preparing for a blow; so, too, does the Hancock subtly shift its bulk, belly dancing high above millions of unwitting Chicagoans every day. Unwitting, I say, unless they're just pretending not to notice, as if saying nothing about it were as much a part of the rules as the rules of physics themselves. Certainly I don't buck the system by mentioning the obvious miracle looming over every single block of the Loop: that we are heading to work beneath the wobble of unimaginable tonnage that somehow never topples down upon us to render all of our appointments moot.

I realize that the woman who kneels before the refrigerator's vegetable crisper is not there to worship the miracle of convection currents, nor should she waste the energy that way. If you come upon a loved one crying in the dark, it is reasonable to assume that it's not the impending heat death of the universe but some more proximate loss that's laid her out. At the faculty party, where everyone is scratching tone quotes throughout the room like so many chickens trying to free seeds from soil, you can bet that nine times out of ten its not a debate over who mans the macrocosm but something sublunary that's got them gossiping. When your child dashes down the hall to find your bedroom in the middle of the night, the chances are pretty good that the monsters populating his nightmare originated with that third slice of pizza rather than from any catastrophe hatched out of atoms. And yet I sometimes think that it takes an unspoken critical mass of faith to keep all of those currents going, planes aloft, and structures up. I suspect that if enough of us on the New York to Boston shuttle suddenly and all at once shut off our laptops, loosened our grip for a minute on our Grishams, and wondered aloud how it's possible that something that weighs as much as all of us, much less the plane itself, could be riding on air, we'd plummet like the totemically stupefied Wile E. Coyote clutching his useless "Yikes!" sign. Perhaps we are sustained by an unspoken consensus of disregard—we are too distracted or inured to question the buoyancy of roughly forty thousand compacted pounds of passengers, who, with so little pleasure apparent in business class, nevertheless assume they're headed for a happy landing. By this reasoning, it is not understanding but unconsciousness that saves us. Such is the oblivion of business class; such is the nimbus surrounding every other preoccupied passenger on the Number Nine bus.

I come to wonder whether every faith operates that way. By which I mean, doesn't faith require a certain absence of certainty? I don't need faith to tell me that my car keys are in my pocket because I can feel them digging into my thigh and with one finger can hook the proof. As to whether the car they start still waits for me where I parked it, however, that I cannot confirm from where I'm standing and have to take on faith. Paradoxically the desire for belief proves only that it's missing. Most of what we know of quarks and positrons and the putative Supreme Being who manufactured them comes from the holes they leave behind. And not knowing for sure that my Honda is where I parked it secures my faith but not my ride.

I wonder just how many empirically challenged worshipers it takes to suspend a heaven, anyway. Consider the sects that contend that instead of each of us having individual ownership of a soul, we are all unconsciously tapped into an invisible aggregate. I confess that my own tendency when I try to conceive of a soul is to think in terms of an essence that's unique and uniquely mine. I do have trouble believing that it resides anywhere inside me, tucked behind some curtain of nerve endings or inside an unobtrusive gland; I sense that the soul can't be contained inside the body just as no significant conversation can be held effectively inside a Chuck E. Cheese restaurant. At the same time, I do lean in the direction of its being some form of personal property, as if this soul were the kite one holds onto gamely against the onslaught of existential wind. But what if the soul were really a global sympathy, an indivisible noumenal network in whose process we all participate like ants submitting their instincts to the colonial whole? Maybe there is no such thing as a solitary spirit, and all esprit is de facto de corps.

This may help to explain why the belief seems to have grown more and more interdisciplinary these days. Slick-handed Elysian fielders might be scouted from any end of the university campus; the newest leak springs from deity, and representatives from the arts and sciences alike are compelled to come stick their thumbs in the dike. Creation is that supernal curriculum where absolutely everything is required. "Why wouldn't the glory of God shine through to the human mind?" asks an Episcopal priest on the eve of his excommunication in E. L. Doctorow's *City of God.* "I look for parity here. I will not claim that your access to the numinous is a delusion if you will not tell me my intellect is irrelevant." Although it may too late to secure for Doctorow's Father Pemberton either a religious post or a scholarship to MIT, it is possible to envision a fruitful collusion, which may lead to a reliably investigative poetry or, conversely, to a scientific sublime. As Doctorow asserts in "The Politics of God," "Eventually even the most fanatic keepers of the faith might have to consider why all human knowledge since scripture is not also God's revelation." After all, captivation may be the most ecumenical quality of our nature. John D. Barrow puts it this way in *The Artful Universe:* "The arts and the sciences flow from a single source; they are informed by the same reality; and their insights are linked in ways that make them look less and less like alternatives." Especially as we set our sights on the greater and greater distances, everything that rises must converge.

Our reflex might be to relegate spiritual exploits to the opposite end of the quad, but recent surveys reveal that approximately as many scientists today believe in God as don't. In this regard the statistics for scientists don't differ very much at all from those taken from any other randomly selected neighborhood. This may indicate that science is just as unwilling to accommodate the notion that we are merely the result of subatomic serendipities. (Thus we read together from the 1954 edition of the *Penguin New Biology:* "Faith seems to be an occupational hazard for physicists.") Is there any professor so smugly entrenched in his tenure that he does not question whether the universe was determined from the beginning to endow him? Maybe we are nature at its most idiosyncratic. (Everything that rises wants to splurge.) The possibility that we result from some lucky scrum of carbon molecules the universe just happens to be conducive to—molecules discreetly, deliberately, expressly mobilized for our being and benefit, by the way—much less the suggestion that the culmination of all existence is our own evanescent meat, is sure to shake more than a few foundations.

On the other hand, cautions the skeptic, a poll that reveals that scientists are no less susceptible to God than anyone else may indicate that where science and religion come together is in their incapacity to take the Creator into custody. As Richard Dawkins, Oxford zoologist and professor of the public understanding of science, maintains, there is no reason to believe that religion can accomplish what science has not. In response to his question about the origin of the properties science has disclosed so far, an Oxford colleague, a professor of astrophysics, directed his man to the chaplain. Dawkins bristled at the reneging: "My immediate thought was, 'But why the chaplain? Why not the gardener or the chef?' If science itself cannot say where the laws of physics ultimately come from, there is no reason to expect that religion will do any better and rather good reason to think it will do worse." It is at best a priestly bewilderment that connects those who labor in the laboratory, the kitchen, the temple, the writing workshop, and the dirt.

This is to say nothing of the little lame literati that, instead of hunkering down with the gardener or consulting the chef, whistle far and twee. Surely there's plenty of room in the universe—in space, space enough—for poets to unpack in, too. So Shakespeare's Lear, after a long night's buffeting by the indeterminate elements levied against him, decides that "'Ay' and 'no' too was not good divinity." So A. R. Ammons, finding the "Overall" out of reach of "Corson's Inlet," turns inconclusiveness into the liberating credo that "scope eludes my grasp, that there is no finality of vision, / that I have perceived nothing completely, / that tomorrow a new walk is a new walk." So Job apostrophizes on his ash heap about the source of light, and neither testament nor textbook appears finally to satisfy his curiosity. I refer now to a God cumbrous and uncompounded and defer to him as well, who exceeds any sonnet we might send in his direction and all we'll ever know of stars. No matter how many prayers or algorithms might fit on the hide of our planet or on the head of a pin, there remains the same vaulted, vaunted absence we can't get over. Everything that rises hits the verge.

Mathematics must provide a relevant property to help determine the highest common denominator. Check the index for Browning's constant, whereby dividing reach by grasp must result in something greater than one. Go figure.

Between fundamentalism and futility, a compromise may be in order. Howard Nemerov posits a viable one. Stumbling upon a consonance—he recognizes how a leaf, a seashell, a fighter pilot working in for the kill, and "certain wall-eyed bugs" working in toward the flame that will kill them all spiral the same way—the poet celebrates the privileged vision. "That is the beautiful / In Nature as in art, not obvious, / Not inaccessible, but just between," he declares, and he goes on to extend the premise, wondering "if everything we are and do / Lies subject to some little law like that, / Hidden in nature, but not deeply so." But if in the end nothing is resolved through "Figures of Thought," nothing is disqualified either. He is left, and leaves us, provoked without being reliably enlightened. In a sense, he is seconding Robert Frost, who finds his attempt to do more than lyrically acknowledge uncertainty and actually deliver "something more of the depths" put off by the very nature he pretends to penetrate. The ambiguous whiteness he glimpses "Deeper down in the well than where the water / Gives me back in a shining surface picture / Me myself in the summer heaven, godlike" is, like that momentary hubris, blotted out by a ripple. "Water came to rebuke the too clear water," and he is left with a very limited consolation: the experience of having witnessed "For once, then, something."

Insecurity seems to govern equally all areas of human endeavor. "The writer is a man who, embarking upon a task, does not know what to do," Donald Barthelme confides in his essay "Not-Knowing." Having done it, he remains in the dark about whether what he's done was necessary or right. Even if one could theoretically compute the universe like a massive set of batting averages, there would be no danger of coming to the end of our inquiries. Such is the integrity of irresolution in all of our disciplines and every enterprise. This is why Nobel Prize–winning physicist Richard Feynman argues that part of the scientist's duty is a respect for and main-tenance of a saving doubt. He extols "the great progress and great value of a satisfactory philosophy of ignorance," which staves off intellectual foreclosure and promises fresh opportunities.

Olber's paradox arises from the recognition that however many stars we identify against the sky, they will never overtake the night. There will always be darkness sufficient to constrain the ruminations it inspires. "The Truth must dazzle gradually," writes Emily Dickinson, with what we may presume is not only her characteristic deference to divinity but also an implicit wink at cosmology. There will always be galactic mirages to conjecture over and, likewise, molten gods. If there's a syntax to existence, its obscurity is assured. If fate is as guaranteed as prescriptive grammar or grooved like a celestial orbit, whether it's science or religion trying to put its foot in the door, it ultimately shuts flush against us.

Life's permutations are so numerous that it is not only innumerates like me who shrug and call them infinite. The same can be said for the explications they've inspired. In developing his uncertainty principle, physicist Werner Heisenberg provided a creed for pretty much every human pursuit. Simply put, regardless of what well-curb you might peer past, whether heaven's portal or zero's rim, your own reflection gets in the way. (Everything that rises is our urge.) You should know that in case of prolonged exposure, the extremities go numb first.

Yet we would cup the physics we swim in; we would read the fortune in God's hand even as we hope to climb into it.

Just last week two young women rang my bell to let me in on their intimacy with the Lord. They were obscenely well groomed and alert for so early on a Saturday. Their politeness, of an order rarely seen nowadays apart from stewardesses and candy stripers, had thanks to months of practice been rendered impregnable by aggravation or scorn. They handed me a free brochure featuring a depiction of a particularly robust, aerobic Christ. To their credit, even after I declined their offer to discuss a fail-safe method of achieving eternal life, they never wavered in their cheerfulness, which as far as I could see an hour later had wafted them all the way down my block.

I am curious why science doesn't likewise deploy representatives in our neighborhoods. Why don't they tuck proofs behind our windshield wipers and insert formulas into the jams of our screen doors? Why don't they set up astrophysics booths on state fairgrounds to compete with the evangelists and the would-be congressmen or waylay us at stoplights and major airports? Although I waved off the insights and affections from those deputies of spirituality, I might very well invite visitors from the research lab into my home to hear more about the Good News of gravitational forces or the trinity of Newton's laws of thermodynamics. Who wouldn't interrupt breakfast for a talk with someone who drops postulates down black holes as casually as one might drop pennies down a well hoping to have his wishes answered? If ten commandments could be obtained from a single summit, how many might be extracted from the cosmos at large? Far be it from me to calculate. But while the prospect of doing probability studies on stellar behavior leaves me as dizzy as handicapping the afterlife would, there are those who gaze skyward each night and discover solid concepts on that milky way. Send them over, and have them bring their pamphlets and charts. Admittedly I won't be able to digest more than a portion of what comes through the door, but I'd gladly sacrifice some of my Sunday for even subsistence-level insight. Grant me this day my ration of understanding, lest everything that rises seem a dirge.

In the closing pages of *White Noise,* Don DeLillo's protagonist, Jack Gladney, brings a wounded man to a hospital, where he converses with a nun. This is not one of those nuns J. D. Salinger's Holden Caulfield pities because she never gets to go anywhere swanky for lunch. It is not one of E. E. Cummings's decertified, desubstantiated nuns, who devolve into "nons" in one of his satiric poems. No, DeLillo's Sister Hermann Marie belongs to the stolid, redoubtable, German variety, whose old-fashioned habit and blocky contours leave Gladney feeling "sentimentally refreshed" by the evidence that someone still believes and, at least momentarily, susceptible to a feel-good faith in a conventional, cumulus-upholstered vision of the afterlife. "Why shouldn't we all meet, as in some epic of protean gods and ordinary people, aloft, well-formed, shining?" he asks himself. In the nun's sober company, Gladney imagines that heaven (which, based on the painting on the wall showing a beatified Jack Kennedy holding hands with Pope John XXIII, "was a partly cloudy place") is at least halfway possible. However, Sister Hermann Marie quickly punctures his assumption, scorning his blind faith in her blind faith. The traditions and the trappings, the doctrine they promulgate and their permeation by the divine are all theater:

> Our pretense is a dedication. Someone must appear to believe.
> Our lives are no less serious than if we professed real faith, real
> belief. As belief shrinks from the world, people find it more neces-
> sary than ever that *someone* believe. . . . Those who have abandoned
> belief must still believe in us. They are sure that they are right not to
> believe but they know belief must not fade completely. Hell is when
> no one believes. There must always be believers. Fools, idiots, those
> who hear voices, those who speak in tongues. We are your lunatics.
> We surrender our lives to make your nonbelief possible. You are
> sure that you are right but you don't want everyone to think as
> you do. There is no truth without fools.

At the hospital, nuns see as much evidence of godlessness as the doctors do. (Like the nuns in their dark garb, their rosaries depending from their waists, the doctors wearing their habitual white coats, with stethoscopes slung about their necks, steel clipboards at the ready, are also submitting themselves to expectation, to keep the patients at ease.) Their calling includes daily confiscation of guns and knives. Into this refuge people do not come imbued but bleeding. Nevertheless, when Sister Hermann Marie's castigation picks up velocity and turns into German, which Gladney cannot understand, he still detects a saving cadence in the mystery. Her words create a storm and a shelter simultaneously. He is taunted and pummeled by her strange vehemence. Yet "the odd thing is I found it beautiful."

Truly these are days of reverence, days of awe. We stand above and under heaven at once. The universe is largesse writ large and, as at least one theory has it, ever enlarging. Science might be excused for checking the penmanship and religion forgiven for wondering if we're remembered in the will, for the very air is thick with integers, the dust of martyrs, the slough of stars. And how do we feel when scientists on television gabble esoterically and reach a consensus as incomprehensible to us as the controversy that called them together? How do we feel when religious figures sit across from us in an airplane? I think the word I want is "serene."

We need lunatics and fools to keep belief aloft. They also undertake the responsibility for the notion that Creation remains unculminated with us. Add to the expanding list of serious and pseudosciences "ufology," or the study of UFOs. (The coinage lends it prestige and consequence, and it indicates its migration from backwoods rumor and swamp gossip to the clean precincts of funded research.) Like other targets lying at the crumbling edge of our instruments and imaginations—like muons and the Almighty, whose respective existences likewise began as virtual —proof of the paranormal looms and eludes us simultaneously. Devotees term these unverifiable sightings, visitations, alien abductions, and close encounters of every numbered level of intimacy "high-strangeness experiences"—everything that rises is encouraged—and their exponential increase over the last few decades has inspired revised evaluations and new commitments to both psychic study and the new physics. According to Jacques Vallee, a pioneer in what admittedly remains for many critics this suppositious discipline, UFOs can be neither dismissed as mirages of mass irrationality nor fully accommodated as "scientific devices having nothing to do with the mystico-religious context." Journalist and communications specialist (not to mention ex–alien abductee) Dr. Joe Lewels also cautions against relying upon any one discipline to provide an accurate, adequate response. He maintains in *The God Hypothesis: Extra-terrestrial Life and Its Implications for Science and Religion* that these phenomena require "each and every one of us [to] become a theologian and a scientist" together. And although he suspects that the growing public fascination with UFOs may be directly caused by our "need to find a wider context for our lives than our earthly existence provides" and one more compelling than conventional institutions have lately sustained, philosopher Paul Davies concurs. As he concludes in *Are We Alone? Philosophical Implications of the Discovery of Extraterrestrial Life*, "This sense of a religious quest may well extend to the scientists themselves." Often as not, supplications to God and searches for the grand unified theory are aimed at the same government. Now more than ever apparently, if a true believer declares in a room full of research scientists, "We are not alone," not only will he not be ushered out as a crackpot, he may find himself preaching to the choir.

The physicists who shared the 2003 Nobel Prize studied supercon-ductivity thousands of miles apart from one another, which is in itself impressive evidence of the theory. Meanwhile, observers in rural England and coastal North Carolina alerted the authorities on the same night about their having seen the same inexplicable light show in their respective skies. Call it mutual insight or mass hallucination, but there's definitely something in the air.

To complete the circle, God is as likely to reveal himself in occult phenomena as in quantum mechanics. So say the proliferating sects of Judeo-Christian ufologists. Rather than to refute reports of alien life-forms, their mission is to incorporate them into conventional theology. Granted there have not been enough rumored Martian sightings by SETI or any-one else to make a *minyan,* and the data supporting the charge that lit-tle green men have been gathering in little green congregations are inconsistent at best. But there is no denying the recent rise in so-called exotheology, which debates, among many other questions, whether the Incarnation might have extraterrestrial consequences (and indeed, other-worldly counterparts). In a representative avoidance of earthly chauvin-ism, Paul Tillich offers a separate-but-equal hypothesis in his *Systematic Theology:* "Incarnation is unique for the special group in which it hap-pens, but it is not unique in the sense that other singular incarnations for other unique worlds are excluded." Depending on which sect's specula-tions one prefers, proof of alien civilizations would represent not a breach but an expansion of religious doctrine. If we focus on the most whole-some theories about Out There out there, transcendent truths are, in fact, interplanetary; salvation as such results from the intervention of space beings whose legendary superhuman capacities strike us as divinely un-derwritten; miracles are the occasionally manifest designs or debris of otherworldly creatures going about their business; the messiah is an itin-erant "celestial," harbinger of past and future evolutionary promise for the human race (with the technology, psychic accomplishment, and ambiguous temperament to back it up). And should we happen to lapse into anthropocentrism about the possibility, in *God and the New Physics* Paul Davies posits Christ as an eternal astronaut whose reach is equal to the demands of the expanding universe and who is thus able to save the aliens as well.

Imagine multiple worlds, each with its alternative Adam scooped from the indigenous mud. Imagine the ecumenical mission taken to its ex-treme, converting the microcosm and macrocosm alike. A subatomic temple. An intergalactic church. At the very least, we'll have to run many more copies of the monthly newsletter and pass the collection plate via satellite.

And when the mail is distributed and the call for contributions sent around, let us not forget to target Reed Springs, Missouri, home of the Museum of the Unexplained. A sort of low-rent Ripley's, the museum contains all manner of high-strange exempla ostensibly culled from other planets, dimensions, and elsewhere beyond the pale. Its contents range from partly plausible artifacts to unimpeachably bizarre testimonies to exhibits that look so jerry rigged they'd make P. T. Barnum blush. The museum's centerpiece and founding incentive is a conical object, about ten inches long, picked up some twenty years ago by Bob White, one of the museum's two founders and proprietors. According to White, the object had been projected by a hovering light "big as a three-story build-ing" and seemed to blaze on its way to striking the side of an embank-ment, where he retrieved it. ("I like to say 'retrieved' because 'found' sounds like you're just walking down the road and then you find it," he tells reporters.)

Inside its illuminated glass case, it rests like a nightclub diva or a prize diamond on a slowly revolving platform. I cannot test its texture or heft for myself, but I can see that it is metallic, split like a fish down one side, and vaguely corrugated. To my untutored eye, it looks like a whelk or a woman's high-fashion clutch bag, but those associations distract from the richer mysteries surrounding the thing, which is formally referred to in the legend next to the case as "The Unknown Object." (Waggish visitors might contend that if anyone were to positively identify it, the object would by definition become ineligible for the Museum of the Unexplained, which would leave an irreparable breach in its holdings.) So far, its provenance has NASA baffled, White claims; its full chemical composition has chemists mumbling to themselves. According to White, more than thirty elements have been identified from samples taken from it, including such rare components as europium, strontium, and vanadium. He insists that a Los Alamos scientist once confided that it was extraterrestrial in origin, a conclusion that the scientist subsequently denied having made.

For his part, Bob White readily admits that there are plenty of hoaxes being perpetrated in the UFO-detection community, a situation that, unfortunately, casts legitimate inquiry into disrepute. (At the same time, White does not apologize for the UFO-themed T-shirts, key chains, and other paraphernalia that are on sale, profits from which help to keep the museum open. He reminds us that while donations to the museum are welcomed, there is no admission fee.) "We hope to show more serious, objective things in the museum and let people decide for themselves," he says.

Assuming that in the face of the uttermost it is our prerogative to assume, I choose to assume that whatever plan or accident landed us here was the universe's effort to contemplate itself. We are the axis of self-reflection: at once thinking figure and figure of thought, both witness enraptured and an aspect of the still water we consider as well. In this, our idols and -ologies might ally before the Overall after all.

And what is the sense that the high and strange horizon we mind is mindful of us as well? What is it that strikes us simultaneously as impenetrable and impending, remote and near? Personally I maintain a principled uncertainty about such matters. But I think the word I want is "holy."

Destiny as a Sentence
by Henry James

Maybe it's the magnitude that distracts us, the regal aura of achievement, the impression of premises met and overcome. No wonder. The New York Edition of his collected works would command three mantelpieces at least. They make an altar of sorts: library shelves in every major university bow beneath them. No one could blame us for granting them supremacy, as well as firmness of belief.

And so, trusting in the great man's standing, we book a first-class passage. Experienced travelers will advise us to pack a map and update our passports before embarking upon a sentence by Henry James. Confronting a capital, we should think in terms of an excursion to come and get something in our stomachs and perhaps use the bathroom before departing. Or like Theseus, we would do well to tether ourselves by a thread, that is, if we ever mean to be extricated and find our way back to the world again.

The tendency is to equate Henry James's style with lavish expenditure, which is in keeping with the richly appointed drawing rooms and ritual teas his characters indulge in. Conventional wisdom tells us to ease deeply into a sentence by Henry James as we would into a piece of upholstered furniture; we should ready ourselves for a protracted, and definitely edifying, stay. It is this reputation as much as anything else that long ago won James the label of "Master." Literary criticism sets him at the head of a long table sumptuously laid, where, by dint of custom and our host's stature, we imagine him carving and distributing rich conceptions for our delectation and amazement. Thus we confront the writer as impresario, orchestrating understandings in a smooth continuum from the insight out.

This is essentially the James whom scholars trust in, defer to, and extol. But how many have come away from James's table with their plates empty because they could not effectively follow the proceedings? His heavily advertised luxuries notwithstanding, the James those would-be readers know remains stingy when it comes to giving the gist. No one in the canon apportions his findings more cautiously or lets drip so little unconditioned giving from his fist. Henry James is at once relentless and diffident. His sentences recoil from certitude as their creator would from today's New York subway, not to mention abjuring the crassness and savagery it contains.

To demonstrate, we might risk a few of his tricky, niggling interiors. Beware: the oxygen is soon exhausted at the higher elevation his characters ordinarily expound from; you can't find anyplace in James, not a servants' quarters, a kitchen, or a cemetery, that will provide a refuge from vocabulary and infectious subordination.

Approaching under advisement, we may consider this sentence from the opening paragraph of "The Turn of the Screw": "The case, I may mention, was that of an apparition in just such an old house as had gathered us for the occasion—an appearance, of a dreadful kind, to a little boy sleeping in the room with his mother and waking her up in the terror of it; waking her not to dissipate his dread and soothe him to sleep again, but to encounter also herself, before she had succeeded in doing so, the same sight that had shocked him." I say "consider this sentence" somewhat ironically, for it could be said that the sentence is bent on considering itself before readers ever subject it to analysis. As so many Jamesian sentences do, this one eddies around the very impediments it puts up against its own advancement. Mention Henry James to most people familiar with his prose, and they will envision someone stiffly held in evening clothes, hardly able to bend over to retrieve a fallen fork. In light of sentences like this one, though, I imagine a suppler fellow, a contortionist in fact, continually risking good sense and his own back.

At the point where our exemplary sentence appears, we find ourselves on the verge of a ghost story—admittedly James's verges often must be measured in acres—and we are forewarned by references to apparitions, shock, and dread. Nevertheless the experience of the sentence is less ominous than lulling. By the time we reach "the terror of it," the cumbrous progress toward the pronoun makes it difficult to discern its reference at all. The appearance of the antecedent is about as ambiguous as that of the ghost lurking several pages ahead. In this one sentence, James expends eighty-one words to ornament the mist. He lets us pull over temporarily —James gives us a semicolon as a kind of rest area just off the highway, where we can collect ourselves, check our itinerary, and stretch our legs— but the fog does not lift. The remainder of the trip is no more forgiving, what with an initial negation ("not to dissipate his dread and soothe him to sleep again") and a brief chronological detour ("before she had succeeded in doing so") yet to be negotiated. In short—a humble phrase, one by all accounts foreign to this author—James's style is overqualified for the job of just delivering the mail.

Later in the tale we find another representative Jamesian sentence taking its long way around what complainants say is a barn without a door. "We met, after I had brought home little Miles, more intimately than ever on the ground of my stupefaction, my general emotion: so monstrous was I then ready to pronounce it that such a child as had now been revealed to me should be under an interdict." The colon after "emotion" seems perfectly suited to what becomes a task of extrusion, an effort of clause after hard-earned clause. It is typical of James, this scrabbling for purchase on the sheer slope of meaning; in truth, "the ground of my stupefaction" is not a promising place to lay in a foundation or stake a claim. All of James's celebrated wrestling with the ineffable seldom concludes with anything better than a truce. Despite the long miles he crosses to bear little Miles home, our speaker is able to proclaim not an epiphany but the injunction against it. With the possible exception of Samuel Beckett, whose own prose features sentences that stretch out their demises the way cigars left to burn extend their ash, no writer is as willing as James to hazard his own failure—to wear it openly and still never wear it out.

Admittedly we would never expect to find Beckett's spectral rat men scrounging anywhere near the estates of James's titled gentry, but they do share an inability to leave off. Not even Joseph Cornell accrued grafts and details more assiduously than James's American dockets; he pocketed no more crap than Beckett's Krapp keeps in his head. You would never confuse the two, but aren't Strether Lambert and Molloy comparably addicted to incidentals, asides, and addenda? They may move through very different fields of inquiry, but they both emerge unkempt and covered with burrs. Remember the blood Hamm thinks is dripping inside his head in *Endgame*? Ignore for a moment the ruined digs and blasted circumstances of Beckett's character, and you may recognize something akin to the unremitting trickle of consciousness common to so many of the flounced and vested inhabitants of Henry James. Despite their obvious differences, Beckett's and James's characters alike display a penchant for complication and an absolute inability to hold their peace.

"Master" implies authority, but James takes great pains to point out that this is precisely the attribute his investigations lack. His sentences bustle with obligations and afterthoughts enough to bloat better than a hundred stories and a score of novels. The paradox is that, no matter how extensive a given Jamesian sentence's intentions may reach, their author forever finds himself "under an interdict." James operates according to a "you can't get there from here" aesthetic. Accordingly integrity takes the form of a refusal to have done with it, to find it satisfactory. Renowned for their psychological amplitude, his tales consist of sentences that recognize every mental state but reconciliation.

Here is the sentence that immediately succeeds the announcement of the homecoming above: "I was a little late on the scene of his arrival, and I felt, as he stood wistfully looking out for me before the door of the inn at which the coach had put him down, that I had seen him on the instant, without and within, in the great glow of freshness, the same positive fragrance of purity, in which I had from the first moment seen his little sister." Leave aside for the moment that rarely can any James narrator be said to have seen *anything* "on the instant," an impromptu, unpremeditated instant being as alien to such a person as spontaneity would be to a clockwork. Leave aside for the moment that this analytical interlude, as well as plenty of sentences before and after, arises not between psycholinguists or conference panelists debating Piaget but between the hired help. What is most striking is that James is basically incapable of traveling light. The man worries everything, and the result is like watching a surgeon cutting himself on his own instruments; to be even less charitable, it is like watching someone pushing a marble along the carpet with his nose. Make the marble in that simile a pearl, and the value of the exertion may increase, but so does the exasperation.

Actually James's obsessives do not chafe by themselves in an isolated corner of the canon. They dither and revise in solid company. Surely we'll

also find Hamlet there, and his nemesis, too. Hamlet is the model of introspection and deferral, no doubt, but in regard to dilation on the stage,
Claudius, for all his activism, comes off just as tortuously:

> That we would do
> We should do when we could, for this "would" changes,
> And hath abatements and delays as many
> As there are tongues, are hands, are accidents.

As king, Claudius is nothing if not politic, and that goes for both his back-
stage machinations and his ongoing justifications for them.

Then there is Eliot's Prufrock, who, when he references his debt to
Shakespeare, practices the circumlocutions he preaches:

> No! I am not Prince Hamlet, nor was meant to be;
> Am an attendant lord, one that will do
> To swell a progress, start a scene or two,
> Advise the prince; no doubt, an easy tool,
> Deferential, glad to be of use,
> Politic, cautious, and meticulous;
> Full of high sentence, but a bit obtuse;
> At times, indeed, almost ridiculous—
> Almost, at times, the Fool.

What a labored attempt this is to edge near the precipice of full disclosure.
In these nine lines, Prufrock stumbles over twenty marks of punctuation
before the climactic petering out of self-regard. "Delayed gratification" is
a common enough phrase, but we are talking about characters for whom
there has never been any other kind.

That is, if "gratification" is ever applicable in James's case. James is
refined, without question, but his is also arguably the most apologetic,
groping prose around, filled as it is with sentences that fidget and fuss in
their evening clothes. There are so many hinges and fittings carpentered
into his arguments, so many disclaimers, hedges, and attenuations to contend with, that the result, often as not, is an elegant ruin. What a lot of
syntactical window-shopping goes on in these sentences. What a cargo of
approximations freights the eminent Henry James, who cannot seem to
shirk or abbreviate anything.

Watching one of his statements unfold, like watching a nervous trucker trying to parallel park a semi, can be twitchy, mystifying business indeed. Witness yet another bumpy avowal from "The Turn of the Screw": "It wasn't so much yet that I was more nervous than I could bear to be as that I was remarkably afraid of becoming so; for the truth I had now to turn over was simply and clearly the truth that I could arrive at no account whatever of the visitor with whom I had been so inexplicably and yet, as it seemed to me, so intimately concerned." It is one more contraption destined to set off the grammar checker—the computer can't abide all that worming through the works. It is one more of James's tenured sentences—one more sentence relegated to the author's extended care facility, one sentence without parole. It recalls a Christmas bill, to which congressmen attach amendment after amendment until the thing becomes too unwieldy to pass. "It wasn't so much yet that," it begins, squeezing out an absence of credentials. James often relies on this method, whereby he sets what he means to convey in relief against the background of what he does not or cannot say. Wyeth never planted a girl in so vast a field of wheat as the abyss of the inscrutable in which James plunges his frail declaration.

One wonders whether being handed a menu of entrées the establishment does *not* serve whets the appetite or sends the hungry patron to another restaurant. In any event, our speaker is finally ready to present the authentic bill of fare: "For the truth I had now to turn over was simply and clearly. . . ." And isn't revelation—the arrival of what is true and simple and clear—worth the wait? But the truth is that "I could arrive at no account whatever of the visitor with whom I had been so inexplicably and yet, as it seemed to me, so intimately concerned." And we conclude in a cultivated shambles, where intimacy does little to solve the inexplicable. As for that courtly "as it seemed to me," this is one of James's signature hiccups. "It is perhaps nearer the truth to say." "As it were." "If I might rightly assess it as such." They are preemptive strikes against being held responsible, codicils to the will. Taken together, such phrases constitute a groveler's thesaurus. Do not begrudge me my splendidly rendered but meager apprehensions, they imply. Indeed you needn't begrudge me because I am already and constantly on record for begrudging myself. James beats the reader to the reconnoitering, then to the recoil.

William Faulkner famously promoted his desire "to say it all . . . between one Cap and one period . . . to put everything into one sentence—

not only the present but the whole past on which it depends and which keeps overtaking the present, second by second." Henry James appears to share in this desire, ceding a sentence its proclivities and dilations, letting its consciousness stretch out like time itself. Like Faulkner, he would define "the whole past on which [the sentence] depends" as not only the familial and social legacy behind its utterance but also the history of the linguistic and intellectual deliberations that went into its construction. But even this burden doesn't account for the tentativeness of its course. More to the point, perhaps, is the conclusion of Donald Barthelme's story "Sentence." ("Conclusion" is too exalted a term, in that the 2,500-word spill merely peters out without earning a period.) "Sentence" begins by noting its own incentive: "Or a long sentence moving at a certain pace down the page aiming for the bottom—if not the bottom of this page then of some other page—where it can rest, or stop for a moment to think about the questions raised by its own (temporary) existence." Any sentiment left out too long will eventually curdle. This one, too, inevitably comes to grief: "a disappointment, to be sure, but it reminds us that the sentence itself is a man-made object, not the one we wanted of course, but still a construction of man, a structure to be treasured for its weakness, as opposed to the strength of stones." Surfing a long sentence can be a heady, splendid ride, but in these cases the enterprise is doomed. Either it will dash itself against a period like a boulder or tear its hull against elliptical shoals.

After undertaking a sentence by Henry James, it is necessary to convalesce. A strict diet of unmodified subjects and exercise predicated by straightforward action verbs is indicated. Stick to a starker economy for a while, whose trappings are spartan and intelligence severe. What's called for is an uncompromising prose, perhaps something in the nature of Hammett's patter. Practice fast rejoinders that crack off cleanly. Swear off appurtenances and spendthrift attachments. Eschew the marbled argument and the larded rationale, which, we ruefully remember, clogged the heart of Henry Marcher in "The Beast in the Jungle" and left at least a dozen other James protagonists gasping for air. Avoid semicolons as you would saturated fats. Restore yourself by banging out a set of subject-verb-object sentences every morning before a sensible breakfast. Strive, in short, for the ripped figure and the leaner look.

Cold turkey is the best way to go. There is something to be said for a clean break, which is that something *can* be said, immediately after which the trick is to push away from the table. And who knows? When James himself finally met his death sentence—"So here it is at last, the distinguished thing"—instead of acknowledging the "occasion" as "an appearance, of a dreadful kind," he might very well have been hailing the humble, unprecedented satisfaction of a full stop.

Staying Away

We keep coming back and coming back
To the real: to the hotel instead of the hymns
That fall upon it out of the wind.

> Wallace Stevens, "An Ordinary Evening in New Haven"

Of the many things that separate me from seasoned travelers, possibly the most striking is my attitude toward hotel rooms. Like others who shuttle between airports or rental cars, I long for absent loved ones and miss the homely aromas I've left behind. But whereas the prospect of staying in a hotel is, by their common account, a drudgery they have to put up with, for me it can be the most enticing aspect of my visit. I think it is that a hotel room brings home to me a rigor more delicious than any home-bound activity ever does. In short, nothing beats a hotel room for putting the "vacate" in "vacation." I'd term hotels utopian, except that the root of "utopia" is "nowhere," while the fact is that you can't travel anywhere in America without running into clutches of them. Ubiquitous and indiscriminate, they represent the essence of accommodation. They take you in as you are.

Certainly compactness is part of the pleasure, having all I am summed up in a couple of suitcases, their entire contents deployable into a closet the size of a London cab and at most three dresser drawers. It does the hotel room an injustice to complain of forced constriction or a constipated decor. On the contrary, this is living light, and in my case about as Buddhist as I'll ever get. I do in a Best Western what Thoreau did in the woods. It's better than back to basics, basically, in the sense that I haven't been so denuded since I slept in a crib. I frankly wonder whether or not to bother unpacking and just dress and redeposit my clothes in and out of the open mouths of the suitcases themselves, arranging and plucking shirts and socks out of their jaws with the expertise of a veterinary dentist.

Compactness is celebrated in all of the hotel room's accoutrements, too. I mean the fundamentalist cunning behind the little complimentary soaps designed to last no longer than the median stay, the perfume vials like anodynes bottled by ancient apothecaries, the encapsulated sewing kits like spring-loaded magician's tricks, the soups for one that appear to have been packeted by NASA. For all I know, it may have taken an entire engineering team to create the one-use shampoo cruet, which, like a pointillist, I have to dab incessantly against my head to get out a single shower's worth of suds. To be sure, living light is the virtual motto of this streamlined environment, and if I am profligate with towels, I am sparing in every other way. And should I stray from this resolve, the housemaid will be able to erase any evidence of my having been here in a matter of minutes. No saint, no second-story man could purge his presence so thoroughly.

The point and paradox of a hotel room is that it resists the occupancy it pretends to invite. A hotel room is a way station only, where nothing settles in. Have you noticed how there is never enough light in a hotel room and no way to increase it? Edward Hopper may get the mood right by bleaching the patrons and premises in his paintings—perhaps his figures vanish into the atmosphere from unnaturally protracting their visits —but he misses the hotel room's ordinary, premeditated dusk, which is critical to the intention of regulating just how comfortable you can be, just how long you can belong.

There is an aesthetic of the unprepossessing operating here. That is to say, nothing in a hotel room possesses you or urges you to possess. I note the contradiction between the bland utility of the furnishings and the heightened security surrounding them: the pictures are bolted to the wall, the television is chained to its hutch like a rabid animal, and the telephone is held by a cable seemingly strong enough to hoist mountain climbers or to lower a bathysphere. The fixtures are, quite literally, fixed. Even the anchoring ends of the clothes hangers totally encircle the pole, irremovable. The implication of value where none objectively exists— who really wants what they work so hard to secure?—has a self-defeating, subliminal effect on people. Treated like potential criminals, they feel compelled to steal the washcloths and load up on stationery they'll never use.

There is a reason why a hotel room hosts liaisons but not relationships, encounters but not commitments. The very atmosphere, flavored by the abandoned stinks and shed cells of forgotten hundreds every year, seems furtive, impermanent. People come to conduct drug deals, to wait out their relatives' hospital stays, or to play all-night poker. But it is a provisional welcome that ferries them from the front desk to their door, which opens onto the utterly generic. Here there is nothing to cherish, interfere, or recall. The room is readily assimilated, but it neither asks for nor answers affection. Nothing in a hotel room begs you to stay or expects you to.

There are exceptions. Think of the New York billionaire who buys out an entire hotel like a private box at the opera, then claims the penthouse, where he holes up alone like a pasha steeped in privilege, bottled up and sumptuous as some unpronounceable wine. (Thus ghettoized and plush, he is from time to time the subject of a segment on the *Today Show* or *20/20*. The televised tour reminds you of an embassy locked down to last out a revolution in the streets.) Apart from the billionaire's rare example, there are also the odd Todd Andrews types. Andrews is the protagonist of John Barth's *The Floating Opera*, who in his far more modest hotel room lives enviably as an oxymoron: he is a resident guest. Andrews pays his bill daily, so as not to presume on his futurity or overestimate his tenancy in the world. He pays out his stay the way a fisherman does his line, letting his catch succumb of its own accord. He writes a check every morning to hold him over until the next breakfast, knowing that every welcome wears out eventually. His preference is to have his wear out evenly, in definite measures. Were the options available, he would even eat and breathe on the installment plan.

Still, the vast majority of hotel patrons are transients, and their lodgings are designed to release them. The eponymous hero of Steven Millhauser's *Martin Dressler* sees this as a fault he means to correct by upping the seductive draw of his hotel. "I want to keep 'em in. I want people to return. I want them to be unhappy when they're not here," he explains, and this is the principle upon which his Grand Cosmo is built. The Tower of Babel evinced no greater hubris than the impossibly fantastic lodgings Dressler establishes to supplant the world.

But Dressler is doomed by definition. A hotel room is the opposite of a painting or a poem, in that it relegates you to surfaces, slick and burnished as the top of the requisite desk near the window, neither of which, desk or window, you will ever use. So much about the room reproves you, refuses to let you linger on or in it. This may be why, whenever I get ready for bed in a hotel room, I consider sleeping on top of the sheets.

On the other hand, I can't help but be tempted by a bed so deftly made. Engineered is more like it, so precise are the angles and pleats. (One enters such a bed like an incision, sliding into sleep like a letter into its envelope or an afterthought between parentheses). It takes real effort to free the spread, the flannel blanket, and the sheets from their systematic packaging; it is a challenge even to find the seams, as if, instead of housekeeping, Brancusi made the bed. But once inside, I realize that it's a brittle fit. In such a bed, you wouldn't crowd the kids under the covers with you to watch a Sunday matinee. It is not a bed to massage your husband's shoulders, to wait out a fever, or to do your dying in.

The hotel room collapses the home it imitates into a bald efficiency. There are no books to individuate the place, nor any shelves to support them if there were. Meanwhile, no magazines rest upon the toilet tank, which is swabbed seven days a week. (Reading takes time, and time is not taken here. You save your expenditures for elsewhere.) The nightstand holds only the most anonymous, ecumenical contents, as does the desk. The bathroom vanity is too severe to earn the name. The chair is too stiff to take your print.

There are several words you cannot use in a hotel room convincingly. "Aura" is one. "Scope" is another. The syllables of "intricacy" meet with resistance, break apart on the carpet. Likewise "aspiration." "Meanwhile." "Whimsy." A hotel room forecloses vocabulary. Save your subordinate clauses for Thanksgiving. Leave your adjectives with the cheese crackers in the car.

There is something about a hotel room that retains its vacancy, that wants us out. The better chains boast of cleanliness and comfort, but a hotel room affords only so much repose. It accepts but does not captivate. (You want to dig in? Try a trench. Choose a church group. Get a grave.) The goods and services that never require more than two digits to summon on the phone are there to expedite your processing; everything from the complimentary breakfast to the automated checkout on channel 55 is conceived to move you along. The furniture consents to anyone who sits, lies, snuggles, or flops upon it. But it is not impressed. All veneers are devised for easy cleaning. If there is wood, it is wood without a burl, dimple, or distress to distract attention or slow the polish. Indeed it is futile to try to personalize a hotel room with your own possessions. Set a framed picture on the dresser, and watch it slide to the floor.

In retrospect you realize how restricted your gestures and how limited your attitudes were during your stay. In a hotel room you make do with no more than half a dozen intonations. Do you know what the record is for perspectives achieved in a hotel room? Seventeen. Less than half of what you can manage in a train station. No more than a quarter of the number available to you in a minor league ballpark.

You presume that the air's aswarm with the thousand chemistries that preceded yours, but they've all been scoured, and the smell of disinfectant presides. Every animal in its own way marks its territory. By souring a place you impose a privacy, you make a space your own. But every day someone comes in to vacuum up your scruffs, danders, and dead cells, to suck out the stinks that wicked from your pits and privates, to mop up and remove whatever inadvertent fluids flavored your wake. Because it does not contain us more than overnight, a hotel room denies the intimacy traveling families travel to recapture and lovers come there for. At once democratic and indifferent, a hotel room always implies our absence.

And this, finally, may be the primary appeal of the hotel room to the general population. It is a reprieve from the pressures of sustaining your own uniqueness. For a hotel room is versus diversity; it assumes some Esperanto of the itinerant, the wayward, the furloughed, the exhausted, and the lost. You are no one special, it says, so live for a few hours anyway in your underwear. You can withdraw into the shade of John Smith, if you wish, and just relax. Inappropriate for prolonged, insistent living, a hotel room abstracts you, assigns you life by proxy, a temporary masquerade. (At the registration desk, didn't you feel the impulse, as you do nowhere else, to go by an invented name?) A hotel room conciliates as it suppresses. Here you have the option to embody an allegory of yourself, an abridged version. You can exploit a break in the narrative. Neither your office nor any room in your home allows you to relinquish so much identity as a Holiday Inn does. By contrast, a restaurant insists on you. A doctor's waiting room holds you to yourself like a résumé or the CIA. But even a low-budget hotel room is a haven. It implies hours to squander, a vacation even from the vacation you may be taking, off the road for a while and out of bounds. More than any other room in any other building does, a hotel room gives you leave.

Call this capacity the apotheosis of room service, hospitality's logical extreme. From salesmen sick on whiskey and too many shrimp, to job interviewees fussing and fretting before the mirror, to kids sprung from the car's back seat and eager to trampoline from bed to bed, to rock bands bound to trash them, hotel rooms suffer us. But, as I said, only for so long.

If they see nothing else clearly, suicides do see this. According to statistics, more than 30 percent of suicides choose to slit their wrists or overdose in a hotel room rather than do themselves in at home. Arguably this is because a home encourages one to linger and lounge, whereas a hotel room suggests departure from the moment one enters it. A suicide's average stay? Twenty-one hours. Especially allowing for the times that the suicide checks into his room immediately after it has been prepared, meaning that, barring a fire alarm or a the sound of a gunshot, an entire housecleaning cycle must pass before anyone looks in on him, this is impressively brief. In fact some psychologists suspect that there is an unwritten protocol governing suicide in a hotel room, so consistent are the data surrounding the procedure. Surveys of hotel staff reveal that the deed is typically committed after ten o'clock at night but before eleven thirty, and about 75 percent of the time in bed. (The shower stall comes in a distant second, at around 20 percent.) A suicide is less likely than the usual guest to overtip or to leave a tip at all; conversely he is more likely to deposit wrappers in the wastebasket and to restore the phone book or the Bible to the drawer of the nightstand. The consensus is that these procedures—they are too common simply to be called tendencies—show the encroachment of oblivion and the longing for chastity, respectively. A suicide's average number of suitcases, average number of calls placed, average number of towels used, average number of pay-per-view movies watched: less than one apiece.

A suicide is also far less likely than other guests to use an alias when he checks in. The seasoned interpreter is not surprised. Unburdening begins by relinquishing one's real name.

What makes a hotel room so appropriate a setting for suicide is that a hotel room certifies that ultimate reduction. A hotel room is a corollary for the escape from superfluity, which describes what often compels a person to take his own life. There is an undeniable quality of held breath about a hotel room, and this offers a sense of commiseration to someone who has made a fatal decision. (This is only conjecture, of course. Suicides don't always leave notes behind, and when they do, they seldom address their motives for selecting the venues they did. Furthermore the hotel room's effects are often so subtle as to be completely subliminal anyway. And since the suicide is understandably too preoccupied to philosophize about the room he occupies, whatever sources of commiseration there might be in the immediate vicinity are going to be minimal, belated, and generally unavailing.)

For someone determined to die deliberately, a hotel room also promotes ritual. Imagine the suicide like a penitent steadying himself against the dresser or with a hand on the back of the chair, slowly unpocketing. He sets his keys down gingerly—it looks like tenderness, but really it is to maintain the spell. He lays out his handkerchief, coins, and comb like the trappings of ceremony. He arranges wadded dollars like watercress. He undresses like a parson, pointlessly fastidious about keeping the lay of his shirt and jacket intact and his pants creased. He is paying himself his last respects, and the hotel room respects this. On the bed he opens his wallet, spreads out photographs, letters, or bills—his last ballast or the inducements to ruin—like relics, like tarot cards.

Anxious observers may infer disturbing links between the suicide's maneuvers and their own. Don't we comparably adapt and empty out in our own hotel rooms? Aren't we as dependent upon the nonjudgmental confines and as self-conscious about the facilities there? Have we been harboring similar symptoms all along, which entering hotel rooms could trigger like allergic reactions? Never fear. There is not one study that proves that there is any causal connection whatsoever. A suicide packs his pills, poisons, and ammunition well in advance of his arrival, not as a consequence of it. A hotel room does not move him to suicide. At most, it grants permission. At best, it forgives.

Yet it must be admitted that this, again, is mostly conjecture. In the end, what brings him to this point and place exceeds understanding. Conjecture. Exceeds. No, the room cannot hold him.

Clothes and the Man

*. . . the vestural Tissue, namely, of woollen or other cloth; which Man's Soul
wears as its outmost wrappings and overall; wherein his whole other Tissues
are included and screened, his whole Faculties work, his whole Self lives,
moves, and has its Being?*

Thomas Carlyle, *Sartor Resartus*

Perhaps it began with your mother. A fair guess: it doesn't take an inspired psychoanalyst to tell you how many of your peccadilloes do. And
doesn't "peccadillo" sound like some spiny, low-lying sort of creature
trundling along the shoulder of the road, which, psychically speaking, it
more or less is. If you mean to trace the evolution of this particular peccadillo of mine, you'll have to imagine my mother, ever restless in her element, laying out prospective pants and shirts, which she'd bought for me
en masse, to inspect and rule upon. Standing by anxiously like someone
awaiting a pawnbroker's appraisal of the last of her heirlooms or, when
she felt certain she'd captured the contemporary taste, like a cat who'd
proudly spread his rat corpses on the floor for his master to admire, she
awaited my verdict.

For my part, it was as close to delivering consequential judgments as
I'd ever been allowed in this household and, really, as close as I'd ever get
until a career choice would decades later land a grade book in my hands.
And although it would have taken relatively little to please my mother
(mothers being what they are), I begrudged her the pleasure (boys being
what *they* are) and, like a snobbish jeweler sneering behind his loupe, gave
her the undiluted bad news that exactly *none* of them would do. Not the

paisley or the plaid, I decreed, no matter what the other kids were wearing; no matter what the catalogs were touting or the local stores stocked, neither the short sleeved nor the long impressed. Certainly nothing earned half the favor of my familiar, faded jeans, despite or, if memory serves, because of the fact that their frayed bottoms ended in tendrils like a *tallis* by now. She did not spare me the complaint that she'd spent a hundred dollars and half the day on behalf of the appearance I was too stubborn to notice when absolutely everybody else—yes, *everybody* else, she informed me—always did. Nevertheless I held my ground. Not the green, I declared, and not the gray. Before I ever heard of Thoreau, I intuited his sentiment that one should "beware of all enterprises that require new clothes," from which set of suspicious enterprises I did not except the selection of new clothes itself. Hence, despite the effort I recognized yet never asked for, not the black and, definitely, not the blue. In my refusal I felt more kingly than unkind. Out of my sight! I cried, like a sovereign dismissing sycophants. Away with the lot of them! Take them away!

If my mother was chagrined, my father was doubly so. Dad's unique purgatory was that he loved fine tailoring, but because of his ample proportions, he couldn't possibly look good in clothes that looked good to him. Barely five foot nine and weighing better than three bills, with a chest that might have been designed by a cooper and a belly the size of something you might find sweating a special vintage in a winery, my father was cursed with refined taste that his body could not accommodate. "I'd kill for your height," he would tell me. "Lucky enough to have your physique, and look how you dress like a bum," he'd mutter, wondering what joke genetics would play next. (First, there was the platypus. Then came his eldest son, who was shaped for tailoring, but who insisted on slogging about in rags no hippie politics could redeem.) "From those washed-out shirts of yours right down to those . . . what are they, loafers? That's just perfect. Shoes to loaf in!" My father had the means and —Chicago West-Side origins to the contrary—the breeding to admire razored pleats and to crave upscale labels, but he was destined to shop in the Big and Tall Men's stores, where "roomy" and "forgiving" were the most elegant adjectives available. Conversely mine was a build that something cultivated could be done with, yet I couldn't be bothered.

And as hard as Dad tried to inculcate the secrets of matching fabrics and hues, instructing me as assiduously as he did about football strategies in all things sartorial, from the subtleties of neckties to the arcana of cuffs, I could not be roused out of my usual slovenliness. I could never understand the anxieties and the passions of people who succumb to the new fall line like an allergy. While some stricken fathers paced the floor over wasted sons who were headed for juvenile hall, mine claimed that I had a problem so profound that only a haberdasher could fix it. That was Dad's word: "haberdasher." Reverence for the trade inspired diction from him that harked back to the days when freshly laundered shirts came back in boxes, individually pinned and sleeved in paper, and no man past twenty years of age would be caught dead outdoors without a hat. And here I languished, squandering my stature. Blessed with dimensions that, if not obviously enviable, were at least sufficient to warrant and benefit from better clothing, I still went out the door each morning resembling something caught midmolt. Whenever the subject arose, I sank back apathetically into my uniform argument: T-shirts and jeans would do me just as well, thank you very much. The rest was vanity. Counsel about formal wear was as lost on me as elocution lessons in a barn, which, according to my parents, from the way I dressed, was where I looked as though I'd been brought up, there in the vulgate of personal appearance, amid the dinginess and the dung.

Some addictions lie beyond the reach of consolation and too deep for words. So my mother may have assailed me like a rabid Santa with shirts and pants in bulk that it wouldn't *kill* me just to try on. My father may have brought home fantastic tales about what the mannequins in the store windows on Michigan Avenue were wearing this season: astounding suits whose details he'd itemize like Homer going over the shield of Achilles, clothes he'd happily *pay* to have me wear. I owed them to outfit honorably the life they gave me. If I wouldn't dress for success, it would content them if I'd dress for redress, and the fact that I refused to must have come from some perversity that, like fashion sense, I never inherited from them. In their view, over which my appearance cast a dark cloud, I cried spite from a homely cocoon out of which I would not be coaxed, reproved, or bribed.

For if clothes made the man, I was inveterately unconstructed, and I expected to remain that way. Unlike so many teens of the sixties, I wasn't making a statement by my stained shirts and deteriorating jeans, at least not consciously. Casualness was not a cause, only my condition, the base-line of my ensemble and my sensibilities. I was chronically unkempt. If "kempt" was even a word, it could never be a desire of mine, much less an option. I may have looked like a campus radical or, if the light was right, like a doddering oddball who prowled the streets for tin foil, but the truth was that I simply treasured ease above all else. Why strangle myself in a tie that made it all the harder to speak or swallow when an open collar was easier and let me breathe freely? Why put on a sport coat that, in the event of a crisis—who knew when a fire might break out, or a burglary, or a swarm of bees—would not allow me to raise my arms above my head? What was the sense in sensible shoes that squeezed, shoes that gave out before they offered any give, when gym shoes or sandals had all of my potential activities and recreations covered? It wasn't conscience, then, but comfort that kept me dressed in that preemployable, antidraftable manner. If it looked like obstinacy against a decent wardrobe or solidarity against an indecent war, so be it. All things being equal, at sixteen or thereabouts I was about as immune to commitment as a tomcat. I left it to others to take their stand. Here I took my slump.

One summer morning during that vague expanse between bar mitzvah and the job market, my father announced that he was making a day of it with me. Just him and his eldest—my brother would have to content himself with his regular rabble of protohoods, who pitched quarters and tore through neighborhood tulip beds on Sting-Ray bikes. Curiosity got the better of me, so like a Labrador that does not see beyond the promise of a ride in the car to the veterinarian he's about to visit, I went along without question. Only when we were almost there did I realize that it wasn't a Cubs game or lunch at Sam and Hy's Deli that beckoned. No, we were headed for Robert Hall, a men's store on Irving Park Road, where I was to be fitted for the suit that, if Dad had his way, would anchor a new set of outfits appropriate to the man he wished I'd become. Or rather, one that was appropriate to the man he believed that, hidden beneath that unprepossessing carapace I wore, I already was.

The full extent of Dad's plot became apparent when he ushered me past the racks to the back of the store, where a platoon of tailors, measuring tapes slung like lanyards around their necks, scissors cunningly tucked into their belts, waited to receive us. "Mr. Saltzman!" said the oldest of the three men and, going by the accidental chalk hashes on his sleeves and trousers, the highest-ranking officer on the premises. "And this is your boy! Let's just see what we have here." With that, Dad surrendered me to their auspices and invasive expertise. (Years later I attended a rock concert where some of the drunken and overly daring audience members launched themselves from the stage into the mosh pit of the equally imbued, who would pass them back and forth above their heads. If the divers at the Chicago Auditorium were more audacious than I was at Robert Hall, they were troubled by less doubt.)

Once I was bequeathed to them, the three men fell instantly to work. They reminded me of those assiduous mice in *Cinderella*, who, despite their handicaps, were good enough to form a guild, or of the Fates in Greek mythology, who, with their awful thread and shears, were essentially tailors, too. And weren't the men of Robert Hall measuring me up for a destiny as well? Out of nowhere, it seemed, Mr. Clevenger manifested an armload of swatches, which materialized like magicians' scarves and which he proceeded to drape one at a time over my shoulders like military epaulettes. After a few deft preliminary measurements of my waist and inseam, Mr. Tillman had me strip off my jeans (no quarter given for shyness or ceremony at Robert Hall) and step—"A foot at a time, please, a foot at a time, that's right," he urged the idiot (how else explain the costume I'd come in with?)—into a pair of pants whose legs lapped over my ankles. Up came Mr. Solomon, conducting a pincer action from the rear. He had with him a contraption that was so ingenious that, I confess, for the moment I forgot my fidgeting. It was a yardstick mounted vertically on a steel block. Attached to it was a kind of oversized atomizer that could be slid up and down the length of the stick. When he'd gauged the proper height for the device, he fastened the clamp and, by squeezing a rubber bulb, fired off several ghostly rounds of chalk against each of my legs for some obscure future reference. Then Mr. Tillman had me slide into the shell of a coat the color and texture of overdone rye toast, and Mr. Clevenger started scoring my shoulders, chest, back, waist, and more delicate precincts with a sliver of soap, inscribing creamy glyphs all over the inchoate garments and leaving me feeling like something readied for butchering.

"You're going to look dapper in this, young man," said one of my attendants, using a word I thought should have been reserved for jockeys, matadors, or foreign ambassadors, but never applied to anyone even remotely associated with my high school. Like "jaunty," "dapper" was for dandies who lived in P. G. Wodehouse, the idyllic and idle Berties and Reginalds and Bingos who lingered on the last syllable of "banal," pronouncing it with an elongated, self-satisfied "ah" for the sheer pleasure of having come up with so superior a word. I mean the sorts of fellows who had fits over fittings or effused over an especially cunning new cut of cummerbund. What could all of that dithering over how a handkerchief might protrude, a collar lie, or a coat's vent settle over one's seat have to do with me, whose sole fashion criterion was whether or not my clothes were too noxious to stand next to for a third consecutive day?

It was somewhere around that point, I believe, in the midst of Project Arthur Resartus, that I began to dream about Garanimals, which my peers may remember as those pre-mated outfits for grade-schoolers. Thanks to an easy-to-follow code, even a child could match any of his giraffe shirts to one of his giraffe pants or unite lion with lion or zebra with zebra when his mother was busying with his sack lunch. Even a toddler could tell that it was fruitless to try to marry a tiger to a horse and that pitting an elephant against a lizard clashed against fashion, common sense, and nature at once. A difficult and tragic weaning, it seemed to me, as the battery of tailors continued to apply themselves to my betterment, their six practiced hands patting and pulling, groping and gashing, fondling and reforming me. Given half a chance, they'd have forced accoutrements upon me or perhaps a camel topcoat so lavish that it came with its own clement weather. It must have been the pain in my face, however, that made my father take pity. "That's enough for one day," he said, and he called the rabidly advancing Solomon, Tillman, and Clevenger off.

Two weeks later I had my first real suit. I'd buy my second ten years later to accommodate the taste and plans of my wife-to-be. And having outgrown the dimensions and deserted the circumstances that the suit denoted, I've now gone many years without owning one. Throughout my college years, I received CARE packages from my mother that included packages of crisp handkerchiefs and Gold Toe socks among the tubes of toothpaste and bars of soap; had she been able to smuggle me a Bill Blass jacket and pants in one of those mailings without wrinkling them beyond repair, I suppose she'd have included them, too. Denied that opportunity, she could only lament over how shabbily I must have been presenting myself out of range of her surveillance. While other mothers worried that their children at college were experimenting with drugs, mine worried that I was trafficking in threadbare shirts and decayed trousers.

I readily confess that one of the primary reasons why I was attracted to a career in college teaching was that it offered a permanent reprieve from dressing up. Certainly when you compare what I currently put on for teaching to the work shirts and battered sandals my own professors wore in graduate school, showing as much solidarity with Marxists and marijuana-besotted grad students as midwestern professors reasonably could, I'm a regular Gatsby. (Actually it doesn't take all that much effort to stay ahead of many of the slackers and grunge devotees I teach, who come slouching toward the required curriculum to be bored.) Paradoxically, in order to compete for a place in the academy among the indifferently dressed, I did have to invest in a corduroy sport coat so as not to clash with the herd of interviewees at the Modern Language Association Convention. When I did manage to secure a job, there was no convincing my parents that the upgrade in my apparel had not trumped anything that could have been confided in my letters of recommendation. You could not have persuaded them that had I not chosen something off the rack and opted instead for something tailor made, I'd have had my choice of Ivy League jobs.

When they earn tenure, some probationary faculty come out of the closet; I purged mine, selling off every vestige of accommodation, including the corduroy sport coat that I'd worn to the interview that landed me here and that I had not put on since. In fact so unstinting is my commitment to casual wear that were I to walk down the hall in a coat and tie tomorrow, I'd be accosted with the concerns of colleagues and students alike, who'd wonder whether I'd been called before the president, which can never be good, or whether I'd come down with a case of administrative ambition, which could only be worse. Or they would suspect I was being ironic. Oh, yes, Saltzman could accomplish in a vest what it took Swift an essay to say. Around my neck, a starched collar could cut into everyone on campus. In short, I can put on a classy suit, but I cannot pull it off. For I am the rumple in plush, the chink in chic.

I like to argue that my raggedy aspect has the advantage of putting people at their ease around me (especially students, who seem to be increasingly prone to intimidation nowadays). Still, it does occasionally put my bosses off their feed. This explains why my department head came into my office on the day before my formal review by the vice president for academic affairs and the dean of arts and sciences to advise me to wear a tie to the meeting. It was a sound tactic: no excerpt from my course evaluations and nothing in my résumé inspired as big a reaction as the tie did. "Well, Art, you appear to be doing very well here at Southern," beamed the dean. "You've been very productive, your supporting materials are quite strong . . . you *look the part* of a professor!" Emphasis his. Whereupon my department head raised an I-told-you-so eyebrow toward me. He would have loved to meet Mom and Dad, who shared his conviction that looking eloquent, imperative, and profound is the advent of being those things. He would have immediately appreciated their insight that even so tiny a detail as the right tie clasp can be the luminous center of a room. Definitely my parents would have been proud, had I given them the satisfaction of telling them just how instrumental dressing well had been in my progress toward promotion.

Thanks to a careful policy of avoidance of occasions that required formal wear, I have had to dress up no more than half a dozen times since that fateful afternoon. And today stands before you a grown man who doesn't own a single a suit worthy of a ceremony. Were a wedding to beckon or, God forbid, a funeral, I'd find myself coming naked before God. Not a legitimate stitch anywhere in my closet. Not one thing decent enough to marry or die in. While it isn't only the clothing that makes me loath to undertake either commitment, I won't deny that it's a factor.

Some parental instruction has stuck with me, however. No one would think it to look at me, but I have a modest reputation as a pretty fair arbiter of outfit alternatives brought home from the mall. Also, whenever my girlfriend is frazzled or late for work, I can quickly, reliably concoct an ensemble for her out of what's left in the closet on laundry day. I have a knack for knowing what goes together with what although I am not interested in any of it going together with me. Finally I have taught at least three sons of divorced mothers how to knot a necktie properly. The trick, should you not be able to get hold of me when the task arises, is not to face the boy but to operate behind him in the bathroom mirror. I find that, that way, I can naturally follow the procedure as I'd perform it on myself instead of having to reverse it in my mind; moreover, the boy can imitate my motions as I perform them. He can even place his hands on my hands in order to develop a sort of physical memory of how to do it, which is the way my father, who passed away several years ago, once stood behind me and passed the talent on. As I say, it's not something I enjoy doing for myself, but it is gratifying to be able to offer that little bit of useful wisdom in the absence of an actual father. In the absence of an actual father, it is consoling to know that I can look the part.

Busy Signals

Busy, busy, busy is what we Bokononists whisper whenever we think of how complicated and unpredictable the machinery of life really is.

Kurt Vonnegut Jr., *Cat's Cradle*

Juggling has never managed very much status among the arts. None of the nine Muses covers juggling, and no university offers an M.F.A. in the field. Juggling has no national laureate, and it has not inspired a critical school or a special collection in any major library. By reputation it has more in common with sword swallowing and shell games than with literature and music. If it is not shadier than these pursuits, it is more frivolous. Even at its most wholesome, juggling does not escape its association with circuses, birthday parties, and clowns. It represents, in short, a shallower aesthetic; it can be pleasant but never profound.

But I submit that there is a poignancy about juggling that belies its reputation, and this is because of all the arts juggling is the most obvious about how it is always postponing the inevitable. The juggler openly competes with the susceptibility to ruin of everything he tries to keep aloft and in play. His efforts remind us of the whole spectrum of entropy that awaits us, from the betrayals that bloom in our own bodies to the heat death of the universe. The poet Richard Wilbur reminds us that the juggler's art and desire is "to win for once over the world's weight." It is but one more form of worship that the juggler conducts, a mass held midair. And it is an implicit prayer: give us this day a little altitude, our ration of uplift. But we join the juggler in knowing what must finally befall him.

His gasping alacrity does not refute but emphasizes his fate. All the while we anticipate the coming collapse, for we know about how bodies operate and how they ultimately do not; we know about the bled energies of the world whose fate they represent. The lesson here is that even someone with a talent for winning for once over the world's weight does not win once and for all.

Jugglers will tell you that it isn't the juggling that's tough. Definitely it's a skill to be reckoned with, but anyone with time on his hands and moderate agility in them can eventually learn to juggle balls. Within a few weeks he'll have his orbit up and running regular as a turbine. And while substituting knives, torches, or sickles for balls vastly increases the chances for disaster, a steady nerve is all that needs to be added to the recipe for success. If you call that success. I suppose there are pleasures to be had merely from staying in circulation, by enduring and denying stresses routinely, with wheels spinning heedlessly in the slick mud, approximating the dream of a permanent revolution. Nevertheless the effect is pretty purgatorial when you come to think about it, like Ixion turning eternally according to his punishment in the underworld. No, the greater art is not juggling several of any one object; rather, it is juggling very different things. A juggler worth the name, as any worthy juggler will attest, is the one who can juggle, say, a gerbil, a bowling ball, and a cricket bat together. It's the negotiation of various shapes and separate hefts that marks the professional—the finding among them of what in the case of successful fiction A. S. Byatt terms "the idiosyncratic arc of connection."

I've watched top-notch jugglers up close, and I have to say that this particular trick, accomplished without fumble or injury, impresses me at the level of the handling of planets in the solar system. Even more so, in fact. Mastering the actions of the planets like that—keeping nine disparate ellipses alive simultaneously—is a singular achievement, beyond dispute. But because the planets being kept cosmically aloft are, in the end, all balls, that accomplishment, for however many eons it's sustained, will not hold an audience for very long. If Mercury were triangular, for instance, or Saturn a stick, crowds might gather to watch the maintenance of their orbits as raptly as they attend upon the fumbly juggler in the park, who invites kids to toss things into his art just barely within reach, and whose maneuvering seems at any second about to succumb to gravity but doesn't quite, doesn't yet.

When Wallace Stevens admires "the things / That in each other are included, the whole, / The complicate, the amassing harmony," it is the orrery of all things he speaks of: the evanescent as well as the evident, the spectral and the solid in concert. He is transfixed by such frail and essential tensions as keep our spirits up and manage by sleight of imagination to lift the material world with them:

> Impalpable habitations that seem to move
> In the movement of the colors of the mind,
>
> The far-fire flowing and the dim-coned bells
> Coming together in a sense in which we are poised. . . .

In their tropes and associations, which venture out and factor back in concert, writers are jugglers, too. They leave the world behind awhile without deserting the premises. Yet it is a temporary success at best: the mundane nature of the given world resists conversion. Ultimately all flights are grounded.

The art lies in testing the boundaries of the contract between escape and return. For while escape may occasionally seduce the practitioner, escape by itself is an insufficient aesthetic to aspire to. "May no fate willfully misunderstand me / And half grant what I wish and snatch me away / Not to return," clarifies Robert Frost, who dreams of being lifted heavenward and returned to earth by a nimble birch tree. Sylvia Plath is grimmer, but she advocates a similar cycle in "Lady Lazarus":

> It's easy enough to do it and stay put.
> It's the theatrical
>
> Comeback in broad day
> To the same place, the same face, the same brute
> Amused shout:
>
> 'A miracle!'
> That knocks me out.

If magicians merely subtracted from the census when they made volunteers disappear from locked boxes and suspended sacks, the effect would not be so satisfying. After the vanishing we want a "Voila!" to ratify the restoration. In the words of Robert Frost, "that would be good both going and coming back."

According to Isaiah Berlin, human beings boil down to two distinct sub-species, the hedgehog and the fox. The hedgehog knows one big thing; his curriculum comprises a single course—javelin throwing, for instance, or the immanence of Jesus. He'll devote his day to the rise and fall of stocks, to honing his ground strokes for tennis, to memorizing all of the five-letter combinations in Scrabble, or to otherwise achieving the zenith of some specific expertise, an isolated promontory from which he'll seldom if ever stray. The fox, however, knows many things. If the hedgehog dwells deep in his only burrow, squatting like a clod of the very earth he's displaced, the fox is inherently itinerant and fidgety. His scampering from subject to subject and from site to site may seem like a trivial pursuit when compared to the hedgehog's devotion to holding the fort, but it is really just another natural disposition.

It may be argued that the ideal juggler performs as a species between them, combining both penchants and capacities, in that he constantly negotiates between the rooted and roaming planes. On the one hand, he manages a hedgehoggian steadfastness, whose essence is repetition—the juggler is dug in, as it were. On the other hand, if he masters his craft, he opens himself up to foxy distraction, coaxing an audience member to toss a ballpoint pen or a tennis racket into the fray he makes. Thus both his hands are occupied, but neither is full for long.

Americans have long been weaned on the Puritan ethic that deems any recuperative hour idle and all idleness unpatriotic. One of the main impacts of American history textbooks is to shame us with the founding achievements of polymaths and multitaskers par excellence. Think of Benjamin Franklin, on whose 1040 form there would not have been nearly enough space for him to list his several professions. Statesman, inventor, author, intercontinental man about town—Franklin makes most of the members of *Who's Who* seem like slackers by comparison. And what discipline didn't Thomas Jefferson have a steady hand in? He'd seem a classic case of schizophrenia were it not for the fact that the egos among which he altered—farmer and architect, historian and surveyor, philosopher and president—were so exalted and so effectively embodied in him. These are the sort of exemplary men invoked by teachers all over the country to chasten and charge the distracted, slumping children in their care, the implicit lesson being that unless their students do not succeed in piling extracurricular Pelion upon homework Ossa, they are not only letting their fathers down, they are also letting their forefathers down as well.

Bad enough to be a boy pressured by conventional gender expectations to score the touchdown, run the company, and fell the elk in order to feed his ego and his family. Nowadays girls are not exempt from such prospects; on the contrary, they are positively singled out for them. As a result, the little girl who contentedly plays house is a budding recidivist, and alert parents will cajole her to upgrade her dream of becoming a mommy by adding an M.B.A. When she naps, they will mix Tonka trucks in with her Cabbage Patch dolls and tuck socket wrenches in with the plastic cookware.

Although the most renowned jugglers, so far as fame is available in circus circles, have been men, outside of the confines of the Big Top, society now conspicuously assigns that job to women. In regard to the laying on of expectation, the media are relentless and merciless. Lifestyle and fashion magazines check each woman out in the checkout line and find her wanting, not-so-subtly instilling inferiority and guilt should she happen to let any option or obligation slip. Not only should she have it all, she is told, as a truly foxy lady she should have it all at the same time.

Magazines like *Cosmopolitan* and *Redbook* prod their readers to know as much about organizing a retirement portfolio as they do about organizing a dinner party and to handle each with equal aplomb. The articles urge them to smooth away anxiety as they iron out cellulite; they instruct them to perfect their capacity for orgasm under couture clothing; they assure them that, with proper exercise, they can attain the ideal, necessary mixture of limberness and stamina. Meanwhile, although television advertising has long been indicted for the impossible models it inflicts upon women, its impact persists despite their knowing better. Advertising keeps them in thrall to motion. Interrupt a woman in the throes of responsibility, and she'll have to judder to a halt, that is, if she deigns to stop at all; odds are she'll hurry past you like a hobo holding a cardboard sign on the side of a highway.

Especially pernicious, as I recall, was a commercial for Enjoli perfume, which featured a temptress in business clothing gyrating to the lines of a trendy siren's song:

> I can bring home the bacon,
> Fry it up in a pan,
> And never, ever let you forget you're a man,
> 'Cause I'm a woman . . .

For every woman who protested that this campaign distorted the feminist cause more than *Playboy* ever did, there may have been one who wondered why, while she tried to help her kid with algebra homework, the spaghetti was boiling over; why, in order to keep up with her bookkeeping, she had to let her gym membership lapse; or why, as she outed the grout around the toilet, her sex drive stalled. Maybe the fragrance has faded, but the memory still stings.

Today an unadvertised version of the Enjoli woman scurries into my American literature class. She is ten minutes late, and that's without her having taken even one minute for glamour. My course is one of five she is currently enrolled in, in addition to the twenty-five hours each week she puts in as a sales clerk at Famous-Barr to pay for tuition. On Wednesday she had to bring her sick daughter to class because her day-care center doesn't allow children with fevers over ninety-nine degrees to be dropped off. At the end of class, while her little girl was corralling her crayons, she came up to ask me if there was any way she could take the midterm ahead of time. Her supervisor wanted her to do an extra Friday morning shift, and frankly she could use the extra hours.

Does she ever think it peculiar how often signs of self-improvement and signs of impending suicide are identical? Losing weight, emptying the attic, dropping ballast, making amends. Strange, too, to discover how resentment leaks, then pools, in the little interims she allows herself. For some women, she knows, this is the run-up to running around or running off. In other cases, it is only an incentive to petulance and petty insurgencies, such as overcooking the roast or buying something frivolous that in another mood she would have passed on. Her wedding anniversary is next week. Although she doesn't say it aloud, I suspect that it crosses her mind that the traditional gift for this one could be weaponry.

Shamed for failings her grandmother never would have recognized as possibilities for failure in the first place, the modern woman cringes as her mandatory personalities haggle. She is all industry and virtuous bustle, counting on the discreet charms of the reconciled account and the scrubbed floor. "Your house is the last before the infinite, / whoever you are," writes Rilke, but he had a less explicitly material residence in mind than the one she lives in, where on her worst days she senses that she's been placed into custody. Before the infinite, she perhaps manages a little spot cleaning between arbitrating the battle in the boys' room over the remote, sewing the button back on Stephanie's dance costume, and finding two minutes' refuge in the garage to remind herself what she needs to bring to tomorrow's early meeting. All this with the day waning and with no detectable end to the claims on her energy and compassion. When Walt Whitman declares, "I loafe and invite my soul, / I lean and loafe at my ease observing a spear of summer grass," she tacitly inserts the phrase "time permitting." More than a little resentfully, she realizes just how long it's been that she's been able to fit her ease in, much less had the house in shape to have her soul over. Who wouldn't like to settle back on ample hindquarters and just ruminate like Ferdinand among the flowers? Maybe one day, when she's out to pasture, she can pick up poetry again. About the time she gets to clean out the attic, she might spare part of an afternoon for transcendentalism.

And sooner or later, the juggler stumbles and grows sullen, the bowling ball having crashed through the breakfront, the hamster having tumbled and scuttled under the refrigerator, the hacksaw having become embedded in her husband's neck. As even the most expert juggler will admit, entropy is not reserved for the cosmos; it also scuttles the staged performance and infiltrates the kitchen. "You making haste haste on decay," offers Robinson Jeffers, knowing that composing poetry is by no means the only neurosis the paradox inspires. It's a poem worth adding to the to-do list.

You should have known Soozie, the first girl in my school to put circles over her *i*'s. when they, along with daisies painted on cheeks and hawser-length French braids, were reigning affectations. Had you known her, you might have guessed that Soozie secretly yearned to add umlauts over both *o*'s, which would have had nothing to do with pronunciation but everything to do with style. And at sixteen she *did* do everything with style, balancing cheerleading, studies, what seemed like sixty closest friends, and the doting attentions of David Goldstein so nonchalantly as to make everyone assume that all of them were weightless anyway.

Fast-forward thirty-five years, and you'll find Susan "Soozie" (Biitner) Nimitz prominently featured in half a dozen organizations ranging from the charities on whose behalf she telephones, to the cultural society whose newsletter she edits, to the parents' association at her twin daughters' high school she bakes for. I imagine her hard at it wherever she is, to the extent of doing butt-tightening exercises when she's stopped at red lights or keeping her financial records on the toilet tank to update during her after-dinner visits to the stool. Oh, she remains a woman of many and diverse gifts, does Susan "Soozie" (Biitner) Nimitz, who has miraculously kept up most of her high school contacts (not to mention her figure, thanks to her Tuesday-Thursday-Saturday early-morning visits to the gym). She is still a blur of talent and activity, is Susan "Soozie" (Biitner) Nimitz, ever selfless yet somehow, magically, always fashionable, so it is only natural that so much falls to her. I mean not only the cascade of proper nouns following mention of her name in the annual alumni bulletin she compiles for the class of '71, nouns that grant her appointments and burdens greater gravity but also exact her service at the helm of the reunion committee. There's her married name on the masthead of the latest mailer: the Soozie I knew is still discernible despite the addition of "Nimitz" and despite the fact that (owing, I suppose, to the limits of her printer) her signature circles have been filled in.

It would suit the thesis to report that Susan "Soozie" (Biitner) Nimitz has on some front dropped the ball. You might predict that one of her girls has written a tell-all memoir of how her mother was everywhere else but there for her, which accounts for that daughter's drug overdose or a youthful experimentation with prostitution. At the very least you might suspect that Susan "Soozie" means to double her weekly sessions with her psychiatrist as soon as she can rearrange her schedule. But this is all only conjecture. Certainly there is no mention of any such thing in the alumni bulletin, which continues to appear, like everything else she's ever been associated with, flawlessly and right on time.

"True happiness, we are told, consists in getting out of one's self," says Henry James, "but the point is not only to get out—you must stay out, and to stay out you must have some absorbing errand." Perhaps, but I doubt that any "absorbing errand" James might have had in mind would have required a drive to the mall. Actually, for the contemporary spouse/ parent/employee, "swamped" comes closer to the mark than "absorbed." In the movie *Parenthood*, Steve Martin's Gil complains, "My whole *life* is have to!" Playing his wife, Mary Steenburgen sympathizes, but not for long, since there's their son to pick up from Little League, their daughter to costume for the school play, and at least a hundred other duties and crises to contend with. She has just as many demands on her as her husband does, with his exasperation thrown in. The instant her head hits the pillow, sleep falls on her like an axe. And by the end of the day, aren't they both grateful for the blade.

A given friend may function like six of the best conditioned and most dedicated people you'll even meet, but not forever and, most likely, not for long. She may purge her vocabulary of qualifiers and abjure the conditional because "maybes," "some days," "mights," and "coulds" collude to undo the project of the self she's embarked upon. She may engage more issues than a caucus, attack more tasks than a squad of moms in their sundry vans, and undertake more missions than a Presbyterian platoon. She may remake herself into a tour de force of resolve. The fact remains that eventually she'll lock her briefcase in the trunk, forget her youngest at Wal-Mart, relegate her family to a dinner of peanut butter and bananas, or trade foreplay for an extra twenty minutes of sleep. Some of her several assignments will crash to the floor the same way that a plate spinner's vaudeville act ends. She will come suddenly awake in the middle of the night, haunted by a bad dream that somewhere a door is closing. And what is that new stab in her back as she hoists herself out of bed? There is a colophon of pain at the base of her spine. It could be anything from an inconvenience to a budding cancer. Either way, worrying about it is an indulgence she can't afford.

She will gird herself again, with "delayed gratification" her mantra, although she realizes that "delayed gratification" is a redundancy. At the end of the day, when she drops from too much duty and solicitude, there is no other kind. Recognizing a predicament peculiar to her gender, Virginia Woolf suggests that had Shakespeare a sister with comparable gifts, she most likely would have gone insane. Despite the relative broadening of opportunities for today's women, throwing in car pool duties and a spin class might remove any doubt on that subject.

Meet Anna H., a patient of celebrated neurologist Dr. Oliver Sacks, who sought out the doctor's help because she was finding it increasingly difficult to keep her bearings. Briefly put, she complained that she could not recognize objects or reliably orient herself in space. And the affliction was growing worse, making it impossible, for instance, for her to continue performing as a concert pianist (she would suddenly find a page of the score she was playing unintelligible) and dangerous for her to drive (she would "miss objects to the right"). For years, through elaborate efforts of improvisation, adjustment, and compensation, she had managed to get by, but over time her coping strategies more and more often fell short. Eventually she found that a photograph of a face would not resolve; she could not make the "mush" of details cohere into anything meaningful. A drawing of a pencil "could be so many things," she said. "Could be a violin . . . a pen." She had no idea what to make of a whistle, while she could not focus at all on a picture of scissors, looking resolutely instead at the white space beneath it. Dr. Sacks does note that she immediately identified a house as a house; however, she once walked off with his doctor's bag, having mistaken it for her handbag. Words, too, had lost their handles. She might have known what a match was or what it was for—"That is to make fire"—but no "match" ever flared in her mind. She was like Eve wandering about the garden before Adam provided the concordance. Not even the condiments she used every day came through any more distinctly than as "little red things," by which she meant the red-topped spice bottles in which the nameless contents were kept. "When I can't say something, I circumscribe," she explained, offering her own unique gloss to the juggler's creed.

And don't we know in advance where all juggling leads? We understand that the act implies the crash to come. One day the juggler will throw one too many unsustainable weights around, and something—the briefcase or the bowling pin, the violin lesson or the volleyball, the cell phone or the cleaver, the morning workout or the raw egg, the appointment to fix the timing belt on the Civic or the flaming ring—will fall too fast and just out of reach. Trying to recover, she will slip or stumble or surrender altogether and hit the floor along with everything else.

Unless there is a countervailing force in the universe, which is, after all, the juggler's intimation and ongoing pretense. Then we might witness a merciful reversal of the fall. And so we pray for the businesswoman's levitation, for the ascension of the working wife and mother, toward a heaven that eternally acknowledges her ambitions and her sacrifices and, as a reward, leaves her nothing whatsoever left to do. We contrive for her a juggler's apotheosis. We wish her risen out of reach of commitment. We flatter her by envisioning one mischievous Fate that understands her perfectly, that grants her a good riddance, good going, and not coming back.

Goodness Knows

Deep in my body the future
Is intact, in smolder, in the very bone,
And I dig for it like a dog, good dog.

William Matthews, "Good"

Money is not the only way in which Thomas Jefferson Independent Day School trumps the public alternatives. Admittedly not having to rely exclusively upon state funding for its existence is its principal and most manifest advantage. No referendum need be floated past recalcitrant voters just to patch its leaky roof, upgrade its video equipment, furnish its library, or keep its teachers within shouting distance of a living wage. A simple flyer sent home to Thomas Jefferson's well-endowed, intensely involved parents is sufficient to rouse their consciences and enlist their fiscal support, from which, as the many doctors, lawyers, certified public accountants, and college professors among them know, all advantages, educational and otherwise, ultimately derive. But as I say, although money may be the major premise of the school's preeminence, it is not the whole argument.

For one thing there is school spirit. Twenty-first-century skeptics may scoff at so hackneyed a notion, but studies clearly indicate that there is a direct correlation between school pride and academic performance. Of course one would predict that children attending a school that betrays no taint of graffiti, illicit drugs, explosives, or miserliness would automatically display greater school spirit than their public school counterparts do. But Thomas Jefferson does not leave even that aspect of its supremacy to chance, lest its students take even one bit of their privilege for granted. Whereas other area schools content themselves with conventional versions of encouragement like an annual Wear Your School Colors Day or Dress Backwards Day, Thomas Jefferson sponsors special student demonstration days on an almost weekly basis.

Far be it from the administration at TJ to miss any chance to turn an event into an opportunity to exercise young imaginations, to urge their charges to trope and scheme. This year alone, there was Dress as Your Hero Day, which saw the elementary school hallways brim with budding facsimiles of sports stars, miniaturized stalwarts from Marvel Comics, and little politicians culled from approved social studies texts. On Wild West Day, the frontier conditions typical of recess were brought indoors, where the boys happily brandished toy guns and dragged about in chaps from class to class. The girls, having raided the secondhand stores for every scrap of crinoline in town, donned bonnets and inserted themselves into skirts so outlandishly large that in their swooshy, cumbrous bustling through the school corridors they collided all day like so many bumper cars set on mute. Future Career Day saw scores of pre-preprofessionals descend in force from their parents' minivans and SUVs, seeding the grounds of Thomas Jefferson with elitism only a country club could compete with. That day saw Jasons overwhelmed by the tailoring of their fathers' cuffs and ties and Jennifers rooting through borrowed pocketbooks for day planners that held no more substantial task than homework and recalled no appointment more pressing than afternoon snack time. Favorite Movie Character Day chiefly featured creatures from science fiction, whose appeal was the opportunity to indulge in makeup and homemade prosthetics. Emerging en masse at 3:00, the ingeniously disfigured kids, clumsy in their taxidermy, their lipstick scars smeared and sundry pusses running, looked as though they'd mutated from some nuclear accident or awful contamination of the drinking fountains.

Strangest and most affecting of all, however, was Fake an Injury Day. I had drop-off duty that morning, so I got to see firsthand the most cheerful triage scene imaginable. All of Thomas Jefferson had been transformed into a shrill, giggly killing field, where kids hung up in crutches and makeshift braces gabbed with temporary amputees and everyone enviously eyed one another's bandaging—those who hadn't opted for blindness as one of their maladies did, that is. Their faces were elaborately tuck pointed, bruised and scabbed with badges of unnamed disaster.

They gasped and groaned retrieving their books from their lockers; on their way to first period, they limped and seeped. "Oh, the humanity!" I might have cried, if they all didn't look so delighted with their manufactured damage and so cute.

I caught sight of the headmaster (the slightly more militant private school equivalent of a principal—think of a principal with epaulets) moving approvingly among the wounded, and I asked him about the idea behind Fake an Injury Day. "Some of the other theme days were basically to give them a good time, but in this case, we thought there might also be a lesson for them about the handicapped. You know, spending a day on crutches or in a wheelchair might make them think twice the next time they encounter someone who actually has to do it every day. They help one another through doors. They sign one another's casts. So while we're giving them a chance to have some fun, we're also trying to instill a sense of charity for people who aren't as fortunate as they are." Thus the good people at Thomas Jefferson believed that they could regulate decency like digestion. "And best of all, at least from the kids' point of view," he continued, "there's the best costume competition for each grade, which really brings out the inventiveness in them." He was right about that: my girlfriend's son had spent the previous evening outfitting his mishap—he'd opted for failing to use his seat belt and being thrown through the windshield in a highway crash—with as much rigor as he did to psych up for a junior league soccer game.

The headmaster then excused himself to settle down a couple of fifth graders who were dueling with canes. Meanwhile, I considered the judging of the contest to come. Whose blood would prove more abundant than whose? Whose bones would be broken more dramatically? Whose chest wounds would suck worse?

At 3:00, the kids sprinted from the building, releasing the energies they'd been suppressing for seven hours. (All honorably discharged, Purple Hearts all.) So much for the metrical procession of mock casualties and ersatz cripples between classes. Resurrected by the last bell, they quickly shed the traces of their suffering. Now their splints, slings, and jerry-rigged constraints miraculously fell away from their newly restored bodies, and by the time they reached their waiting parents, their former vigor had been completely restored.

I wonder if, despite the official optimism, the sensitivity the administration had hoped Fake an Injury Day would inspire actually lasted past the parking lot. Returned to their homes and regular health, did the children retain their sympathy, or did it fall away as readily as the rest of the trappings of their masquerade? I appreciated the headmaster's incentives, but his "Learn to Hug, Hug to Learn" did not exactly correspond with the children I knew (much less the child I'd once been) beyond the confines of the school. At his behest, the kids had played at cowboys and comic book characters, but no matter how resolute their pretense, they were never taken in. Why assume that they would succumb to mandatory compassion permanently on their own?

Not that my own university is any less hopeful in this regard. In addition to complying with our catalog's insistence that requiring coursework in the arts and humanities will invigorate the latent virtues of the undergraduates, the honors students must complete a special component of the core curriculum: mandatory volunteer work. Especially gifted and bolstered by grants, honors students are expected to give of themselves especially, and for a grade. Cynics among us have suggested that mandatory volunteerism is not only inauthentic but also self-contradictory. But just because noblesse oblige may not come naturally, that does not make it any less noble or obligatory, or so our deans declare. The homeless whom our seniors feed at Souls' Harbor Mission, the tornado victims whose debris they clear and whose roofs they repair, the indigent whose Goodwill clothing they fold and box, and the nursing home residents whose stories they sit still for do not complain that the students have interned with them for credit. If need is not finicky, neither should sympathy be.

In case anyone wonders, in order to earn A's, the students are expected to devote at least fifty hours apiece to a community activity chosen from an approved menu provided by the honors program. (Students must document their contributions and must keep journals detailing the nature and impact of their experiences.) The most dedicated, most visible volunteers are honored by having their names etched onto a plaque for permanent display. Once again there are some who question this practice. They recall, for example, that according to the Hebrew idea of *tzedakah,* the highest form of charity is anonymous since it does not further humble its recipient or aggrandize the giver. But the consensus is that if we are going to broadcast the accomplishments of our top athletes, we should commemorate the efforts of these students as well. So there are trophies for star halfbacks and for star humanitarians, too.

Scheduling pressures being what they are, it is not unusual for a few honors students to find themselves having to scramble at the end of the semester to live up to their contracts. Then the greater Joplin area is positively *bombarded* by philanthropy, and it seems that no cripple can approach a curb without being accosted by aggressively well-meaning students. Bums are lifted bodily from their benches and shunted into free lunches. With summa cum laude on the line, procrastinators fight about who has dibs on manning the Salvation Army kettle in front of Smitty's Market or swiftly descend upon the last unclaimed illiterate adults at NALA. When local desperation gets depleted, some sympathetic families graciously submit to the care of several anxious degree-seeking students at the same time. For it is not always only the needy that are in need.

And if school projects cannot implant sympathy by themselves, the government is glad to take up the slack. I do not mean those controversial entitlement programs that keep a considerable percentage of Americans treading water at the shallow end of the pool, although even hard-shelled Republicans will agree that altruistic desires lie behind them. I am referring instead to the proposal made by the first President Bush for a national resurgence of volunteerism. He famously envisioned "a thousand points of light," by which he meant all of the heartfelt, unheralded efforts of individual citizens serving up and doling out, picking up and pitching in all over America. He maintained that the forces of fellowship would be self-perpetuating (by which he implied they'd receive no additional funding), leading to a veritable epidemic of aid. Here was a touchstone of what came to be known as "compassionate conservatism," a concept that has managed to endure well beyond President Bush's term in office and will undoubtedly persist for quite some time. Candidates present and future can rest assured: there is plenty of squalor to go around.

For what it's worth, sympathy training also precedes children's exposure to formal education and political campaigns. Although they are notorious for the ways their plastic weaponry and gruesome video games contribute to the coarsening of American children, toy manufacturers do market items designed to inspire gentility, too. For instance, it has probably been superseded by fancier toys by now, but I remember that back in the sixties my friend's sister, Bonnie, had a doll that delivered wholesome messages whenever she tugged the ring that hung like a loose vertebra from its back. "I love you." "I'm sorry." "Hope you feel better soon." "Oh, excuse me!" "Give me a kiss, please!" "Thank you very much!" I can't recall the doll's complete repertoire, but I can still hear its bright ardors and squawky solicitations, all of which were delivered (until the mechanism wore out) with the same exaggerated zeal. I realize now that this doll—Luvvy, I think it was called, unless that was just the name Bonnie chose for it—was created not only to provide companionship and comfort when no friends visited or the night noises came, but also to condition kids to perform the same courtesies in the world beyond their bedrooms (where, to be sure, those sentiments were needed even more frequently). My own daughter, who when it came to good manners was always, I am proud to say, something of a prodigy, charmed as many adults with her sweetly delivered "Excuse me" or "No thank you" as she did with conventional little-girl endowments like her gurgling laugh or her naturally curly hair. Her mother and I would be complimented so often on what a polite and thoughtful daughter we'd raised that I came to think her etiquette an achievement that would forever outshine any other achievement of hers; it had already apparently eclipsed anything her parents could affix to their own résumés. I suppose that in the unlikely event my girl ever turns to delinquency, her polished "I beg your pardon" would persuade any judge to suspend his sentence.

While I joke about our Elizabeth's good manners, saying that we've taught her that since we are not rich and powerful, we need to be polite, I confess that I am still surprised by their general rarity. I am a full professor at my university, and however you might rate my stature, I believe that, regardless, I still merit better than a "Hey, I didn't get a syllabus" barked from halfway down the hall. "Where are your parents?" I feel like saying whenever I'm so impertinently accosted. (That "Where are your parents?," like the phrase "impertinently accosted," would betray more years than I care to disclose stays me, but only barely.) But where *are* they or, rather, where *were* they when the critical civilities should have been planted in their children's minds while those minds were still loamy and arable? I mean, do you *eat* with those mouths? I know that public school budgets are constrained, but what would it have cost to sponsor an Etiquette Day, anyway? Because the cost of not having done so is glaringly apparent.

One definitely detects it in that common solecism "I could care less," which is typically uttered with equal parts impertinence and ennui. Obviously the dismissive speaker means that he *couldn't* care less, but the attitude behind the comment deflects any impulse one might have to correct him. On the other hand, it may well be that "I could care less" is precisely what he'd intended to say. Don't think you've arrived at the rock bottom of my indifference—there's a subbasement you haven't seen yet, an essential vacancy beyond whose first step no tenderness survives and the sun doesn't touch. That is the literal meaning of the claim: immunity to otherness. A sand crab's accomplishment, a spider's utterly centripetal life.

The unsettling aspect of this kind of unflappable affect is that it may be as natural to people as nurture, maybe more so. Do not underestimate the wish or the ability not to be bothered.

In his wistfully titled literary anthology, *The Book of Virtues*, William Bennett assumes a clear, causal connection between righteous texts and right conduct. What we need, he contends, is a moral reference and ethical compendium. Nobility in, nobility out: purify the input, he implies, and we can dissolve all of that postmodern sludge that's been clogging the progress of the ambivalent and the lost. Once we are properly reconditioned, we will overcome our consternation when we are caught behind the handicapped driver who hugs the middle of the freeway at forty miles per hour, replacing surliness with sympathy. Once we have absorbed the loftier abstractions that captain Bennett's chapters—"Compassion," "Responsibility," "Self-Discipline," and so on—we will transcend those inferior reactions—irritation, impatience, guilt, and so on—we have toward the images of starving, staring Africans and tattered orphans diaspora'd over the television channels after midnight when we're searching for something decent to help us get back to sleep.

Frankly I think it naive to suppose that a charitable heart can be cultivated just like a champion rose. Yet however misguided spiritual courses like Bennett's seem to me, it is not because I've tested out of them, goodness knows. My students cannot reconcile the unsavory biographical notes accompanying the stories and poems in the Norton with the notion that reading them will prove any more redemptive to them than they were to the drunks, abusers, and suicides who wrote them in the first place. For once, I'm tempted to side with them. Doubt may be another one of the deadly contaminants William Bennett blames our insensitivity on. But it's fair of university students, for whom every tuition dollar is dear, to ask, first, how the boorish and corrupt were able to withhold their better impulses everywhere but on the page and, second, why the writers remained unaffected by what the Academic Policies Committee insists will benefit the people forced to read them. If we really are going to book on our virtues, it is incumbent upon us to countenance our vices at the same time, not to mention those of the canonical authors whose saving graces didn't dependably grace or save them personally.

And what is this hypothetical repository of goodness, anyway, on which administrations rely? It hardly exalts us to think so, but much of what we call virtue might really come down to a failure of time management. We are not too moral but too mortgaged, schedulewise, to stray. Consider daytime dramas, in whose collective rolling boil characters constantly—violently, inadvertently, sexually, and even, more often than you might believe, amnesiacally—collide. Track them as they bind and break along every conceivable surface and couple according to every possible option in the matrix of the cast. Desire and revenge are seldom merely mutual but soon evolve into triangular and, when ratings warrant, quadrilateral or pentagonal phases. (Note that even the most notoriously depraved among the characters are still admitted to every private party.) What keeps the fans enraptured and compels the skeptical to tune in is the prospect of watching how everyone, not excepting the upright, eventually gets down and dirty, only to rise perpetually glamorous from his or her neighbor's bed.

What strikes me as most incredible about this fictional economy is that everyone involved gets to have world enough and time to get involved with everyone else in town. No one has to get the kids off to school, balance a checkbook, mow a lawn. No one has to take the car in, visit the dentist, stop at the grocery. Oh, they purportedly have jobs, most of them, and elevated ones at that. They are doctors, lawyers, corporate magnates, ostentatiously titled protagonists. But no one actually *works*. No one moves paper with a fraction of the fluster folks who actually do those jobs have to. Admittedly it's hard to imagine theme music accompanying our own quotidian efforts, but it's just as hard to imagine those of us taken up with those responsibilities dirtying so much laundry so operatically so often. But if we are in this one way superior to the sexually fluent and ideally abbed, the trendily coiffed and relentlessly co-opted characters on television, it may simply be that it's our schedules, not our ethics, that prohibit it. We are not necessarily too principled, just too busy. While they elongate their glares and extend their sighs, we have to take the dog to the vet and get to the dry cleaner before it closes. They linger, gossip, plot, molest, and chide while we, with real jobs and families pressing, cannot. Transgression requires not so much evil thoughts as it does hours we haven't got.

Nevertheless we have to keep our sympathies on alert for whenever the odd hour does present itself. Toward that end, temples all across the country encourage their congregations to practice the spirit of *tikkun olam*, the repair of the world. That sentiment has always been a staple of Judaism, but the idea of making a tangible contribution, of manifesting faith in the form of humanitarian deeds, has become increasingly popular these days, perhaps because in these harried times we are so much more aware of all that needs repair. Under the auspices of so-called Caring Committees and Legions of Love, blood drives are on the rise and gift baskets are more ample than ever before. More and more meals are being distributed, clothes collected, and pets adopted. Disparage if you will the youth of today, but I challenge you to find a square mile of contemporary America that remains untouched by *mitzvot*. If submission to sin is in our nature, so is the performance of durable goods. As the statisticians might say, we are trending sympathetic. In short, the fix is in.

In other houses of worship, the impulse goes by different names, but it is *tikkun olam* nonetheless. And when it comes to gathering canned goods, visiting shut-ins, or writing cards to victims of poverty overseas, it's the children who are the most enthusiastic. There is undoubtedly a lesson there, too, as any rabbi, minister, or headmaster worth his homilies would tell you. Children are hungry for special days, you see, and eager to believe in them. Give them another task to look forward to—that's the key to making learning relevant to the young. Turn the chore into a calling. That way, although they complete the latest philanthropic round of delivering foil-wrapped dinners to the elderly or wrapping presents for hospitalized toddlers, of soliciting donations door to door or holding bake sales in front of Wal-Mart's door, of bagging trash for those who haven't or walking for those who can't, they understand that they will never be finished. And this awareness brings them down and uplifts them together: the opportunities and the urgencies are unending. They will never be finished for good.

Let's Be Realistic

Some high schools positively glom onto their most renowned graduates, graduates that, to be honest, their alma maters did little other than endure during their pre-esteem years. Some eagerly take credit for having spawned state senators or sports heroes, who return for commencement exercises to shower the gathered with mottoes, homilies, or acronyms to rise by. But notoriety can be a mixed blessing. For every school that celebrates an eminent grad, there is one that makes the evening news for having unwittingly harbored an embezzler-to-be or for having weaned a future drug dealer. Apart from the credits or crimes of the students in their temporary care, there are also high schools that suffer media attention for misfortunes they did nothing to contribute to. They are filmed for having stood in the path of a tornado, for example, or for having provided a wall for a bus whose brakes went out to come to rest against. In these ways a building can build a reputation and a résumé. A given high school may find prominence either as the birthplace of accomplishment or as the backdrop for disaster.

I went to Niles East High School, which closed in 1980 due to the vicissitudes of demographics and the local budget. For several years the building lay barren, holding only the ghosts of school years past and students passed on. The consolation for its closure, however, was that this perfectly viable high school could be used as a movie set. The next time you rent *Risky Business,* force yourself to look beyond the puckish good looks of a young Tom Cruise to take in the school he's attending, and you'll see the school I attended, too. Admittedly when students go home in *Risky Business,* they return to better, more cinematically attractive neighborhoods than I did, like the gated roads of Kenilworth or the

sculpted, grove-cuddled hush of Highland Park. But do not be fooled by
the director's creative license. To go to Niles East, Tom Cruise had to live
in Skokie. Deal with it.

Sixteen Candles, too, was shot at my school. Check out the Niles East
windbreaker on a teenage John Cusack. Those halls and grounds were my
halls and grounds, and although my classmates and I may not have chafed
and shuddered at the sight of them for millions to witness on the big
screen, we chafed and shuddered unacknowledged all the same. The establishing shot of the high school that opens the movie also greeted my
friends and me each morning for four years, for four years establishing
my friends and me as well.

So my high school's greatest claim to fame is, basically, that it looked
like a high school. During my stay, the place was unselfconsciously iconic.
The lockers looked the way lockers looked in movies and as lockers in
movies always would; the cafeteria ladies appeared to have come to us
from central casting; the custodians were cloned from the cells of the
originals of that unobtrusive and dutiful species. In fact every detail, from
the blackboard erasers laid out in measured lengths along each chalk tray
to the dented stainless steel paper towel dispensers in the bathroom, from
the perforated ceiling tiles to the unvarying linoleum floors, had the quality of the Platonic about them. Not that any heaven worthy of the name
would include a high school anywhere in its blissful vicinity, but if it did,
it would be the quintessence of Niles East, whence all high schools, to my
way of thinking, derive.

Speaking through his blue guitarist, Wallace Stevens tries to entice listen-
ers by promising that "things as they are / Are changed upon the blue gui-
tar." But the people clamored for a less transcendent number: "But play,
you must, / A tune beyond us, yet ourselves, // A tune upon the blue gui-
tar / Of things exactly as they are." As it happened, the old man had neither the instrument nor the wherewithal to play requests. How could he?
Imagine the prospect of encountering things precisely, exclusively as they
are, and you will find that the imagination inevitably intrudes. "Yet the
absence of the imagination had / Itself to be imagined," Stevens says in
another inevitably decorated venue, the point being that the so-called
"plain sense of things" is a contradiction in contaminated terms. At least,
so the imagination, protecting its turf, reassures itself.

But if a pure, uninflected performance were possible, how would it appear? How would we perceive a scene unimpeded by ornament or preconception? Comedian Steven Wright once deadpanned that he'd had a dream in which everything had been replaced by an exact duplicate. I submit that such a dream might best have been realized at my high school, where in the translation to Hollywood not a molecule varied from standard issue. Everything was exactly and unwaveringly itself, from the routine cheers at the basketball games to the clichéd decor of the gym. Despite the poet's contentions about the tenacity of the imagination, you could just about forget about metaphor making inroads in such a place, where a rose was a rose was a rose and never aspired to rise higher. To what I guess would have been the consternation of Robert Browning, at Niles East, reach and grasp never lost touch, as if they'd pledged their mutual commitments in the pages of one another's yearbooks. On that closed campus, tenors went flat, and vehicles stalled; "like" was laid off and "as" banished. Like aliens missing the proper papers—I have analogized freely ever since graduation, with an ex-con's compulsion never to take any license for granted—tropes were indefinitely detained at customs. Newborn figures were smothered at birth in their beds. Movie reviews to the contrary, mimesis was never much of an achievement at Niles East, for no art whatsoever could escape the orbit of the evident there. There every thing-in-itself could not be disguised as a thing outside itself; every ding an sich hewed closed, stayed unflappably intact.

"Reality is only the base," Stevens writes, then immediately insists, "But it is the base." And it was a base we seldom strayed from; cautious runners all, we kept our leads short. Or shift to vertical terms, and you'd find us hugging the ladder's lowest rung.

Another way of describing Niles East is that my high school was immune to exclamation. By all means the halls were loud and rowdy enough —force 2,500 teenagers into any enclosure and the place will echo with their cries, complaints, and agitations all day long. But just try placing an exclamation point after any statement made in secondary school, and it will sound secondary anyway. I saw Laurie leave after fourth period! There was an announcement over the P.A. system about band practice! Shrill, childish stuff—in retrospect, news that was hardly worth the bother of punctuating or passing along with half the fervency we brought to it. Certainly nothing to distract from the premise of any movie you might want to make there. And that's as it should be, I suppose, since in a movie you don't want anything to obstruct the stars.

Nothing at Niles East ever did. Nothing there ever even threatened to. Theodore Roethke mourns the sight of the "duplicate gray standard faces" he encountered in school, where pupils were so inured to desolation, sealed between walls the color of nothing in nature, petrifying like the blisters of gum beneath their chairs, that they never missed the light. The fact was that Niles East was not especially conditioned to being unexceptional because nothing in any high school was *ever* unique, nor was it meant to be. Not the lunch trays or the lines to the buses, not the pastel hall passes or the dingy trophy cases, not the scabby, buckled textbooks or the dreary cafeterias, not the photographs at the back of every yearbook honoring the untimely deaths of kids cut down by leukemia or killed when they rolled the family car—nothing startled the bureaucracy or stretched the imagination one bit. So far as any of us could tell, schools all schooled according to the same push-me–pull-you system of inhibit and edify, balk and imbue. The result: model citizens. (Think "model" as in modeling clay, which is absolutely malleable before it's fired into permanent shape.) By definition and decree, students were treated as reptilian—incurious, lidded, tucked and ducking under daily protocols like desert climate—and, little wonder, we came to resemble the creatures they presumed us to be. Everything settled into preconceived categories, nesting steadily like the chairs the custodians stacked at the close of each day. In the end, high school seemed anathema to any fantasy other than getting through it.

And as we neared the finish, our college counselors, such as they were (the two we had did double duty, one as a gym teacher, the other as a health instructor), singled out the requisite percentage of students with college potential, such as we were (the ACT exam, regular attendance, and a relatively drug-free record being the chief criteria). Urging us, as the middle-class kids of middle-class parents, to be realistic about our chances, they advised us to attend one of two schools: the local community college (for the homesick) or University of Illinois at Champaign-Urbana (for those sick of home). Both were state-funded institutions, meaning that our parents were already supporting both with their tax dollars, so it stood to reason that we should be sent to cash in on what was already a mandatory investment. Wherever we ended up, we would be groomed for middle management, our names and titles never climbing more than halfway up the employee placards that adorn the entryways of hundreds of downtown office buildings. Even those of us who saw ourselves as up and coming would, statistically speaking, come up only so far. Hence we were designated for conscription, written to fit.

Hollywood reserves its accolades for players who make the top of the bill. But let's remember the character actors they play against and whose dependable company sets them off. Think of Jack Elam, born to be the slightly crazed yet companionable old guy in a hundred westerns, as if the West could not have been opened without his totemic presence to authorize the site. The man was the very definition of grizzled. You'd think he came wizened out of the womb. And there are a hundred others equally noteworthy for not being *too* noteworthy. I mean the utilitarian talents, the useful types. I mean the stalwart unsensational, the film equivalents of soy. I mean the Arthur Kennedys, the Strother Martins, and the Charles Lanes; I mean the Jack Wardens and the Ward Bonds and the Jack Carsons and the Harry Dean Stantons and the scores of other oh-yeah-*that*-guys, all of whom add anonymous ballast to the screen. (Believe me, only research accounts for my knowing their names.) Regular and necessary as the cinder blocks everything else is built upon, they do not seem to mind that we are not mindful of them; on the contrary, they make solid careers out of standing aside as soon as the stars come out. So although in one sense they are hardly regardable at all, the fact is that they gird and guarantee the credibility of so many movies that there probably wouldn't be a Hollywood without them.

Second bananas? Heck, they hardly climb even that high up the bowl. But this is not to suggest that character actors are not good actors. On the contrary, believability is their stock and trade, not to mention the key to their modest fortune. But they are good the way mailmen and referees are good: their virtue is a product of their being at the ready—ubiquitous is more like it—and utterly unpresuming about it.

In this sense my Niles East was the character actor of high schools—simultaneously unassuming and integral. Bastion of born coat holders and also-rans, of the inherently unclimactic and the mundanely preordained, of students who seldom if ever tested the premises they occupied. Now and evermore, gold and blue, we're true to you, just down the block from consequential. Watch us jostling behind the ropes as celebrities waft by. Watch us being interviewed as innocent bystanders who caught a glimpse of the criminal as he sped off or saw the semi as it over-turned. We just happened to be in the vicinity, for we are the ones who make the vicinity such as it is. If we aren't necessarily compelling, we are always convincing, like pencils stacked in their boxes, which Roethke says are inexorably sad (and sadder still because they are insensible to their state), or like anyone penned in parentheses, or like students inserted daily into their desks. Look for us in the background of the next feature you see. Thanks to years of instruction, we look exactly, exactly as you would expect us to.

Driving Concerns

. . . and all that road going, all the people dreaming in the immensity of it . . .

Jack Kerouac, *On the Road*

Visiting a friend one Saturday afternoon, I happened upon his fifteen-year-old son, Ron, who was sitting in his father's parked car. Squeezing the wheel at ten and two o'clock, he seemed to be gazing wistfully at the headliner, as if mesmerized by the pattern of perforated stars. Certainly he was too preoccupied to notice me until I rapped on the window to ask what he was up to. He did not shift position at all, except for the slightest sorrowful shake of his head. "I'm waiting for my life to begin," he answered.

Your high school civics class to the contrary, America is an autocracy. Take the term literally: ours is a country ruled by cars. "These dreaming vehicles of our ideal and onrushing manhood," John Updike calls them in one of his stories, and the epithet holds true outside of fiction. If you buy into the commercials—and the sales figures prove that most of us, our sophistication about the deceptions of advertising notwithstanding, still do—cars are at once the means to freedom and the embodiment of that freedom. This may be the only thing that for all their whiny promotion of sun and sand the Beach Boys got right. Surfing takes us only so far, until we run aground, our bodies grown brittle and our aspirations grown up. On the other hand, as the band attests in at least half a dozen songs, an open stretch of road remains unassailably sublime.

The way Ron idles inside his dad's Accord is the way millions of American boys imagine their manhood: the seduction of uninterrupted fifth gear on an impossibly untrammeled expressway. Sex may be the essential mystery separating youth from adulthood, but driving is the indispensable means of transportation between them. (Even in the event one does find a young woman with a low threshold of amenability to the ragtag charms of a teenage boy, it still takes a car to carry the seduction off.) Once I got my own license, I no longer cursed and cooed at pinball games or contented myself with all-night poker with companions as stationary and predictable as the machines at the arcade. Although pinball is passé and, by his account, no one under thirty plays poker anymore, I predict that Ron will discover that his pastimes are rendered just as paltry and just as outmoded as mine were by the sensation of starting up his first car. He'll put away childish things, whether experimenting with pot or gliding through cyberspace, in favor of cravings more appropriately hormonal, such as throaty V-8s and virile torques. Instead of World Series–winning home runs, he'll fantasize about spine-jarring overdrives; instead of touchdowns, turbochargers will fill his visions and define his dreams.

"Nobody with a good car needs to be justified," insists Flannery O'Connor's Hazel Motes, whose own rat-colored, rattletrap Essex would seem to belie his confidence. But if Motes, the itinerant antipreacher, claims to be clear sighted about Christianity, he still succumbs to worship of the automobile, which represents a religion that, in America at least, is no less pervasive. Some psychologists and school principals—those who aren't making payments on pricey throwback Thunderbirds of their own, that is—say that an obsession with cars unnaturally protracts adolescence when, according to the obsessed adolescents themselves, they seek only to give it a classy ride.

In his poem "I Know a Man," Robert Creeley's speaker stammers to his friend, "the darkness sur- / rounds us, what // can we do against / it, or else," to which his friend offers this brusque reply: "drive, he sd, for / christ's sake, look / out where yr going." The metaphysical implications of this interchange merit considerable class discussion, but let us not neglect the sage advice that lies on the surface: that is, a working automobile rather than an overwrought consciousness may be better equipped to convey us out of malaise. In short, don't philosophize, floor it!

Now, far be it from me to want to pop the clutch of this essential American mythos, but as a man in my fifties I must report, not without shame, that the mystique of cars still persists for precious few of my peers.

"Just get me there" is hardly the sort of motto to inspire a multimillion-dollar ad campaign, but it's basically what our vehicular desires have come down to nowadays. Buyer surveys reveal that men in my age and economic bracket name "reliability" as the primary feature they are looking for when they look to buy a car. Reliable: it's a pretty dismal adjective, I admit, befitting dime-store clerks who give correct change or mail carriers chugging ten feet at a time in their shapeless vans. Reliability is about as stimulating to a teenage driver as a Saturday morning cartoon; reliability doesn't rev the senses or flutter the blood. Yet apart from the occasional midlife crisis, which is conventionally appointed by a sports car whose bucket seats fit a bit too snugly below the belt, yearnings tend to shift down into a less adventurous gear. When did driving our cars become extensions of the work we did to pay for them? When did travel become just one more way to spell travail? Remember the time you asked about what the warranty covered before you wondered about horsepower? Those priorities switched places at least a few miles back.

And so I am reduced to a commuter, a runner of errands. The sensible cars I consider today are as indistinguishable from one another as so many sofa cushions. The contrast to the richly individuated, uniquely truculent cars I lusted after during the sixties is startling—humiliating, really—and a fatal mitigation of my Walter Mitty–ish reveries, now decades out of date. Back then, we boys believed our irrepressible prospects (no matter the fact that we were socioeconomically swaddled in the suburbs) would soon be conducted in undomesticatable cars. None of us could concentrate on studies, not with the high school less than fifty yards from the street. A whiff of gasoline, its honest, unmistakable stink on someone's jeans, soon rerouted any conversation; needless to say, the French Revolution and binomial equations could not withstand it. Was it gears under duress that made us so digress?

There was a dealership on the way to the ballpark where we played, and the models we ran our hands over whenever we passed it provided all of the longing and all of the poetry we thought we'd ever need. There was the Charger, named for a horse but looking more like a wicked fish, whose grillwork extended the sense of predatory menace. There was the Challenger, sleek and mean and aggressive and spoiling for a race. There was the Corvette, that embodiment of aerodynamic urgency, whose retractable headlights were like the seeled eyes of falcons and whose hyperpronounced front end represented an evolutionary leap on the order of the enlarged brains of Homo sapiens (enlarged, we might have assumed back then, to contain the images and statistics of cars). Charger, Challenger, Corvette: bodies and power trains to salivate over, and these were only the *C*'s! There were dozens of other "high-performance cars" (a transparent euphemism for zoom, possibly designed to allay parental concerns) whose stat sheets we argued over, all of which sported curves like expensive courtesans and seemed eager to be had. It wasn't *Playboy* but *Motor Trend* whose hot new models aroused us and adorned our walls.

This all sounds pretty lascivious—a textbook case of displacement it doesn't take Freud to detect. But I submit that there was a spiritual commitment to our hopes as well. If sex was the overt lure—the "buy a sports car, get a girl" causal logic of almost every advertisement—transcendence was the subtle one. There was the promise of going from zero to sixty in mere seconds: that sort of escape velocity could snap a Sufi into a higher state of being faster than any stay-put ritual he might practice. There was the vision of breaking from the jammed pack of traffic to experience a form of liberation no Founding Father (and, for that matter, no driver who had to hazard the glacial progress of the Dan Ryan at rush hour) had ever known. And there was the totemic sight of the motorist sent from the skies in the Hertz commercial, who inexplicably eased directly from heaven into the driver's seat as the car cruised at highway speed. Admittedly he did not captivate my friends because he wore a suit and tie and wasted his magic on a rental. But for me he was nevertheless the avatar of driving, the supernatural validation of the amalgamation of human and vehicle. The wildest hybrids out of Greek mythology could not compete with him and never commanded so fierce a faith.

The Camaro, by the way, should have qualified for esteem, seeing as it was as sporty a *C*-car as the aforementioned aims of my affection. But since my mother drove one, it was disqualified. True, my friends thought it cool. While their moms shopped in station wagons or in midsized family vehicles whose safety features and unambitious engines left them no more attractively rabid than a housebroken cat, mine tooled around town in a zippy red Camaro, a car renowned for how very close to the asphalt you sat your ass to operate it. Bad enough that such intimate anatomical considerations might be visited on my mother instead of on some fleeting, anonymous blond—worse that my mother had contaminated a perfectly good car for me, and I had to scratch the Camaro from my wish list. Let's suppose that instead of trading hers in on a new car she bequeathed it to me. No matter how pristine she'd kept the jet interior, no matter how provocative the exploits I might plan for it, I'd always feel as though I were bringing home groceries or picking up my kid brother from school. Better to take the bus or to double with a buddy with a junker whose soul was wholly his than to be seen idling at a stop sign in a car once owned and lately spurned by a housewife.

Strangely no one I knew had his dreams of speed slowed by the splatter films we were required to watch in Driver's Ed. Designed as cautionary tales, films like *Signal 40* and *Wheels of Tragedy* were bloodier than revenge tragedies and, because of their documentary explicitness, potentially more traumatic. In fact, thanks to the intervention of kinder, gentler PTA's, mine was the last generation of rising drivers to be exposed to them. The stronger indictment, however, was not that these films made us afraid but that they made us arrogant. The same clownish bravado that caused some of us specifically to target in our simulators the blind guy with the cane or the kids who always ran out into the virtual street after the soccer ball carried over into these screenings. Interjections of "That's *gotta* hurt!" and "*That*'ll get your license revoked!" were as predictable as the catastrophes that inspired them. In other words, blood didn't deter us; warnings were lost on us. They might as well have tried to sell a school of sharks on vegetarian fare as hoped to instill an instinct to hesitate in a bunch of sophomores crying out for ignition.

Actually I felt a little sorry for our poor Driver's Ed instructor, a gym teacher who must have committed some unspeakable crime against pedagogy to have had this extra task inflicted upon him. Indeed, Mr. Byrum was a man whom no one remembered ever having cracked a smile, much less hazarded a joke, in his whole career; the guy permanently resided ten degrees south of dour. But the reason I sympathized with him was not that he suffered us, which every high school teacher had to do anyway. (At least we were hungry for the subject. Special dispensations should have been reserved for those saddled with grammar and remedial math.) No, I felt sorry for Mr. Byrum because the thrill of driving had been ruined for him. To adapt Wallace Stevens's phrase, instead of bringing requital to desire, driving was a part of labor and a part of pain. In short, it was a job like any other—worse, really, when you consider the writhing, raucous, incorrigible fifteen-year-olds in whose daily presence he had to perform it. The professional golfer who sighs about having to haul himself over another eighteen holes at Pebble Beach and the movie actor who must

kiss his gorgeous co-star in take after take might have some notion of the
exasperating conditions Mr. Byrum faced, with one of life's profoundest
delights distorted into a chore.

For weren't we born to cherish our cars? We may complain when the
toaster gives out or the air conditioner goes down. We may derogate our
refrigerators and telephones when they suddenly implode into useless
hums, then contrast their treacheries to the quality of their ancestors,
which we somehow remember as superior. We may contend that the ap-
pliances of the past accommodated us better than the supposed advances
of the current generation, in which a congenital obsolescence manifests
like hemophilia. Yes, we may recollect all of the other machines of our
past and even, when the dishwasher dies or the computer crashes, maintain that we prefer them. But it is only our lost cars we truly eulogize.

And as I say, it is not only the cars we lose but the means of loving
them as well. It is a secret even to us just how we turn into the people who
rail against those rotten kids who race down the blocks we're trying to
manicure or even, like John Irving's Garp, chase them through the neighborhood to avenge the assault on our safety and equanimity. This, when
we were once the would-be racers; this, although we then became the racers ourselves. Somewhere along the impacted highway leading to maturity
—the road that knows no turning—the Indianapolis 500 became nothing but loud and NASCAR baffling, a worthless purgatory of left turns.
At some point our passion for acceleration subsided, and instead of
breathing heat behind the wheels of Porsches and Ferraris, we became the
parents who shake our fists at whoever does.

Age brings no more vicious predicament than this. People who once
vowed to drive nothing Mario Andretti wouldn't approve of find themselves stuck with the Fords they can afford. Deny it all they want, they
now have Volvo souls, which, tragically, are almost never convertible.

There was a time when the trappings of romance included a willing-
ness to be trapped on the interstate for the sake of one's beloved and, literally, to go the extra mile. I was a Chicago teenager, which meant that
meeting a girl at a club or a concert might have required a commitment
of many hours and many miles just to keep a relationship alive. I was
from the north suburbs, but she could have been from the hinterlands of
Schiller Park or Berwyn. The course of true love never did run smoothly
past the Stevenson interchange. Yet that would be no obstacle to conscientious affections. Romeo and Juliet had but family prejudice and half a

stage to cross to earn their embrace; we might have downtown traffic and half a dozen toll plazas to traverse. But couples who could construct an entire night's entertainment out of cruising up and down Sheridan Road would have welcomed the chance to be confined together and would have been grateful for the privacy. (Considering what alternative settings were available for teenagers to ply their troths, or at least practice their techniques—a friend's cellar, a hedge next to the elementary school, a bedraggled patch of lawn behind a local factory—the interior of a four-door sedan seemed as luxurious as Hefner's penthouse.) Love of one another and love of driving would combine to sustain us . . . for a while. Then, suddenly, unaccountably, distance turned from an opportunity into an aggravation. Prospective relationships were sunk at the outset because they were NGF: not geographically feasible. Then Tinley Park might as well have been Thailand or Addison above the Arctic Circle for all the intention I could muster to undertake the trip. What? You're from Elgin? But you speak our language so well! Wheaton? Wouldn't I need to update my inoculations to go there? Dolton? *Dolton*? Does Dolton even make the freakin' *map*?

Maybe my disenchantment has to do with the way I currently have to insert and extract myself from my car in stages. I used to slide cleanly into the front seat like a bullet into its chamber and ease out without contortion or complaint, or so I continue to tell myself. Now I cannot get in without grunting; now astronauts strapped into their capsules and anchovies tamped tight in their cans come out with less effort than I depart my compact car. Then there is the car itself that, by virtue of my teacher's budget, I've settled for and settle into every day. Try just once peeling out in a bottom-line Honda, and you'll see how ridiculous a drag racer's impulses become. Not even squirrels scurry for the curb when a Civic approaches; no pedestrian respects my impending approach behind one hundred and six horsepower, much less is struck with fear and awe. And not even the dealer can say, "Chicks dig Civics" with a straight face.

Once, having the reflex if not the means, I must have stopped at the magazine rack to pore over the latest issue of *Car and Driver*. I must have responded to the gleaming cross-section of a cam assembly the way I would to a glimpse of breast or a flash of thigh. But if ever I lusted and lingered, I no longer do; dutiful as any husband filling a take-out order for his family, I pass the new Jag as I do the nubile cashier, undistracted, undeterred. "I am perhaps the first American ever to give up automobiling, formally and honestly. I sold my car so long ago as 1919, and have never regretted it," wrote that formidable curmudgeon H. L. Mencken. Is it only the absence of sufficient public transportation in my town that has kept me from getting as old as *that*?

But growing old cannot explain that revision alone. Clichés about the aged are insufficient. Maybe in our imaginations, instead of blazing off like James Dean, the old are going out like odors, rusting out like hulks of abandoned cars. Their mobility, or such pitifully delineated movements as remain to them, is strictly observed, cautious and muffled as Sunday meals. Yet among these senior citizens, barely able to produce enough saliva for a decent spit, there are some nonetheless able to savor the details of bygone automobiles. Those happy few fill their shelves in the nursing home with more samples from their vintage Hot Wheels collections than they do with pictures of the grandchildren, and memories of uninhibited motors fashion their sleep and discharge their snores. Not every retiree succumbs to Florida just to toddle out on the patio for his few final after-noons or to bake away to sand on the sand. For Florida is the home of Daytona, the Holy Grail of Winston Cup racing, and a dozen other speed-ways as well, where, cheering on the supercharged, old men might lever-age their own absent dash.

And rumor has it that half of the members of Congress were model car enthusiasts, and a good many of them secretly continue to be. Who knows that as high a percentage of Supreme Court justices don't take breaks from legislative sessions to debate the alleged upgrades in the Sub-aru Impreza WRX STi. And what about the rabbi who hurries home from Sabbath services to take his rest beneath the chassis of his '69 Firebird, with his wrenches laid lovingly beside him like a second set of *tefillin*? And what about the minister on his knees before his '66 Mustang, who emerges from his labors with a sheen of grease like the requisite aura of rose and gold worn by saints in Renaissance paintings? (Woe to the man who takes his car to Jiffy Lube instead of proving his virtue himself. Redemption must be especially elusive to the driver who cannot diagnose the sounds beneath his own hood or perform the catechism of the over-head cam engine.) And what about the billionaire who willed that he be buried in his 1970 Challenger, plutonic purple and slick as a cigarette case? No pharaoh can be traveling through eternity so lavishly as that; no mythological hero ever arrived in paradise in such style.

As I write, this nation is in the midst of war in the Middle East. In a rush of patriotic support, trees in my town wear bright yellow sashes around their middles, as though the maples were winning advanced degrees in judo and samurai oaks were readying themselves for a last stand. Kentucky Fried Chicken announces "Back Our Troops—8-Piece Dinner Only $8.99," as if to sustain our soldiers overseas with the knowledge that, in their absence, their families were being fortified by the most celebrated chicken the world has ever known, complete with two sides at reasonable prices. Pride swells in every breast. A local motel proclaims, "God Bless America! We're Pet Friendly!" The sentiment is too substantial for anyone to bother with the non sequitur. Suffice to say that God is exhorted to love our country and our kittens together and with equal zeal. And above a set of ATM lanes is a banner that reads, "Pray for America Drive Thru." W. H. Auden called poetry the clear expression of mixed feelings, but there is as much sincerity to be found in the mixed expression of clear ones. Better yet, here is a core myth made overt: America is a massive drive-through, and religious worship in this country is best demonstrated by a road trip.

An aged Yeats wrote off his native land by complaining, "That is no country for old men." Would that he had a muscle car to counter that mood—a car souped up enough to outstrip affliction, a car as eloquent as any canto could ever be. No one in a classic GTO remains forlorn for long. Would that he had not just an anthology to mark his departure but a badass Barracuda to floor. Because, as Ron might remind us when we feel impeded, predictable, or just plain bourgeois, once one's life has begun, it must be brought up to speed.

Only Just

"*Everyone strives to reach the Law,*" *says the man,* "*so how does it happen that for all these many years no one but myself has ever begged for admittance?*" *The doorkeeper recognizes that the man has reached his end, and, to let his failing senses catch the words, roars in his ear:* "*No one else could ever be admitted here, since this gate was meant only for you. I am now going to shut it.*"

Franz Kafka, "Before the Law"

Any good lawyer knows that it's not what you believe that counts; it's what you can prove. Nevertheless, in recounting my formative experiences with the law, I ask that you depend on hearsay. As in love and politics, so, too, in testimony. I know my parents are my parents because my parents told me so, and that's the story I'm stuck with and the one I have stuck to. Why should anyone's subsequent story be any better sustained?

I refer to "any good lawyer" without irony, for I have not succumbed to the spate of lawyer jokes that have become conversational standards over the years. On the contrary, I grew up a lawyer's son and an eventual lawyer's brother. My mother, though officially a housewife, was an occasional legal secretary (working for Dad pro bono, of course, as indeed so many wives did). As she quizzed and cajoled him through his studies, my father would grudgingly attest that Mom could have passed the bar exam before he managed to. In any case, she, too, contributed to the generally legislative atmosphere of our home.

Judge not, lest ye be judged? Whoever crafted that axiom never sat at our dinner table. I grew up admiring Clarence Darrow, Louis Nizer, and selected stalwarts from the Supreme Court, whose biographies added gravity to the living room shelves and commemorated the influence of the profession upon the majority of the family. While other kids doted on cowboys, I studied Raymond Burr's basso profundity as Perry Mason, who weekly redirected misaimed accusations against his client to their proper target elsewhere in the gallery.

Actually, because my family was too aware of the inaccuracies of conventional television depictions of the courtroom, I watched the lawyer shows alone. My father in particular couldn't abide those moments when the competing attorneys expatiated past one another's objections and the judge's gavel. "You know when they have the judge rule, 'This is a bit irregular, but I'll grant you some latitude for dramatic effect'?" Dad would ask. "How can you *watch* that crap? 'Not in my courtroom, counselor.' *That's* what he'd say, that is, if he didn't just cite the guy for contempt. You might as well stick to cartoons, son. At least when Bugs Bunny tap dances across the bench, no one takes it as authentic procedure."

While my friends scripted their fantasies to reflect films about pirates, spies, and sports legends, I was urged to worship Gregory Peck's iconic Atticus Finch in *To Kill a Mockingbird,* Spencer Tracy's hard-bitten Henry Drummond in *Inherit the Wind,* and Jimmy Stewart's shambling but sly Paul Biegler in *Anatomy of a Murder.* My upbringing led me to believe that a deft cross-examination trumped stolen treasure and that points made during a closing argument were more significant than the six you got for a touchdown. And while other boys purportedly settled in with their families on rainy evenings for backgammon or Monopoly, the four Saltzmans sat down to something called Point of Law, a game whose object was to see how often you could rightly ascertain the decision in a hypothetical civil or criminal case, at which I'd lose repeatedly.

The way a carpenter's child considers strapping on tools of his own some day or a butcher boy's fancies inevitably turn to cuts of meat, I naturally entertained the notion of becoming a lawyer. But only just. "Stand up, your father's passing," the preacher in *To Kill a Mockingbird* admonishes Scout from their cramped vantage in the courtroom balcony, for Atticus stoutly embodied both fatherhood and the law. My brother rose to my own father's example. But the first son hunkered down, held back.

I sometimes think that what triggered my turning away from exploring a livelihood as an attorney was the forbidding image of my father's law books—thick tan volumes belted in red, they lined his downtown office like a heartless division of Roman soldiers. Taking one down and drawing open its oddly warped cover was like prying open a crypt—the blackness within was that unremitting. There was something repellent and more than a little frightening, frankly, about those airless, convoluted confines, and I would lift up dizzy from the plunge. As I say, I grew up in the midst of litigators present and future, but while they extolled the law for its limberness, I found it unyielding; while they basked in statutes like beacons of democracy, I remained in the dark.

More likely though, my swerving started during one of those Point of Law sessions, when, because I always voted according to some intuition of what was fair instead of recognizing the point of law that real courts were guided by, I regularly found myself on the wrong side of the decision. Meanwhile my father, mother, and younger brother, holding properly with the majority, looked at me dumbfounded by my idiosyncratic findings, whose only legal precedent was my track record of judicial error over the course of play. "No, Art. You have to focus on the *point of law*," my father would repeat, as if everything democracy was defined by lay in the name of the game. But the point of law remained an indigestible quiddity for me. "But that's not *fair!*" I would bray, reacting to a given decision the way a boy might complain that his brother had cheated him on consecutive evenings out of the bigger dessert. And my emphasis on fairness, or (to be fair) on my *perception* of fairness, demonstrated beyond all doubt my childish priorities, whereby I maintained that the presumed point of law might be the point of law according to the *game*, but not according to *my* lights, which, truth to tell, I have continued to navigate by into adulthood. Clearly ill suited to the business of bringing suit, an ongoing catastrophe at case law, and in my estimation hopelessly hobbled by common sense, I was irrevocably headed down a dangerous path, where lay radical self-indulgence, leftist propensities, and a humanities major.

Or possibly my disaffection toward the law stemmed from the trials we conducted in fourth grade. This was a generation before metal detectors at school entrances would become commonplace, mind you, and decades before homeroom would focus on frisking and confiscation. Approximately once a month, under the weary juridical eye of Mrs. Seifert, who by seventh period was no doubt ready to sentence the lot of us to solitary confinement far from her hallway, we practiced an adolescent version of the legal system. Mrs. Seifert was a prodigious figure for all of us: imperious and outstandingly fat, she sashayed about the room like an eminent heifer who, if our prayers ever penetrated the walls of Middleton Elementary, would one day prove a roast sufficient to cover twenty dinner tables in hell. She had a real draconian streak, did Mrs. Seifert, who was known to clap kids into detention for failing to distinguish between a peninsula and an archipelago or for misspelling "Czechoslovakia" (the country she came from) during the weekly bee, where it unfailingly appeared. She was always the judge—her desk was the bench and homeroom represented her chambers, this or any other role playing notwithstanding—and she rotated the choice roles of prosecuting and defense attorneys, leaving those who were not being tried, had not brought suit, or were not on the witness list to serve as jurors.

More often than not, Bob Feldman was under indictment and the whole day's docket. Moreover he was always already guilty. His plea was superfluous, and judicial protocol was observed simply for the sake of appearances and dissolving some of the seemingly endless afternoon. Prejudice may be anathema to the American justice system, but in this case—in Bob's cases—it was expedient and accurate. Feldman was a prodigy of malfeasance, a precon, if you will, whose reputation preceded him and followed him, too, like a stink bomb, whose detonation in the school cafeteria, by the way, was another anonymous accomplishment everyone immediately knew to add to his rap sheet. A notorious bully and incurable practical joker, Bob was always the first and usually the only suspect when a pair of glasses was broken in the hall, a missing math book was found in the toilet (the girls' restroom may have been the crime scene, but even a ten-year-old's sense of forensics could not be long distracted from determining the culprit), or blood or tears were shed at recess. Evidentiary procedure was a formality, if that term might be applied to the ramshackle, rowdy progress of our court toward his conviction at the end of the period. (In this sense, it could be said that Mrs. Seifert never heard a civil case.) This excerpt from one of the trial transcripts was typical:

Prosecuting Attorney Billy Spies: Mr. Feldman, did you on the
     afternoon of March 4 give Van Schwab a wedgie in gym class
     in front of everybody? Did you then say he was a retard?
Defendant Bob Feldman: Did I say what to him?
Prosecuting Attorney Spies: Did you say, "Van, you're a retard"?

Defendant Feldman: Could the court reporter read that back?

Court Reporter Linda Putziger: "Did you then say he was a retard?"
   "Could you read that back?" "Did you say, 'Van, you're a retard'?"

Defense Attorney Debbie Seidman: Shouldn't that be "alleged retard,"
   Mrs. Seifert?

Plaintiff Van Schwab: I object, Mrs. Seifert! Make him stop calling me
   that!

Defendant Feldman: You can't object, retard!

Prosecuting Attorney Spies: Well, *you* can't object that he can't object!
   Only the defense attorney can object that Van's a retard.

Defendant Feldman: I'm not objecting that's Van's a retard. It's *fine* with
   me that he's a retard, actually. Let him be *king* of the retards for all
   I care.

Plaintiff Schwab: Mrs. Seifert!

Judge Seifert: That'll do, boys.

Prosecuting Attorney Spies: (*Giggling*) Can you tell us *why*, Mr. Feldman,
   you called Van a retard?

Defendant Feldman: Just look at him! And only a retard wears his
   underwear outside his gym shorts.

Plaintiff Schwab: You pulled them out!

Defense Attorney Seidman: Objection! That hasn't been established.
   Only "Van's a retard" has been established so far.

And so the verdict would come in just ahead of recess: Bob would be found guilty beyond a reasonable doubt, which deceptively implies that there was even a single juror with reason to doubt his guilt. Shakespeare wrote that the quality of mercy is not strained; Shakespeare never had to put up with Bob Feldman, who could exhaust the patience of a Portia. Our court jinx and jester, Bob made a mockery of all pretensions to the therapeutic effects of jurisprudence, insofar as fourth grade was ever conducive to it. He was remorseless and recidivist to the core. Mrs. Seifert would have had better luck trying to rehabilitate a torpedo. Neither punishment nor leniency, neither a two-week sentence to washing blackboards nor the promise of parole deterred him, and he ended fourth grade with as many crimes to his credit as Mrs. Seifert had class periods to devote to disclosing them. As his inevitable sentence was read—it varied only in terms of the length and location of after-school detention—

Bob would be probing his nose with a pencil or quacking merrily away like a caffeinated duck. Frailty, thy name is Feldman!

Bob would eventually matriculate from brat to bum, graduating to official misdemeanors that would earn the attention of the local police, but he would remain a perpetrator of petty crimes exclusively. Too crude for tax evasion, too bumbling for arson or racketeering, too ill bred for embezzlement or the grandeur of grand larceny, he would stockpile inferior felonies relegated to inferior courts. Basically his regular consignment to the custody of the assistant principal at Middleton Elementary augured both the nature and the scope of his future infractions. Originator of low-grade rampages, a persistent itch in the justice system, he would irritate the authorities but never in any significant way threaten the peace.

Or so I presume. I have not precisely kept up with Bob Feldman, but his fate is not relevant to the issue at hand, which is my own steady disenchantment with, disinclination for, and incompatibility with the legal profession. I needed commit no crime to run afoul of its vague auspices, which fascinate and forbid me still. The absurd version of "time served" that Franz Kafka provides in "Before the Law" strikes me as no great stretch. As his parabolic doorkeeper says, "If you are so drawn to it, just try to go in despite my veto. But take note: I am powerful. And I am only the least of the doorkeepers. From hall to hall there is one doorkeeper after another, each more powerful than the last." Weaned on and warded off the law by Saltzman family practice, finding the language of *Black's Law Dictionary* as murky as its title warns, and blocked off by the immovable magistrate Mrs. Seifert bulking at the gate, it's no surprise that I withdrew.

My own intersections with the authorities, however ordinary, have likewise discouraged me from approaching the bench from any direction. I am relieved to report that my adult run-ins with the law have never escalated very much beyond the level of indiscretion handled in my elementary school courtroom. In other words, I've committed nothing that I might be extorted for were I to run for public office one day. With apologies to the cognoscenti at 3M Games, I have come to appreciate that the real Point of Law is, if at all possible, to steer clear of it. Despite my brother's confidence that the reason that most people who get arrested *get* arrested is that they are *guilty*, my handful of experiences in traffic court, for which I was counseled to promise never to do again what I didn't believe I'd done in the first place, have made me wonder. "But, Officer," I've said in response to the odd, arbitrary citation, "I was driving the same speed as everybody else. Why do *I* get a ticket?" "Because *you're* the one I caught." Add to that the proliferation of class actions, slap suits, and outrageous settlements making news nowadays, and while I would not go so far as to side with Shakespeare's often-quoted strategy—"The first thing we do, let's kill all the lawyers"—not the least reason because considerable Saltzman blood would be shed, I confess that I find myself shying from the connection. At the very least, the profession can prosper without me. Family may have plied me with heritage, and a half-dozen friends from high school prosperously opted for the J.D., but I stand by my aversion and will not be courted.

So allow me my embroideries and elaborations, the prerogative of the literary, while attorneys keep to the brief. "Lawyers find out still / Litigious men, which quarrels move," argues John Donne. So let me love elsewhere and otherwise and have done with it.

To tell the whole truth, I have not earned complete immunity. Like everyone else, I buy into the clamor whenever a celebrity gets arrested; like everyone else, I'm a sucker for the offenses of the famous and the photogenic, whose trials more than hold their own in the Nielsen ratings. Along with you, I tuned in to the *Tonight Show* to see Hugh Grant explain away his arrest for having solicited a prostitute, all the while manifesting his signature stammers and tics, his famously amiable form of Tourette's. Along with you, I eagerly seized upon every atom of evidence and commentary surrounding the O. J. Simpson trial and grumbled about the general demise of decency and sanity indicated by the verdict.

Worse yet, I am set apart from my flagrantly educated friends by my admission to the guilty pleasure of watching afternoon TV small claims court programs. I mean the ones that feature judges who go by their first names, thereby making the proceedings seem more familiar and entertaining, in the manner of the talk shows they compete with, a fact that in itself makes it difficult to take these judges seriously. Surely even Mrs. Seifert would never have allowed the liberty of addressing her by her given name to go unchecked in her courtroom. To this day, in fact, I don't even *know* her first name, much less imagine having the gumption to use it should I ever cross paths with her again. In view of the antics of the litigants, the outrageousness of the complaints, the incinerating sarcasm of the judge, and the game-show suspense of the judgment following the commercial break, there's plenty to keep fans fascinated and to guarantee John Donne's prediction that there will be sufficient business to see all of these courtroom shows safely into syndication. In a single week, the diligent viewer might be treated to a controversy over a contract scrawled on a candy wrapper that barely took the ink, as well as see enough drunken depositions and illiterate affidavits to fluster a Solomon and inspire him to take the sword not only to the disputed baby but to everyone who's taken the stand. There might be a dozen deadbeat dads to deal with and just as many undisciplined dogs indicted for assaulting neighbors' legs and lawns. Broken fingers, broken windows, broken promises, broken hearts—it's a virtual carnival of domestic wreckage.

Each trial seems better suited to a locked ward somewhere, one even more isolated than fourth grade. Daily frustrated and used to screwings they can't understand except to know to expect them, the litigants are perpetually on the verge of obscenity or tears. The plaintiff whines and rails, strewing her abused history about the room. (The judge warns her to stick to the point, but she is convinced that everything is the point, and everything sticks.) The guy whose son bounced stones off her car hood or failed to pay child support isn't the only one who's wronged her, but he's the one she caught. The typically underdressed defendant—he trudges up in overalls, and he'll suffer judgment in a half-buttoned work shirt and frayed shorts—is at home only beneath a truck chassis. He has cultivated a perpetual two days' growth of beard over sunburn and acne scars, which looks like a spice rub on a piece of steak. Regardless of the sentence, he will beat the shit out of some blood relative before the week is out. As he is unceremoniously dressed down, the guy writhes dully in the box, confused and blinking like a sea creature dredged up from countless fathoms below.

It all ought to be more reverential somehow, the low-level desperation and steady evidence of ruin. The saying isn't "sober as a judge" for nothing, and as in tennis, another game designed for a court, points should result from savvy and power, pace and depth. Especially when the program focuses on the academically, culturally, and socioeconomically deprived, so that defendant and plaintiff alike, regardless of this half hour's outcome, are in the larger sense doomed, it should be at least as serious as Seifert, but television militates against it and makes that argument moot.

In *Born Yesterday* William Holden passes on his father's advice: never do anything you wouldn't want to show up the next morning on the front page of the *New York Times*. Watching the televised contestants bear witness, I wonder what's happened to shame as a mitigating factor. Is any exposure worth enduring if the reward is getting to be on TV? To my mind it would be bad enough to be involved in a dispute that demeaned or humiliated me; it would be worse still to suffer it publicly. But "suffer" is wrong, apparently, for these people are desperate to beguile us into their grievances. Like kids at a ball game who mug for the cameras between innings in the hope of picking themselves out on the miniature sets they've brought along with them, the antagonists depend upon the air for definition. Granted the American system of justice may ensure every citizen the right to a fair hearing, but I suspect that these broadcasts do not so much extend that opportunity as dissipate it.

Only here and there, perhaps after too many consecutive tapings have worn away her resolve to accept the premises of televised court, one of the judges who go by their given names alone shouts down the gallery for laughing. Her show drones for her, and it feels as if there's a crack in the brainpan, a short in the immune system that usually prevents her from recognizing what a mockery legislation has evidently come down to. She drifts a little, and she tries to think just how long it's been that she's been leaking self-respect. A baseball umpire has greater stature than I do, she thinks. A crossing guard does. A wrestling referee on the show that follows on the very same channel that carries me. She envisions a California earthquake sufficient to fossilize her in this posture, here in her seventh season on the air (after twenty numbing years of family court), brittle and obsolete. She lets herself wish that she could bundle the next flannel-backed slacker off to San Quentin or give the next scraggly debaucher the chair, putting him out of his misery or, at any rate, out of hers. There's a growing incontinence under her robes. Who else suspects?

In a dream of dignity she thinks it blasphemous of the gallery to react —we're not handing out refrigerators here! she thinks—and, ratings be damned, she gavels them back to silence. In a demoralized moment, maybe, she thinks justice matters too much to entrust to an audience. Giving in to a flicker of wistfulness, she thinks that she's a *judge,* rather than the host of a show, that the trappings of the camera are outweighed by the trappings of the court, and that the point of law is the point of law. Maybe

for a moment she recalls her adolescent faith in fairness or John House-
man's audition for Mount Rushmore as Professor Kingsfield in *The Paper
Chase,* whose gravitas she'd intended to cultivate in her own courtroom.
Who can guess what pretrial motions moved her to embrace the bench?
Maybe it was the recorded eloquence of a certain chief justice she'd studied in law school or the aura of eminence arising from the courtroom
itself—with its enduring rituals and mahogany rows, not so very different from a church's—that appealed to her.

My own opinion on the matter is merely that, and it likely has little
bearing on the case. Of the poet, Montaigne writes, "He is always beginning afresh, always persisting, and always reconsidering; and is all the
firmer and more inflexible in his opinion for being the only man interested in maintaining it." The poet has always worked pro bono, I suppose, and it has always been debatable what sort of community service
he might practically be sentenced to. Like him, I conjecture fondly and
freely, my opinion unencumbered by the consequence of a Louis Bran-
deis and denied the reach of a Learned Hand.

But there was an undeniably desperate something in the judge's countenance that day, something that said, I am only the least of the doorkeepers, and no amount of moral clarity or regret gets me through the gate,
though it was meant only for me. Or so I imagined, as my family knows
I'm accustomed to do during cross-examination. Anyway, it was only for
a moment, and only just.

Afraid So

At the banquet honoring his retirement, the star pitcher admitted that it wasn't the money that had made him throw so hard. It wasn't his devotion to the team or the prospect of reaching the World Series. It wasn't anything so sentimental as honoring the memory of his father, who had spent so many summer evenings coaching his son without bothering to change out of his good shirt and tie after coming home from work. It had nothing to do with not letting down the kids who had posters of him rampant and bearing down upon their beds from the closet door. It was not pride, glory, or revenge, much less love of the game. These were all proven motivations for other players, but they were not at the center of his efforts on the mound. No, what put the extra oomph into his delivery, what carried him through the late innings when he'd lost his good stuff and through the heat of August during those blighted seasons when the team was merely playing out the string, was fear.

It was fear that had forced him to do the extra laps around the bases and the extra reps in the weight room. It was fear that had kept him from resting on his laurels and that had kept him from believing that those he'd earned wouldn't wither. Between the dugout and the mound at the beginning of an inning, he'd be ambushed by it; between the mound and the dugout at the end of an inning, he'd be waylaid again. He fretted, not only from start to start but from batter to batter, that the batters would solve him for good, taking the food from his table, scuttling his plans to send his children to tonier private schools. He worried that some assiduous sportswriter would discover that he'd had a gambling habit or had committed some indiscretion with drugs. Neither was true—a weekly poker game and the occasional toke at a college party had been the extent of his transgressions—but somehow the thought dogged him nonetheless.

During his playing days, he refused to elaborate; pressed on the issue, he'd grow fidgety, until an alert coach corralled him and ended the interview. But now he confided that on the nights before he pitched, he would come gaspingly awake from bad dreams in which he watched himself pitch into metaphysical jams that no amount of coaching could counter. His curveball wouldn't bite, his slider by some inimical magic caught the meat of every bat or fell mortifyingly short of the catcher's mitt, his sinker sank into an abyss too deep for Dante to recover, and his fastball fattened like a Thanksgiving turkey on its way to the plate. When his wife would ask if it was the same nightmare again, she knew what his answer would be: "I'm afraid so."

When President Roosevelt declared that there is "nothing to fear but fear itself," he meant to calm the country, and only cynics, fifth columnists, and sticklers for clinical psychology might have corrected his claim by noting that "fear itself" is at once the core and the compass of any intimidation anyway. My guess is that the preponderance of injury and illness at the hospital is the only real disincentive for the doctors who work there, and that few policemen would focus so exclusively on their retirement dates were it not for the crime they encounter on the job. I speak from experience when I say that apart from the paperwork, writing is a rather palatable way of spending one's time. Saying that fear is all we have to be afraid of, so as to buck up America, is like saying that sick people are all we have to cure, criminals are all we have to arrest, and papers are all we have to compose to motivate the professionals who contend with their respective demands. Under scrutiny, the president's statement doesn't seem like much of a consolation or much of a stretch.

And even if it did settle the case to say that fear is all we have to fear, that single menace impends from so many directions that it's like saying that the Hydra was just one monster to dispatch. Research confirms that the list of likely and unlikely phobias is, for all practical purposes and for all we are able to do to dispel them, infinite. Who knew that trembling had so extensive a set of etiologies? Who knew that so vast an assortment of quakings could shake us? There are the more celebrated fears, such as those caused by spaces that are too expansive or too closed in. So many of us are afraid of flying or afraid of the dark that it's been years since either phobia has inspired a new journal article. And there's nothing newsworthy when people confess a fear of being burned. As kids, they shivered at the sight of counselors feeding campfires as gingerly as they would newborn calves; none of the ghost stories that sent the campers skittishly to their tents affected the budding pyrophobes among them so profoundly as the sight of the fire around which they were forced to close in to hear them. Today, as adults, they would curse the darkness all night long rather than risk lighting a single candle. Meanwhile mice, spiders, and snakes have inspired shudders and support groups all over the world. Cars backfire, and millions startle. By a conservative estimate, 10 percent of the visitors who ascend the Empire State Building cannot look down to seek how far they've come for fear that they'll see how far they'll fall. And the uniformed professionals we bring in to deal with urgencies— cops and generals, exterminators and ushers—unsettle a good many of us as badly as the problems they're summoned to handle.

But it is also possible to be more strangely afraid. For instance, to freak out more obliquely, you could suffer from batrachophobia, which is fear of amphibians, or from selachophobia, which is fear of sharks, or cymobphobia, which is fear of sea swell. Avoiding the water altogether may stave off these conditions, but it won't protect you from merinthophobia, which is fear of being tied up, xenoglossophobia, which is fear of foreign languages, or keraunothnetophobia, which could be fear of long, unpronounceable words but is actually fear of falling satellites. It seems that no fear is too exotic that no one could succumb to it. The literature reports and finds terms for fearing blushing, crowds, and clowns, for fearing tasting garlic, going to school, and encountering ghosts. And where can the barophobic hide from gravity, the aurophobic from breezes, the acarophobic from itching, or the ophthalmophobic from being stared at? (Obviously the man who is afraid of Latin better not even open up the reference book to check out his particular malady.) Colors, clocks, and novelty spook enough victims to earn their own vocabulary words, as do wrinkles, snow, and animal skins. There are ladders and tunnels, microwaves and drains, algebra exams and public speaking, swallowing and fluorescent lights and modern art out to get enough people to require support groups for each concern. One friend of mine from college recoiled from corners, while a second sought them out as refuges against

strangers in the room. A third currently refuses to look through a tele-
scope because, from his perspective, the sky is chiefly composed of bumps
in the night. A fourth can't abide anything sharp in his pockets, so he
keeps his keys on a belt loop and his pens in a drawer; this same poor fellow shies from the barber when he approaches, scissors hissing, from
behind. Ferris wheels unstring a fifth friend; public fountains paralyze a
sixth.

There are enough superstitions spooking any randomly selected community to fill a textbook and to keep ten psychologists per square mile
in business. Those unnerved by the least hint of acrylic warrant mention
separate from those who can't handle wool. Feathers are evidently plot-
ting against at least some of us, while others are upset because they will
some day feel the fatal pinch of digits in the number thirteen. "One of
Catherine's neuroses was a horror of maroon," we learn in Alan Hol-
linghurst's novel *The Line of Beauty*. "It outdid her phobia of the *au*
sound, or augmented it perhaps, with some worse intimation." There are
those who are never more creative than they are in the matter of founding fears. Perhaps the AMA should sponsor grants to enable the most
promising of the afflicted to develop their disquiet into a truly pioneering alarm.

Elevators wait in ambush for a select group of sensitives; they hum
idly as if they intended no menace whatsoever, but those phobic about
them know better or, at any rate, more intensely, what conspiracies they're
up to. Some can sense an assault at the sight of a beard (pogonophobia),
a bridge (gephyrophobia), or an imperfection (atelophobia). And though
some can ignore it, who can doubt that legions of viral agents gather in
any given vial of spit, semen, or blood? We all fear the void, no doubt, but
it looms largest and hourly before the kenophobic among us, while hell
prepares for no one so terribly as it does for the stygiophobic. Meanwhile
it's enough to have to open his eyes to send the optophobic back under
the covers, where one can only hope a new phobia, such as a fear of the
fabric or a fear of being smothered, doesn't break out.

Nothing to fear but fear itself? It'll do.

A phobia is usually referred to as an irrational fear, but only by those
who think their own fears sensible. In fact what Emily Dickinson calls
"Zero at the Bone" feels just as cold if it's due to north wind or inner
weather. Anyway, the diagnosis that says it isn't external factors but one's

own biology that's treacherous simply gives the afflicted one more thing to be anxious about. And given the many forms that the body's treason can take, frozen bones aren't the half of it. Spots of blood on the toothbrush or in the toilet bowl would turn anyone's blood to butter. They say that there are no atheists in foxholes, but neither will you find one behind any curtain in the hospital emergency room. What is the Merck Manual, after all, but a compendium of threats so dastardly and various that they'd send Poe into a panic and usurp Stephen King? Each edition just extends the body's repertoire of mishaps and infidelities. (That the thousand shocks that flesh is heir to make up so massive a volume must increase the count to a thousand and one.) As for life's final perfidy, the thought of spending eternity in a sunken box or not equally terrify. Robert Lowell mourned how "the downward glide / and bias of existing wrings us dry," realizing how our defeats all come down to the final demise of the body: "this urn" in which "the animal night sweats of the spirit burn." "And in short," as Eliot's Prufrock put it in a rare succinct moment, "I was afraid." In my case it doesn't take poets or physicians to formulate implications frightening enough to unman me. My amateurish understanding of my physical situation suffices.

Fear has been formalized for us in post-9/11 America by color-coded levels of threat. Calamities both actual and anticipated come in assorted colors like the new fall line. Every intimated covert operation, whether situated in some hidden niche of the Internet or conducted from a Middle Eastern network of caves, cries its peculiar hue. Rumors of anthrax in a Virginia mailroom have to be sorted out as assiduously as the mail itself, then colored in for public consumption. Anyone passing through an airport, train station, bus terminal, or bike shop that fits the profile gets painted. Thus the government discomposes the population in stages, much the way that flight engineers incrementally pressurize astronauts to prepare them for radical changes in the atmosphere. On any given morning, we awaken to learn what level of threat—low (green), guarded (blue), elevated (yellow), high (orange), or severe (red)—to gird ourselves for, much the same way as we dress to comply with the weather report. (Note that no absolute calm is ever called for. Ours is perpetually staged fright. There is no living without risk anymore, if indeed there ever was.) It has been argued that citizens will come to dread the designation of dread as much as they will the potential danger occasioning it. On the other hand, as we become inured to the official cries of "wolf" issuing from the Department of Homeland Security, complacency may overcome the caution that's called for, and warnings of coming attack have already begun to blur into the same negligible background as have the hazard labels on diet pills and cigarette packages.

But credit the government with sparing us for certain from one fear, which is the fear that we won't be appropriately afraid. The use of colors ensures that even the illiterate will always be guided to the requisite intensity of anxiety. In fact simple semaphore can clue us in to just how terrified we should be. "Be afraid. Be very afraid," goes the movie cliché. In the even more concentrated parlance of the Department of Homeland Security, that translates as "Orange. Red."

Unfortunately the enzyme reactions responsible for our fear cannot be readily subjected to categories. Many live in the grip of an arbitrary, unanswerable chill, as rigid as climate. Free-floating anxiety can light on any brain stem like a buzzard on a branch, where it fastens as relentlessly as it chooses. Faced with the same crisis, one man's adrenaline will barely mist his cells like cologne while another's will spill out uncontrollably as though the bottle had broken. Similarly the shift from jitters—a sudden pluck at the nerves, a sideways knock at equanimity—to full-scale panic, from fire drill to live ammo mode, is impossible to regulate. A chemical cascade saturates the neurotransmitters, and no message more intricate than "run!" gets through to the body.

Then the multisyllabic battle is joined: against the insurgencies of serotonin, catecholamine, natural opioids, and dopamine, the pharmacy launches its reuptake inhibitors, benzodiazepines, and neuroleptics. Our panics are answerable to prescription, so never fear. We are the stuff that drams are made on. There are also prophylactic nostrums out there, and more cunning ones always being developed in time for the next medical symposium, which dampen the synapses and dull us down in a general way. However, we are still nowhere near the point of being able to make our impulses permanently get with the system.

Where biochemists have had considerable success, it turns out, is in simulating the substances that our bodies produce under siege. Apparently the experts have been stressing out lab rats and traumatizing chimps for some time now. It may not be long before we'll be able to dope opponents' aquifers with enzymes that will disarm them before the battle ever begins. On a humbler front, imagine having someone smuggle his way into the opposing players' training facility and dousing their cereal with serotonin, leaving them too freaked to take the field for the kickoff.

Knowing that my own panic attacks are due to a chemical shower is not in itself sufficient to relax me. Situated somewhere between regular beneficiary and full-blown addict, I am fluent in the features and side effects of Zoloft, Paxil, Valium, Ativan, and perhaps half a dozen other well-advertised, commonly prescribed lifters and inhibitors. (To reword Prufrock, who might have done better had he turned to drugs instead of abstruse divagations, I have known the pharmacists already, known them all.) They do help to modulate the treble and the bass of mood, but something dire still seems to thrum inside me, too deep for them to dial back.

What's more, I am the suggestible sort. Now that I'm on the down slope of fifty, I am more susceptible to an impressive array of infarctions, clots, and stoppages than I was only a few years ago; more to the point, I am more susceptible to the news bulletins that call my attention to them. In my most vulnerable moments, I am aware that any metal on or about me can attract the next bolt of lightning; that there's nothing but probability protecting me from one of a thousand drunk drivers in Missouri tonight from running a red light or leaping the median in my direction; or that, although in Joplin I'm reasonably safe from cyclones, floods, and suicide bombers, a forgotten lead mine could open beneath my feet and end me that way. These worries do not supplant my other fears but add to their store. In the back of my mind, for example, there is still the image of the weird amoebic industry I discovered in a drop of water thanks to the microscope I received one Hanukkah, the thought of which intervened for about a month afterward whenever I tried to take a drink. There is the memory of the rubbery puddle of mucus I stepped in barefoot in the shower at a public pool, which decades later retains enough visceral impact to guarantee that I always approach the shower at the Y with my eyes pointed at the floor. The tornado that touched down within blocks of my house, a violent cloud of starlings like a mile-long band of rasps and hammers, the odd alley, most animals off their leashes, every telegram, and any surgery whatsoever are old traumas ready to detonate.

Only last week I read that Aeschylus died when an eagle dropped a turtle on his head. A few seconds' sane consideration would assure me that the chances of death by plummeting reptile are about as great as my being clobbered by a shard of deteriorated space station . . . and now both

perils are added to my paranoia. They are stored in the same file as mete-
orites, compacted excrement jettisoned from planes, and pennies cast
from skyscrapers. I know it's crazy, but from now on, although I am a
thousand feet below them, I will probably duck where eagles dare and
flinch at any turtle I see on the sidewalk, imagining that it's just plum-
meted to earth, missing me by mere moments, mere inches. Batracho-
phobes, move over. There are reptiles after us as well.

Most fears, I fear, are not so much irrational as they are inconvenient.
As I say, like everyone else, I'm afraid of going senile or of going blind, of
internal pains and the outer dark. There's that ever-growing gauntlet of
cancers that I wonder if I can pass through unscathed, not to mention
several syndromes that have inspired telethons and countless others that
sneak in more anonymously. And even if by magic I never aged another
day, I'd still have my daughter to fear for. As any parent worth his apprehensions knows, children widen the perimeter of vulnerability. Therefore
there's a part of me that forever waits for Fate to phone in with its ran-
som demand: "Listen, buddy, we've got the girl." For there are more ways
for the world to get at you when you launch a child into it, and all prior
proportions have to be recalculated. "I see my flesh and bedding washed
with light, / my child exploding into dynamite," wrote Lowell, and would
that it were only a nightmare he could be reassured out of. That my
daughter might be betrayed one day by friends she trusted is worse than
basements, worse than bats. The dissolution of the ozone layer dissolves
before the idea of her going loveless for any length of time at all. Irregu-
larly shaped moles and vengeful ghosts fade as her fever crests, while the
depletion of oil reserves and of the bee population needed to pollinate
the orchards our diets depend upon must wait for her test grades to come
in until they can be attended to. The sun could flame out, physics collapse, or God forget us entirely, but if a traffic accident, CAT scan, or child
abduction happens close to home, any cosmic glitch in the offing is
eclipsed. And when some disappointment I can do nothing about casts
my girl into a gloom she can't find her way through, what color does the
government provide for that?

The world won't survive us, or it will. This is all there is to existence,
or a species stands beyond. The question is, what gets you back to sleep?

As a child, I liked to pretend that I was a spy. In order to give the private game juice, I invented enemies out of strangers and imagined that
people I knew, or *thought* I knew—teachers, the bus driver, my friends'

parents—were double agents, whose ruses it was only a matter of time and diligence before they were exposed. I'd stiffen each time Mom or Dad started the car because the engine might have been booby trapped (a procedure even grunts and gunsels in detective films knew how to manage). Strollers in the park concealed not babies but bombs beneath the blankets. Traffic signals were cameras in disguise. Cats and dogs were bugged. There was no point in alerting the police, since they were just as suspicious and (knobby, ruthlessly shaven, sleek and blunt as the bullets in their guns) just as forbidding as anyone or anything I might report. In this way, I cultivated consequence. I upped the ante on even the most ordinary gambits, so that every street I crossed on the way home from school was climactic; every house, a lair to cower from; every tree, a villain to circumvent.

These days, though, I find that just making my way through the mundane more or less exhausts my heroic capacities. And whereas I suppose that I am as likely as the next guy to find some untapped resources inside me if I happened upon a crime in progress or some fellow creature in readily amendable distress, that's only if the next guy isn't wearing tights and a cape. Basically my swashbuckling doesn't wash and tends to buckle under duress. So you can forget about my joining the ranks of the unwitting in horror films who, buoyed by curiosity and formula, investigate the dark at the top of the stairs. I'd never play the soldier you see in war movies who bursts first off the landing craft the second it scuffs the beach or the one who volunteers to parachute behind the lines into unmapped, unpronounceable territory. It will never be in me to stand stalwart and foursquare with the men of *Braveheart* while the arrows rain down, holding there, our terror turned galvanic and moving through us, shoulder to shoulder, bracing us against the worst. I'm afraid not.

Still, while fear may not be the fundamental instinct behind our backing up our hard drives and our loved ones, it is certainly among the most dependable incentives we have for taking pains and taking care. Fear does not consecrate what's dearest to us, but fastening seat belts, locking the front door, keeping up with the insurance payments, getting regular checkups, and otherwise battening down the essential and the evanescent as best we can is no insult to faith. Rather, it helps to instill the vigilance that sustains it.

Does it help us much to say as much? In an online forum sponsored by *Speakeasy Magazine,* a group of writers were asked what they believe to be the relationship between fear and the imagination. They confessed to being threatened by fraudulence, irrelevance, and silence. They were afraid of remembering and afraid of forgetting. They were afraid of facing the page and of forgoing the confrontation. "Fear keeps me writing," said Luis Rodriguez. "Fear also of the next work, the right word, the wrong word—of the warning in most words. I now evoke the darkness in front of my computer." There wasn't one who didn't understand the question or who couldn't relate. Writing may be a form of therapy, but it can also be a disease.

Love is a double agent, too. Internal security is laxest nearest the heart. When I'd come home famished from a hard day's spying, I would huddle over my lunch like a poker player concealing his hand. By dinnertime I was too hungry to wonder if the woman who called herself my mother had put poison in the chicken salad, and I plunged in. For the five minutes at most that it took me to finish, Mom would assail me with her own predictable anxieties: I would choke, I would gouge my tongue with the fork, I would spill the food or smash the plate on the clean floor. I never took her seriously, which is a boy's prerogative; certainly these concerns would never register as any color recognized by contemporary protectors of homeland security. They belonged to the same category as her horror whenever the doorbell would ring before she'd had a chance to clean. (I will show you fear in a handful of dust.) For her favorite admonishment, she had to reach deeply into our genealogy: "Look how you're eating. You'd think that the Cossacks were coming!" An obsolete figure, an inherited fear, but it showed how, when it comes to perils closest to home, the reflex is to grab on to something durable. Anyway, in a sense, there is always some sort of siege to withstand, which means that no apprehension is really very far off. Something is always closing in.

Are the Cossacks really coming, to make me so afraid? I'm afraid so. That, or something comparable. Come what may, it's enough to keep this kid's back against the wall.

Captivities

At three years old, my daughter was rabid for animals. She was transfixed by movies about the adventures of heroic dogs and savvy cats that relied for survival on nothing else but their native courage and bon mots recognizably voiced by human actors of the second rank. From her bibs to her sneakers, from her blocks to her cereal bowls, everything she owned sported at least one teddy bear, chick, dinosaur, or duck. (By an unspoken consensus of designers, this was—with the odd robin or lizard occasionally thrown in—the acceptable menagerie of the lovable.) She had an entire toy chest stuffed with stuffed animals, which also heaped her dresser and crowded her, according to her own demand, in bed. Lizzie was basically the St. Francis of the preschool set; if she weren't accompanied by a furry or feathered companion before we left the house, she simply refused to go. On the other hand, we could persuade her to visit the pediatrician just by giving her a glimpse of the barnyard stickers that would be her reward if she submitted without a fuss.

However, when it came to Saturday outings, it wasn't the local zoo she pined for. Admittedly, even in the context of a town with a modest tax base and a limited array of wholesome activities to choose from, the Dickerson Park Zoo was a second-tier attraction at best. By even the most lenient standards, its offerings were pretty paltry. A couple of indifferent giraffes emerged every so often to lip at the lofted straw. Two apparently boneless lions lay listless and splayed over a heap of tractor tires. The ravine that ringed their domain implied a threat that had evidently been bred out of them; possibly they were just too bored to bother with the dads that bore exhausted toddlers on their backs or the dutiful, diaper-bagged, worn-down moms. A scabrous camel surveyed its vicinity and, going by its expression, found it wanting. Dickerson was down to one stunned-looking monkey, which would thrash about in its hammock for half a minute, then, defeated by circumstance, would slump against the smudged glass. A hornbill, looking totemic with indigestion, cast a somber eye and could not be prodded to react to anything. In half of the cages you couldn't find animals at all: some had died off and not been replaced, while others, rejecting the premise of the zoo or just desperate for relief, slunk into blind corners and tucked themselves into the available shade, awaiting therapy.

Moreover the zoo facilities were primitive: gouged and splintered picnic tables that hadn't seen paint for several seasons running, communal bathrooms designed by Dante on a bad day, and vending machines that dispensed stale birdseed garnished by dirt and rust, which the indifferent ducks ambled over, grudgingly, to accept. The gift shop's holdings were, shall we say, unimpressive, and because the zoo administration couldn't afford to hire clerks, the shop was often as not locked anyway. The snack stand's sandwich meats were untenable and, like the zoo residents, stank of resignation and mange. Parents desperate to quell their kids would risk only the overpriced snow cones, which bled their questionable, indelible chemicals through cheap paper cups.

Now, three-year-olds can invent pleasure almost anywhere, and even this denuded zoo offered charms sufficient for my animal-mad daughter to coo over. But it was no contest: while she'd never refuse a trip to Dickerson, she much preferred a trip to the Bass Pro Shop. Touting itself as the largest outdoor sporting goods store in the world, the Bass Pro Shop advertises its own immensity as much as it does its merchandise. Indeed it annexes more of the adjacent acreage every few years, and there must be several citizens of Springfield who suspect that one day they'll awaken in the midst of shotgun ammunition, golf clubs, and knives, their bedroom decor having been supplanted by camouflage. Without a doubt, the Bass Pro Shop is Mecca for the camping and flannel crowd, and not even Wal-Mart boasts as many busloads of tourists on its premises.

As a displaced Chicagoan whose outdoor adventures had essentially been bracketed by "L" stops, I never did contract the seasonal fevers that afflict hunters and fishermen. Like someone who grew up in Vegas and never placed a bet, I keep my indifference and my distance from Bass Pro, or at least I did until my daughter pleaded to see it. And once she did, she was hooked: not by dreams of masterful casts or tales of stopping power, not by the displays of a hundred means of outfitting oneself to face every conceivable variety of wilderness, but by the taxidermy to which fully one-third of the main floor had been dedicated. Mounted high above us were heads, horns, and severed and sewn halves of animals culled from jungle, desert, forest, and sea, with dozens of carcasses peculiar to Missouri propped throughout the store. Scores of stuffed birds were suspended like model airplanes, harking back to their previously vital force and capacity for flight. Installed upon the man-made cliffs and inserted into the artificial clefts was a strategic composition of antelopes, wildcats, moose, bucks, and boars. In short, we shopped under surveillance by perhaps a thousand delegates from the animal kingdom—some entirely present, others represented solely by parts and pelts—permanently attending upon and petrified by it all.

But these were not the creatures that pulled my Lizzie into the crowd. Rather it was the land-based animals that had been arranged behind restraining ropes at eye level that enchanted her. Some seemed entranced, glassy eyed, for, of course, their eyes had been traded for mibs and aggies. Others were rigged in assorted tableaux of killer and kill, deployed on apt landscapes and apparently complying with James Dickey's "Heaven of Animals": "If they have lived in a wood / It is a wood. / If they have lived on plains / It is grass rolling / Under their feet forever." Jaws wired open and teeth set at the very instant before purchase, the predators were forever homed in on eternally acquiescent prey and hinted that there was still a vestigial spirit that would bring down the claws, sink the fangs, tear every last gawking one of us to pieces if they could. But that bloody fantasy didn't hold up very long at all in this context. Rather, all of the inhabitants were dependably, picturesquely glazed, good citizens of a peaceable kingdom open from nine to nine daily, all manicured and cordoned off and, whatever the attitudes conferred upon them might have implied, serene.

And certainly that serenity had a lot to do with what set off my daughter, who, almost predatory herself in her fixity of purpose, dashed through the masses, dodging adult legs as undeterred as a deer scampering through a stand of aspen, to reach what she called the Pro Shop Zoo, where domestication had been taken to its final extreme. If the animals' natural aura was dulled by proximity to so much naked consumption, not to mention by whatever wadding had supplanted their innards or by the synthetic texture of their dry-cleaned hides, it never bothered my daughter or slowed her toddler's safari through the stylized brush. Objectively speaking, this was an emporium of corpses, beasts with all of their biology scoured out, and manifesting Robert Frost's "Desert Places"— "All animals are smothered in their lairs." But to my daughter, it was paradise: an aphrodisia of species and, notwithstanding the Astroturf savannas and the faux glens, an uninterrupted dream of Elysian fields and streams.

Like a movie star or a mob boss used to special treatment, Lizzie would duck under the ropes to rush up to the animals and hug them. Not one among their rigid ranks failed to earn my little girl's adoration. The frozen polar bears next to the ATM delighted her into darting, with all the intrepidness of Eliza in *Uncle Tom's Cabin,* onto their makeshift ice floe for a bout of heavy petting. The rampant Kodiak, in whose stuck clutches families took turns mugging for the camera, inspired Lizzie to launch a full frontal assault: she latched on by boarding one of its paws with both feet and drove her nose into its scurvy flank. The stopped wombats and weasels, the stunned badgers and seized wolverines all met with her effusive approval. For Lizzie was omnivorous in her affections and undiscriminating, ignoring neither fish nor fowl, each of which was accorded posthumous honors: an embrace, a nuzzle, a stroke, a tickle, a kiss. It was touching, once you got past the fact of her infractions, and no matter that it was probably so much careless, aggressive love that had already worn down the fur of a recumbent fawn until the scalp showed through and had broken off a piece of a mountain goat's ear. Lizzie giggled amid the bobcats. She offered jellybeans to the lemur and a sip from her tippy cup to the great horned owl, staying them from the departures they'd been posed for—the pounce to the shelf where the bowling bags were kept and the flight to the rotary fan overhead, respectively. And with the lion and the lamb she lay down together, and she never wanted to leave.

Whether reclusive or vicious in life, the animals were cuddled in death and, by virtue of Lizzie's ceremony of innocence, redeemed in ways their vital counterparts at that other zoo they call "the zoo" would never be, not while they breathed. For that was the advantage of the Pro Shop Zoo: its inadvertent hospitality. Here you could *feel* the animals, which, if they could not reciprocate one's love, suffered it without repercussion or complaint. Let no one tell you different: that is as much love as any other kind.

"Be careful not to touch Nana's things," I tell her in advance. We have just arrived in Chicago, and eleven hours in the car have left me bent out of shape in every sense of the phrase. But I don't know how much instruction Lizzie has managed to take in, because she is fairly bursting at the straps of her car seat. The passion she and my mother have for one another is ferocious, absolute; having no agenda other than their mutual affections, they positively charge one another the second Lizzie's been unbelted. When my mother turns her attention to my wife and me, Lizzie zooms into the house, flailing her stuffed monkey by its tail.

"Careful!" I call after her.

"Don't worry," my mother assures me. "I've put up anything she might hurt herself with."

"It's not her getting hurt so much as what she can smash," I say, but I'm happy to learn that Lizzie's protection and her pleasure are both higher priorities here. This is news. When I lived with her, Mom flinched whenever my brother or I even so much as sat in her living room, a tidy trinket museum reminiscent of Laura's glass menagerie in the Tennessee Williams play. Lizzie couldn't have understood that Mom's having without hesitation given her an unconditional run of the house was as much a sign of how completely she doted on her as any of the clothes, toys, or special desserts she had waiting for her granddaughter. Regardless, I was relieved to see when I made my way inside with the suitcases that everything in sight had survived her.

After dinner, with Lizzie collapsed in front of a Muppet video and pinching half an ice cream sandwich (something I'd never have been allowed to eat in a carpeted room, by the way), Mom asked us to follow her downstairs, where she had some things to show us. Since our taste in decor seldom coincided with hers, we girded ourselves to compliment her on a new vase or on the undetectable way she'd rearranged the furniture. However, that was not the subject tonight. Instead, she explained, she wanted us to go through her possessions and tell her what we wanted after she was dead. More than a few of her friends had recently passed away—for some reason the northwest suburbs had suddenly become a hotbed of metastasized cancers, organ failures, and infarctions—and one of the results was that it now seemed to her imperative to get her bequests in order.

"But you're perfectly healthy. This is grotesque."

"Listen, honey," she said, "when the time comes, I don't want there to be any confusion about who has what coming to him. I especially don't want there to be any hard feelings between you and Jeff over anything you might particularly want."

"Mom, I don't want to do this."

"There must be *something* you can use."

"I mean, I don't want to do this *now*."

"How often do you come up to Chicago, Art? Now is what we've got."

And so we went through the stuff, with Mom looming over us as we considered what to want without seeming greedy, eager, or condescending. She worked us like a salesman trying to waken and shape our craving. I picked up what looked like a jade ashtray, and Mom gave me the history of its acquisition. Marla slowed before a quilt, and Mom laid out its provenance for her. I fingered a candy dish, and Mom whispered the appraised value.

"Doreen asked to have the Chinese chest already," she warned me as I happened past it. Otherwise, though, we were free to stake our claims, secure in the knowledge that my mother's eventual death made these deals irresistible. And so, uneasily, tentatively, like comparison shoppers wary of hidden catches, we admitted that, yes, that mirror would go well in our bedroom, and no, we didn't have a coffee table and could really use one, and truth to tell, we'd always admired the cherry nightstand.

"Really? Why didn't you tell me before? Take it with you when you go back."

"Mom!"

"The nightstand is not that big. You could fit it right next to Elizabeth in the back seat."

"Mom, we don't want it now. I mean, we want it, we'd love to have it, but not now," I explained. "*Some* day. In the *very* distant future. Then I promise we'll take it."

"You will?"

"We'll back up a truck to the front door. Trust me. There'll be nothing worth anything left when we get through."

And so, with her major holdings now apportioned, she was content. Apportioned, that is, with one exception: the mink coat. My sister-in-law wanted no part of it, and my wife had both political and sartorial objections to wearing real fur.

"What are you talking about? It's gorgeous!" she cried, draping it over the couch (which had already been spoken for by my sister-in-law).

"That has nothing to do with it, Mom," Marla said.

"Art, talk to her." By now, Lizzie had wandered in to see if we were in fact up to something more interesting than her umpteenth viewing of the Muppet video.

"I'm not getting into this," I said. Having snagged the nightstand, three lacquer boxes, and a cloisonné vase, I'd met my quota. "You're on your own."

"Forget it, Mom. It would just sit in the closet," Marla said.

"That's all it's doing *now* is sitting in the closet!"

"I just don't want it in the house. Please!"

"Well," my mother huffed, "maybe *you* wouldn't want it, but Elizabeth might want it one day. What do you think, sweetheart? Wouldn't you like to wear a real fur coat?"

By way of reply she plunged into the coat, tumbling with it onto the floor, and began a clumsy impersonation of a bear (what did she know from minks?) trundling her way toward us. I would have scolded her, but once again Mom seemed oblivious to a transgression that, had I tried anything like it years ago, would have won me punishment. She was clearly so pleased that Lizzie had gotten into the spirit of this valedictory ceremony—had thrown herself into it, as it were—that lint and misbehavior were beside the point. Here was a level of domestic bliss I had never experienced in my mother's company. Without my input or sanction, the two of them had revised the terms of the contract that, so far as I knew, I was still bound by. Or maybe it was simply that the principal business of the evening—the disposition of love and death, the impending dispossession and departure—had rendered old stipulations irrelevant. There would be plenty of time for abstinence once she was gone, and nothing much else. In any case, it's practically impossible for any grandmother worthy of the name not to indulge her granddaughter's joy when it's right in front of her and hers to give. Because now is what we have.

Inside the fur, Lizzie was all smiles and writhes, as if being digested like that was the best joke she'd ever heard.

"Just look at that sweet little girl," Mom said. "How can you not . . . ?" And she couldn't stand it anymore but gathered her up, coat and all, into her loving clutches. And in return, as was typical of her, Lizzie hugged back just as hard. Say what you will about heaven, but my guess is that the dead would give anything and all they have to be held like that, to hold on.

Spitting Images

Negligible in every other way that was available to us, Mr. Hessman was in one way gifted: he was the most versatile, prodigious, and downright impressive spitter any of us had ever seen. Because spitting was the sort of pointless, limited talent one was likeliest to perfect in prison, we all assumed that Mr. Hessman had done time—enough time to establish an unparalleled arsenal of spitting styles and effects. Based on the number, variety, and sheer technique he commanded, we figured that he must have committed a pretty substantial crime. Either that, or he had been a hostage somewhere. Possibly he'd been a professional baseball player, that being the only career we could come up with that accommodated the daily attention to spitting someone with his abilities required to master it. No occasional spitter—an accountant trying to remove the lingering effect of stale coffee on his way to the car, say, or a secretary startled by the belched remnants of a chef's salad—could have managed a fraction of his repertoire. Such spitting was the stuff of local song and story—ours, at any rate, and in keeping with what little kids could compose. To the untutored, Mr. Hessman may not have merited a moment's notice, but the young wantons and wastrels of Kimball Avenue knew better. The man had status and glamour, raising him above the common run of fathers. Other men, from their dull workdays to their weekend dozes, were just ordinary. But this man spit myth.

Even as a child, Mr. Hessman told us, he was precocious about it, and he could dimple a cheek or stud the back of a neck from halfway across the classroom. Early on, he became a spitter's spitter, resplendent at recess, where for commanding interest he was easily the equal of any cartwheeling girl or any boy with soft porn swiped from his dad's dresser drawer.

His classmates knew not to cross him, for if he took offense, no ear was safe, nor could any eye hide forever.

Eventually he said, there was no sluice or flume he couldn't manage. He could produce a junior high kid's loogie or an old man's leak. He could spit assiduously or absently, thoughtfully or balefully, in anticipation or in retrospect, with satisfaction or with regret. His spew was encyclopedic. He could work up a projectile globby with mucus or debris from his most recent meal or send a wire-thin stream like water shot through a dentist's jet. He could arc, dribble, stipple, splash, or spray. He could spit sludgy or spit clean, fire bullets at tree bark or let wet necklaces depend from the leaves. He could flatten an ant to the pavement or sting a bee in flight.

Mr. Hessman could let his spit slop, an event which he'd herald with a throat-purging prelude that sounded as if he were scraping wallpaper or preparing to pronounce Hebrew consonants. But he could also aspire, rendering aesthetic spits, transcendent spits, and spits as extravagant as any courtier could do, could one envision one of the elegant letting fly. He could rain filigrees and festoons, decorating the grass with slimy diadems and dripping corollas more arresting than any accident of morning dew. He could trace columns, arches, volutes, helixes, and (supplied with a pitcher of iced tea) whole entablatures on the floor of the porch with sufficient precision to charm an architect. Or he could spit for sheer power. Legend had it that he could take the tarnish off of silver, blast gum wads from the undersides of patio furniture, power wash the wooden deck one square inch at a time. He could flick twigs from the verge into the gutter or riddle lit cigarettes to death.

Should the challenge arise, he could outspit any competition. No matter how many contestants laid out dimes on the sidewalk to aim at, he'd always hit the most money and in ten minutes sweep up enough change to buy lunch at Morry's Diner, with enough left over for a moist tip. For he was the Robin Hood of hawkers; of expectoration, the contemporary William Tell. From ten feet away he could douse your pinkie while keeping every other digit dry. Packing his mouth with watermelon seeds, he could ping the Hessmans' wind chimes a dozen times running. Without moving from his chair, he could mist the petunias that lined the porch railing. Then suddenly, changing targets, he could shave a dandelion before bisecting the bare stem.

Mr. Hessman spat with matchless alacrity and versatility, easily filling the gamut from spurt to burble. He could spit for accuracy or distance, through pursed lips or bared teeth, to prove or refute, to start an argument or suspend one. He formed the most suggestive saliva you'd ever seen, which could come out dripping with sarcasm or thick with judgment. His spit could be incisive or roundabout. He could spit staccato or spit legato, spit to corrupt, spit to cleanse, or spit to cling. He could do in drool what Titian did in oils. No carom, bank, or ricochet was beyond his spitter's ken. With but one unannounced burst he could blot, denounce, purify, dispel, or undeceive. A Stanislavsky of Method expectoration, the man could spit to embarrass or to emboss, to scoff or to scold, to insinuate or exhort, to seduce or deride. He meted out more and subtler moods in liquid measures than Hollywood's most honored actors packed into a career's worth of roles. And where was the Oscar for that?

Mr. Hessman could spit iconically. No one's spit was richer in connotation than his. On request, he hacked and spat to suggest the spirit and image of a cowboy or a coroner, a kid in detention or a cop on patrol. Just by spitting he emulated a train conductor, a bank president, an auto mechanic, a pimp. The range the man could manifest rivaled Shakespeare himself, who through his thousand invented mouthpieces showed no greater scope than Mr. Hessman did. To commemorate a wedding, he could cast a fountain over the head table. He could splash pleasure and exaltation or send forth a stream of balm to anoint the multitudes—well, as close to a multitude as the neighborhood kids who drew close could be said to have mustered. And we imagined that, facing death, he would have left a transient epitaph on the wall of his hospital room. If Keats's words were writ on water, Mr. Hessman's legacy was similarly liquid and just as subject to dissolution.

That was what Mr. Hessman was for us, who implied adages in miniature and sermons spit small. His spit was as bristling with expressiveness as an orange is full of juice. He spat with rhetorical emphasis and visionary gleam. Definitely he could creep out even the brashest kid if he chose to. From the edge of his porch, he could, with one wet dart heavy and rancid with tobacco, indict any one of us, dampen our extravagances, discover our hypocrisies, cover us with shame. He spat acid and grease, curses and blood. With a single broadside, he could turn away wrath. With one protracted drizzle, he could change your luck or ruin your digestion. Against compliments and contradiction, against missing buttons and tears in his shirt, against the summer's humidity and the winter's teeth, against meddlesome relatives (his sister-in-law, specifically) and government in general, against the scourge of company and the scourge of loneliness, against every late-inning blown lead by the White Sox and his own mortality, he spat and spat and spat again. From the gouts he dropped between his feet, he could read the fate configured there. And his slobber could break your heart.

I cannot attest to Mr. Hessman's reading habits, but were I to meet him again today I'd urge him to consult Cormac McCarthy's Border Trilogy, which so far as I know represents the paramount achievement in the literature of spit. Indeed it could be said to constitute the true spitter's bible. McCarthy's hard-pressed, hard-bitten characters are the foremost practitioners and true aficionados of the art. They spit to complain of the weather or to test the wind; they spit leaning over their saddles or twisting off of their bar stools; they spit for commentary, sarcasm, and commiseration; they spit to interrupt the silence or to pay their respects to it. In *The Cities of the Plain* alone there must be thirty separate instances of spitting. It is at once eloquent and austere, the way McCarthy's knowledgeable spitters spit, in disappearing glyphs leaving their mark, punctuating the dust they'll ultimately come down to.

Whatever their motives in so dedicating themselves, don't McCarthy's cattlemen, as well as all studied and kindred spitters, emulate the sacramental ejaculations of God himself, who on the third day of Creation spat the oceans of the globe? (Science tells us today that when God turned his efforts to us, he made our chief component water as well.) Of course, when human beings sullied the earth past saving, he extinguished the lot by letting loose a flood. Whereas once the Creator salivated over our prospects, he eventually drowned us out with his now-dismissive spit.

Clearly the Lord is otherwise distinguished, and it would be wrong to suggest that Mr. Hessman wasn't as well. There was the way his mustache attached to the beard that lined his jaw, which looped over his ears to join the remaining fringe of hair at the back of his head, making a kind of widow's walk about his skull. There were the moles he wore openly in summer, which were grouped over his right shoulder blade like the Pleiades, any one of which might have indicated the onset of an enigmatic disease. There was the quality of his voice, which sounded like something heavy and rusted dredged up from the seafloor. Think Everett Dirksen with a head cold if you can, the ancient senator having by now faded so far from public consciousness. For evaporation finds the eminent and the Hessmans, those with seats in Congress and those anonymously parked on suburban porches, all the same.

Or we might honor Mr. Hessman's backhanded way of spanking ash off his trousers. We might recognize his tendency to divide boys and girls into "little shits" and "tiny tits," respectively, and irrespective of their behavior or of his recognizing them as regular infestations of his own block. We might recall his manner of loading every one of his sneezes with rancor, turning the concluding "choo" into "you dirty" to curse the cause and effect of the discharge together. I am sure that as a husband, a father, a brother, an uncle, a son, and a friend, he made and answered claims, memories, and desires that we had no inkling of whatsoever nor, frankly, that we had any particular interest in. Who knows whether or not what engendered his expectoration was a hole in his bank account? Who can say whether or not what really lifted his spit was a wish to traverse the gap that had grown over time between himself and Mrs. Hessman? There must be a million men on a million porches comparably inclined, their own spit heated by related sources of smolder. Hence, whatever his intentions happened to be during a given display, perhaps Mr. Hessman spat for the masses.

No doubt he had complaints and satisfactions, gainful employment and closet hobbies, dreams and disappointments that exceeded what we saw on his porch. And today I maintain that it is a cruel and arbitrary fate that grants one man millions because he can put a puck in a net or a toss a ball through a hoop while letting a man who can just as unerringly spit lemon seeds into a wastebasket go begging. Surely the shooter's and the spitter's dedications must be similarly Hasidic, their eyes equally keen. Hath not a Hessman hands, organs, dimensions, senses, affections, and pastimes on a par with other athletes and as artful as any prospective Hall of Famer's?

Unfortunately precious few of us get to dictate the angle from which we're regarded, much less the terms of worship. Truly we make the future, but we do not know the future we are making. Mr. Hessman may have had a passion for Italian food, light opera, or young boys. Who can say? *He* never said, not to any of us, the offending shits and noisome tits who, like flies and allergens, kept up our attendance until he'd shrugged off the rest of the afternoon and gone back inside, or school started up again, or no one under ten years old was left to linger. Out of sight and off his lawn,

I suspect that we ceased to exist for him, leaving him that much less to suffer. Against these sentiments and all allusion, out of his gnarled self-involvement spits the ghost of Mr. Hessman.

Is "destiny" too expansive a term to apply to him? Possibly so, since I assume that like most old men he did little else but grow steadily more wizened and dry. It has been more than forty years since I watched him do his ablutions at the end of our block, so it is hard to imagine that he is anything other than gone now. One cynical thing they say of the dead is that they aren't worth spit. For what it's worth, I am here to confirm that, whatever else he might not have been—and it's no small community of falling short that includes him—Mr. Hessman was.

Why I Don't Write Best Sellers

Write without pay until somebody offers to pay you. If nobody offers within three years, sawing wood is perhaps what you were intended for.

Mark Twain

There was a time when even William Faulkner found William Faulkner exasperating. With Faulkner forced upon them, stricken undergraduates might manage to lift themselves from their mandatory struggle with his prose to joke, "It's tough enough having to read the stuff. This poor guy had to *write* it!" But regarding the author's own vexation with himself, I am thinking of the years before Faulkner had secured a first-class berth in the canon, before Malcolm Cowley's edition made him more portable and palatable. I am thinking of the years when he was still unable to persuade the English-speaking world to speak highly of him or, for that matter, to speak of him at all. And so he set about to produce a sensation, a potboiler that steamed with shocking (and, he presumed, shockingly profitable) sex and violence, thereby following the theory that if he could not enchant the critics, he might at least for once cash a fat check.

Well, have you read *Sanctuary*? Despite its reputation in the academy for being just about the most decadent entry in the Faulkner canon—the novelistic equivalent of a Snopes tracking mud about his master's otherwise venerable mansion—it is rife with literary ambition, associative verve, and depth of purpose. It is immediately recognizable, inescapably traceable to the same pen that produced *The Sound and the Fury* and *Absalom, Absalom!* and inspired their attendant testimonials and term papers. The author's bastard book, it has nevertheless garnered almost as much exegetical attention as its so-called legitimate brethren have. It is, in other words, another Faulkner novel, for, evidently, Faulkner could produce nothing other.

During World War II many American factories were transformed in response to the growing military imperative, so that, in a typical case, laborers who had just the previous January been stamping out kitchen utensils were molding shell casings by June. Should it take a crisis of global proportions to persuade an ignored writer similarly to bend his own machinery toward a more practical direction? You might think that having mouths to feed would be motivation enough, and maybe it would be, were motivation the only factor involved. For you can coax, plead with, or threaten a cow, but strain as she might, all she can do is calve. That was Faulkner's predicament as well. Despite having a family to support, he could not alter what he could deliver from the only system at his disposal, and his fiction came out Faulknerian as predictably and irrevocably as Bossie's issue comes out bovine.

Fortunately director Howard Hawks took the accursed novelist in hand and, at least in material terms, saved him from himself. So for some time posterity was transferred to the back burner while Faulkner took up screenwriting, an occupation (with apologies to Hollywood) about which he consoled himself by believing it never depleted his genuine gifts because it did not tempt, employ, or require them.

My mother occasionally wonders why I don't follow suit. By all means, I should do my thing, agreed, but to increase my means beyond meagerness, would it kill me to do *their* thing, too? (In my copious spare time, presumably.) Who am I to balk at what Faulkner himself embraced? I could say that it just isn't in me, alluding to how, for instance, Sousa couldn't produce music that didn't march to save his life. The fact is that, when it comes to literature, my love is deeper than it is wide. What I treasure, I treasure zealously; the rest might just as well be returned to pulp. It is not an attitude conducive to crossing over.

Fantasy, for example, is more popular than ever, to the point that bookstores these days are pervaded by more alien-oriented than earth-bound books, and it would be sensible of me, creatively speaking, to hitch a ride on the next interstellar transport out. I concur; I just can't comply. E. A. Robinson's Miniver Cheevy missed "the medieval grace / Of iron clothing," and I am quick to recognize the poet's irony at his sodden character's expense. From my perspective, the medieval conditions of so much fantasy literature are less impressive than pestilential, and knights errant go bad in their cans. And as far as outer space goes, it has always left me cold. Part of the problem is that in fantasy absolutely anything can happen at any time, as if the universe were one massive convenience store. Just take a look—one can hardly avoid them—at the movies made from these novels, or in many cases, the movies that will spontaneously generate the novelizations to come. The characters seem little more than carriers for genealogies, which they recite at regular intervals—"I am Ararat, son of Andiron, grandson of Ampersand, heir to the throne of Arachnid, next-door neighbor of Amphetamine"—as if they were freshmen undergoing a fraternity hazing. Out of nowhere, these unshaven, square-jawed gallants are assaulted by conceptual art. Out of no comprehendible narrative necessity, a battle is waged between what appears to be an army of luggage and oversized, irate dental equipment. Indeed fantasy's penchant for piecing together exotic creatures holds about as much appeal for me as the back of a butcher shop. Nor does its fetish for weaponry trip my trigger. As for the archaic inversions, which are evidently the coin of most otherworldly realms—"To the temple you shall take them!" "Ascend the Mountain of the Third Doom, you must!"—I find myself more interested in ironing out the diction than in following the difficulties they describe.

All right, suggest well-meaning relatives and friends, what about Victorian-style romances, with their dashing suitors and dashed hopes, their passion-swept lovers and windswept heaths? This summer, like every other summer, bathers will block the sun from their eyes with scores of florid hardbacks the way they'll protect their skin with lotion. A hundred descendants of Cathy will sacrifice their better judgment and their virginity on the sand; a hundred replicas of Heathcliff will stud the beach. Why not get in on the action?

The truth is, I soon tire of the paid-by-the-word verbal fretwork of those novels, whose sentences so often betray the taint of forced labor. The method is easier to emulate than to savor:

> When she awoke, swimming out of that winter's drowse that had
> claimed her the evening before, she realized that it was no longer
> Sunday, but rather Monday, one day after, a day admittedly very like
> its immediate predecessor, similar to all appearances save that it lay
> one day distant, so that it was reminiscent of its nearest ancestor
> in terms of days yet was nonetheless undeniably distinct from the

weekend of which Sunday had been so significant a part, concluding
as it had the week heretofore, whose events, harmonies, and, it may
be said, very tides, which presided over the course of those seven
lately expended days, were now belied by her dawning awareness
that it was the aforesaid Sunday no longer, and that this subsequent
Monday, which she now inhabited and to which she was becoming
steadily attuned, would likewise prove ephemeral, that is to say,
would succumb to the selfsame oblivion toward which every day,
no sooner begun than attenuating, tends, no matter how she might
wish otherwise or disbelieve, in but twenty-four hours' time.

Whatever plot travails Tess Durbeyfield had to endure were undoubtedly
made all the more difficult by her having to make love amongst the tun-
dra of unkempt clauses. No heroine dilates upon the heather, delicately
collapses into her overstuffed chair with her overstuffed novel, or lan-
guishes in predictably fragrant meadows as protractedly as the sentences
describing these activities do. Trying to read such meandering is like trying to eat spaghetti without utensils. Then there is all of that Olympic
yearning, with all of those ill-fated heroines forever bursting by turns into
tirades and tears. One reads with sharp intakes of breath, as if the subject
of the sentence before him might be coaxed toward its main clause by
force of suction alone. What ultimately does me in isn't empathy but
hyperventilation.

Spy novels, too, cannot tempt me. Many of my friends consume them
ravenously, but I've never developed the taste. The first obstacle for me is
a fundamental disqualification: I simply can't keep the principals straight
or their tensions untangled when I read the books, so I can't imagine having better luck in trying to concoct them myself. Fans of the genre seem
altogether blissful in the rigging of a John Le Carré, while I'm left franti-
cally backtracking to find out how the felon I thought had died in chapter 11 somehow has his laser trained on our favorite agent in chapter 24.

Although even the most steadfast aficionado would call them ridiculous, I am grateful when the characters flatten into readily separable cartoons, whose physical abnormalities, diction, and tics identify them as
indelibly as DNA from scene to scene. Remember the movie versions that
once took up our Saturday afternoons? It would be only a few minutes
from the climax, and the outlandish evildoer had the hero at his absolute
and voluble mercy. Typically sheathed in black—shellacked in black says

it better—and perhaps sporting a waxy, protruding mustache through which his very wickedness seemed to wick, he was as much a staple of the matinee as the wildlife documentary that preceded the feature, and as crucial to the movie's moral equilibrium as our man's ultimately overcoming him. For without the counterweight of corruption, the good guy's goodness would have gone bad, his guns rusting, his prowess seizing up over long disuse as surely as his knees would. Nobility needed a nemesis to stay relevant and to hone itself against. More critical from my cloudy point of view, he provided the service of explaining the plot to us. His expository rants came from a bravado that would betray him, but I couldn't help approving of him for doing me the kindness of bringing me up to speed. As the acid oozed nearer, the rope frayed to breaking, or the tiger closed in, my concern was that civilization would be saved or the spy would die before I understood how we'd arrived at the crisis in the first place. But thanks to the bad guy's irrepressible garrulousness, I usually eventually knew: Oh, *that's* who you are and who that was and who you came in with and why any of you did what you did and now are preparing to do. My companions may have groaned because this dissertating obviously gave Bond time to unbind, but in my own way I was as dependent on the evil professor's hubris as the hero was for definition.

The point, then, is that I would compose best sellers, or at any rate better sellers, were it in me to do so. I cannot without considerable hesitation produce a sentence that refers both to Faulkner and me in the same clause. Nevertheless, whenever I'm asked why I don't write best-selling novels instead of the apparently unimbursable stuff I do write, I flatter myself to imagine that I have some inkling of what Faulkner was up against. In fact Faulkner might have been better positioned than I am to withstand oblivion because he must have sensed that for such a talent as his, oblivion could only be temporary, and renown, when it inevitably did ripen, would not ripen only to rot. Definitely, as it was for so many leads in Restoration comedy who had only to wait for greatness to find them in the last act, Faulkner's fortune was on the come. Frustrations notwithstanding, Faulkner was a ticketed passenger who had simply arrived too early for his ride; I, on the other hand, tend to suspect that I've missed the last bus.

When I began writing literary criticism some twenty-five years ago or so, I toiled beneath what was, so far as I knew in the culturally buffered

Midwest, a prestructuralist sky. At any rate not all of us freshly minted Ph.D.'s had as yet been outplaced by theorists, nor had we as yet detected their smoke on the horizon. We persisted in believing that there were still jobs available for honest sentences to do and, a savagely constricted job market to the contrary, that there remained tenurable occupation for their makers. We assumed that we could still go climbing, carving, tunneling, sculpting, and spelunking in stories and poems—this was when the pretexts of interpretive treatment were pre-"texts"—and use the tools we'd inherited to our advantage. Some of us even dared to imagine that our own language, as though enriched by context, occasionally lived up to the level set by the language that set us analyzing. And that was the sort of writing I would devote my professional life to for a couple of decades, until the limited publishing world of lit crit made it clear that a sea change had occurred, and all that had been solid enterprise had melted into error. Or rather, I should say, into obsolescence. "A few years ago we'd have jumped at the chance to publish this," a representative rejection letter might have begun. What usually followed was a form-fitted apology that the university press had lost the limberness to jump at much of anything that did not make its way in the often clunky but inevitably modish poststructuralist armature of the day.

Once society traded in horses for cars, there was no point in trying to perfect the manufacture of buggy whips. In deference to the times and to the unabated insistence on publication, I did consider tailoring my tendencies to suit new methodologies; however, I quickly realized that I wasn't up to the challenge. Try as I might, every passage, page, and fingerprint I produced upon them was indelibly me, undeniably mine. Furthermore I could not see myself spending half a career retrofitting my prose to accommodate the new requirements, nor did I eagerly anticipate shifting my reading diet to trendy French cuisine. What's more, I knew myself to be recidivist at the core. While the ostensibly reformed alcoholic keeps a flask beneath his mattress and gin-filled aspirin bottles tucked back in his sock drawer, I would secretly imbibe from a stash of smoothly intoxicating sentences. I might rinse with Ricouer or gnash Derrida like anise seeds to cover my breath. But by my wistful expression and my wobble, you'd know what contraband I'd been sneaking.

Of all the crises occurring at the close of the last millennium, the embattled status of my writing career aroused relatively little public notice. So it was with nearly inaudible fanfare that I pulled up stakes in literary criticism and resituated myself in the largely undiscovered territory of the lyrical essay. And if at first the challenge was to convince prospective publishers that the field existed, later it became to secure amid the sudden popularity of memoirs a plot of my own to cultivate. After all, the market was positively bristling with confessions and cautionary tales, with arch criminals and addicts reformed and relapsed. In a society where the number of personal Web sites is actually greater than the number of persons to supervise them and where "talk show host" is among the top ten dream vocations chosen by high school seniors, certainly there was room for one more writer to capitalize on himself by capitalizing himself. Today, the "I's" have it, and why shouldn't my personal pronoun stand as tall as anyone else's?

Or so I reasoned until I learned that the gooey alluvium of my particular mind was not what the market would choose to build upon. The problem was not my presumption that my writing style and general sense of things had mass appeal, as if the whole room would be relieved whenever I moved my bowels, for that presumption regularly earned shelf space at the local bookstore. The problem was that my essays failed the formula; the problem was my predilection for idiosyncrasy and the odd donnée. Whatever I called it, whether lyric essay, creative nonfiction, literary nonfiction, personal essay—wrestling with designation is like trying to get comfortable on a pull-out bed—I came to realize that unless my collection revealed how to satisfy a sexually frustrated partner, offered revolutionary diet tips, exposed corporate malfeasance, or worked the abs, literary agents and reputable presses alike were loath to back it. I'd be little better than an interloper at Barnes & Noble or seized as an illegal the moment I crossed Borders. Unless I exposed some novel affliction, signature perversion, or telegenic mayhem, unless I produced a book whose cover a swastika, stab wound, or prodigious cleavage could adorn, I would be doomed to compose and complain beneath the radar. "Lovely stuff, but how can I tout this, and to whom?" So echoed a chorus of acquisitions editors. Whatever its intrinsic value or artistic brilliance, I'm afraid your manuscript will do its shining in a drawer.

William Gass, a contemporary author whose critical esteem has always outpaced his sales, once said that he didn't want everyone loving his books just as he didn't want everyone loving his daughter. He wished he could restrict both to worthy suitors. One could argue that as the sales of one's books sag so far that no bookstore will stock them and as one's daughter's dateless nights compile until it seems that she will never leave the nest at all, it becomes increasingly difficult to be so discriminating. Even if one could customize a reader like a sports car, much less adjust a son-in-law to one's specifications, that would be only *one*—arguably sufficient to last a driver or a daughter, respectively, for a lifetime, but not enough by any means to support a publishing run.

Still, serious and unsung authors and anxious fathers alike may take solace from Gass's desire . . . or they would if his assertion had appeared in a book more of them had bought. One thinks of Emily Dickinson's determination to remain a "nobody," obeying a kind of "you can't fire me, I quit" conviction: "How dreary—to be—Somebody! / How public—like a Frog— / To tell one's name—the livelong June— / To an admiring Bog!" she announces, in what could be construed as the quintessential expression of sour grapes on record. That this repudiation *is* on record—that it is canonical, in fact—proves that she could not dispense with the marshy din and fug of reputation after all. Then there is the command that concludes Rilke's poem "Archaic Torso of Apollo," which honors the transformative authority of that statue's magnificent remains. The closing line is not "How may I serve you?" but "You must change your life." According to this "the ball is in your court" poetics, the burden is placed on the perceiver to live up to the demands of the work of art, by which one might rightly mean either the Apollo or the poem. Better literature wants us to be better; better yet, it believes and demonstrates that we can be. Would that half the people I knew were as well made, nimble, and resolute as the best sentences I've seen, Gass muses. If I might be permitted to squeeze my way into a paragraph with these elitists, I, too, wish that certain books read and edited more of us.

A tough choice, getting stranded or getting swamped, especially when the artists themselves do not get to do the choosing. Artists struggle with audience in part because they cannot predict what posterity will look like, not to mention whom it will look *at* at all or even mention. On the one hand, we have Vincent van Gogh, anonymous by default during his lifetime, who could not have won critical attention had he severed *every* appendage of his at high noon in midtown Amsterdam. What would he now make of the paradox that facsimiles of his paintings grace everything from calendars to linoleum floors to mouse pads while Japanese conglomerates buy his originals for millions at auction only to seal them in vaults with their other investments? On the other hand, just imagine the reaction of ancient Egyptian craftsmen who intended their works to be tucked forever out of sight in a pharaoh's tomb, but because archaeology could not abide that desire, their creations tour museums all over the world, with posters, postcards, and earrings duplicating them on sale in the gift shop. Some artists cannot get a showing for trying; others shun the public in vain. Posterity has always been fickle.

It has been said that writers write the books they want to read. Gertrude Stein widened her own prospective audience a crack when she declared that she wrote for herself and strangers, but the royalties that that precious circle promises won't register with any acquisitions board nowadays. (Like so many modernists, Stein wrote a prose so rare that few readers dare enter it unaided by annotations and ibuprofen, evidence of integrity that nowadays would make the sell tougher still.) Borges offered that he wrote "perhaps for a few personal friends," and I'm with him, grudgingly, in that it ends up being primarily a few friends who read and do not begrudge me my writing. "Any writer, I suppose, feels that the world into which he was born is nothing less than a conspiracy against the cultivation of his talent," said James Baldwin. Nice to think, despite the negative incentive, that at least the world's on the alert for him.

Some writers are buoyed by the notion of a receptive clientele gratefully awaiting their forthcoming pages like those (possibly apocryphal) devotees crowding the dock for the arrival of the next shipload of Dickens. John Cheever was that type of author. He gleefully envisioned literate divisions of Cheever legionnaires: "The room where I work has a window looking into a wood, and I like to think that these earnest, lovable, and mysterious readers are in there," he confided. On the other hand, there are writers like Gabriel García Márquez, who said that the prospect of putting his work before "a million eyes" just "upsets and inhibits" him. Some, like Eudora Welty, claimed to have written for "the pleasure of *it*," while others, like Joseph Conrad, said they did so for the cleansing integrity of the pain; either way, during the composition process, other people were roped off outside the study. Philip Roth declared himself spurred by the thought of the hypothetical anti-Roth reader (not so hypothetical, given Roth's controversial legacy); John Updike, by the anonymous teenager who'll happen upon his books on a library shelf situated in "a vague spot a little to the east of Kansas"; Joan Didion, by the prospect of "selling somebody out." Joseph Brodsky said that he liked to picture Auden or Orwell over his shoulder while he was hard at it;

S. J. Perelman winced at the picture of the neighborhood grocer over his. "I've always tried out my material on my dogs first," John Steinbeck once told an interviewer, which is to say that he did not test the literary establishment before he risked offending the ASPCA. The most common comment you'll find, though, is that writers write for themselves. Which in the end, whether we like it or not, is for most of us closest to the mark.

When in *The Living End* Stanley Elkin's Lord God found himself relegated to that lonely status of discovering no audience to understand him as he thought they ought to, he busted up his Covenant before philistines could sully his Creation further. In frustration writ large, he destroyed the universe like a bad draft. "All right, that's it! *Kairos!* Doomsday!" Religious readers may have been aghast, but other unappreciated artists—fellow solitaries, if you will—commiserated.

I tend to imagine myself imitating the final trial of Odysseus as prophesied by the ghost of Tiresias that the hero would have to carry an oar so far inland that he would encounter someone who did not recognize what it was. There he would fix it in the ground and offer many sacrifices to appease Poseidon. In my case, and if the presumption of referencing Homer didn't disqualify the dream, I'd carry the latest best-seller list from the *New York Times* until I came upon a community of readers who did not recognize a single name on it. There in those Un-Pilchered, Mary Higgins Clark–less climes, where Nora Roberts had never ventured nor Janet Dailey ever dared trespass, where jacket photographs of Danielle Steel earned not a glimmer of recognition, I would stake my claim. Then Koontz and Krantz and King better scurry.

It is Saturday morning, and like the old lobsterman who lives where the waters are fished out but who cannot abandon his routine, I set out my traps anyway. At the library I snag the copy of my book from the local authors section, where it has been communing with a compendium of off-color Ozark humor, a self-published memoir of a life devoted to regional politics, and sheaves of a Joplin-area minister's sermons bound by a small religious press. I place my book on one of the reading tables at the front of the library and insert a note: "This is fantastic stuff! You HAVE TO READ THIS!" Next, I patrol the online booksellers to see how far down in the hundred thousands my sales are languishing. In lieu of unsolicited customer reviews, I e-mail colleagues to ask that they post on my behalf, a kindness that I promise to repay in kind. (Sometimes while driving or drifting off to sleep, I've contrived exemplary reviews I hope to discover appended to my sales data some day, a hope I consider answering by submitting the reviews myself under various aliases.) Incognito, I call the local bookstores to request that they order my book, knowing that when I do not show up to buy it they will add it to the shelves, where some chance contamination might occur. Then I visit the bookstores in person to tape up photocopies of the cover and strategically excerpted reviews near the entrances and on the bathroom doors. Then I check each outlet to make sure that the one copy of my book it carries is prominently displayed, with its front cover instead of its spine facing outward. (Far be it from me to turn my back upon the populace.) If the book has sold—the world has not exhausted its miracles yet—I not only immediately replace it, I also ask the store manager for the name of the patron. I want to call him, to thank him, to congratulate him, to urge him to urge the book upon his friends, and to offer to personalize his copy as part of a special "meet the author" event to be held the moment I hang up the phone.

And it is while I am there at Books-A-Million that I ask myself not, whom am I kidding? but rather, why try to change, anyway? Here in Middle America I go to bed each night under America's right wing, where the Wal-Mart lines are long and fuses are short, where more citizens will have their skin tattooed than their passports stamped. Stanley Elkin, that same audience-haunted writer who imagined a God so outraged by his public that he scrapped mankind and manuscript together, was astonished that only a couple of hours west of his home in St. Louis he could find himself caught "in some redneck video game—in the walnut-bowl belt, in roadside zoo land, cavern and cave country." And although in my bleaker moods I'm ready to grant all of these knee-jerk condemnations and worse, in this chain bookstore that two years ago was a Hobby Lobby I come upon books depicting Greek desserts and painted Mexican doors. In the act of finding what will suffice, I find anthologies of poetry witnessing the wonders of nature and the horrors of war, the beginnings of promiscuity and the deaths of pets. In this unified field and most ecumenical council, scientists and spiritualists quite comfortably convene. A barber to six U.S. presidents discusses what he heard from whom as he styled their hair and swept up after them. Next to him, an usher from the Belasco Theatre tells about a lifetime of proximity to the great men and women of the stage. A guy who immersed himself in excrement to get into a modern art museum professes next to a guy whose parents stuffed him when he was three into a steamer trunk to get their boy out of East Berlin. Gamblers and embezzlers, prophets and strippers, hoaxers and stowaways among the shelves weigh in.

Yes, the place is replete with memoirs. There are collections of recollection galore. I have entered a veritable potpourri of remembrance. People who would never be caught dead together in public cozy up between the covers like Christmas commuters stuck at the terminal. Here is the complete consort dancing together: congressmen do their remembering on the very table that reformed porn stars do; syndicated and fifth columnists recollect in concert, their enmity put away for the sake of sales they hope to share; army generals, music promoters, and batting champs in the selfsame remainders bin recall. Here celebrity divas bed down with radio therapists, and a self-styled Spiderman who scales buildings with minimal equipment crosses paths with an "urban diver" who parachutes from famous roofs. Here the lying C.E.O. (now subdued and supplicating) shall lie down with the serial killer snatched from the lam (now in custody and available for consultation). And the 9/11 firefighter and the rose gardener are one.

I come up abruptly against massive tomes—real cockroach crushers, five pounders if they're an ounce—devoted to the graffiti found on walls around the world, to the scarves of movie stars, to facsimiles of animals made entirely out of food. Hundreds of pages and untold shade trees have been sacrificed for this very store alone to handle the history of European footwear, color coordinating tips for the den, dog-a-day desk calendars, coffee table pictorials of Coca-Cola advertising through the ages. In this eccentric welter, how can my book fail to be germane?

I have heard the merchants singing, each to each. I do not think that they will sing to me.

Folks in these parts—and by "these parts" I again refer to a region where folks refer to "folks in these parts" as a matter of course—have an expression for the way that they have adapted their guns to ensure that no one else can fire them accurately or, more to the point, against them. Rifles whose sights have been deliberately distorted are called "Kentucky winded," the result being that only the rightful owners can reliably reckon their aim. I am inclined to call the drafts I hazard Kentucky winded, too —that is, if my neighbors would not mind sharing the term with a displaced and unarmed ex-urbanite like me.

All right, long winded may be more like it. Either designation keeps Faulkner-phobic readers from handling the merchandise and Stein-estranged ones from making off with property. An exotic wind, in any event, a sirocco, which so many figure to be poisonous.

So I'm content to be compromised out of sight so long as it's not out of existence. Denied a major splash, I'll accept a discernible ripple. Does my writing come from humbler blood than royalties require? Then I'll aim my aspirations elsewhere than the throne. Mark me forever, inveterately, "not available in stores" so long as I'm not eradicated altogether. Secrete me if you must in the deepest reaches of the Internet, the way lead-lined barrels are kept at the bottom of the sea, there in the digital inchoate to be conjured solely by a doughty few. Consign me to a shrink-wrapped stash in the back of my closet, which, like an illicit drug, I can press upon the occasional prospect who accidentally wanders off from the herd. (Coleridge's Ancient Mariner "stoppeth one of three," and what author wouldn't gladly bargain for a tenth of those odds?) For the alternative, I fear, is not posterity but a potter's field of the unpublished, where all who scribbled, typed, or clicked and saved in vain are destined to spend eternity beneath a quarter ton apiece of illiterate dirt. From dust to dust, beneath a final dust cover, undiscovered.

That way lies despair—it is the kind of thinking that can put you off the keyboard permanently. Because there is no profit in it, I rouse myself with happier imaginings and a more wholesome muse. For no reason other than that it keeps me at it, I wish for good news in the next mail. I let myself hope that the next phone call will at least reward my impulses if not be my making. Having no alternative, I trust in the page.

Which Reminds Me

It is the stars,
The stars above us, govern our conditions.

William Shakespeare, *King Lear*

Its name sounds as if it belonged to a Greek god, and were there a god of afterthought, there would be a place reserved—at the last minute, most likely—for Asterisk at the table where Olympians preside.* Yet of all the mythological promotions from the mundane to the immortal, his apotheosis would undoubtedly have beaten the longest odds, so unprepossessing a figure does he cut.

For there is something mincing, something apologetic inherent in any asterisk, whose very emblem, attached in the upper corner like the sentence's epaulet, was won not for boldness—precious little risk in "asterisk," really—but for vexing in the field, at once unstinting and discreet. The asterisk represents the hedged bet, the nervous playwright's waving at the actors from the wings. It is the heraldic insignia of the person who stops his car halfway down the driveway to go back into his house to check for the second time that the oven is really off.** Perched on the shoulder of a sentence like a cartoon conscience, it whispers in the ear of the last word, insisting that the last word is not the last word after all.*** It calls to mind a confection, a sparkler, or a dandelion puff, any one of which implies frivolousness, I suppose, little more than a serendipitous flick at the reader's awareness. One could contend that the important thing is that it *does* trip awareness; it *does* call to mind. By that standard the asterisk is a sort of lagniappe of delight, that little something luckily come upon and tucked into a shirt pocket because . . . well, just because.

But you won't persuade those who tout concision and the unadulterated clause. Were it up to detractors, asterisks would be swept up like so many dust balls and disposed of before company comes. A nick in the fabric of argument, a dot of jam stuck in the works, an itch that the declaration it battens on can't quite scratch—for them, the asterisk is ultimately an esoteric bother and, plainly put, the most nebbishy aspect of any academic pursuit.****

Were a signer to include punctuation for the deaf, he might indicate the asterisk with a quick backward brush of the hand near his eye, complete with wince, as if he were shooing a gnat.

For almost forty years, American boys first encountered the asterisk in the context of Roger Maris. It disputed the Yankee outfielder's accomplishment of eclipsing Babe Ruth's single-season home run record of sixty by reminding them that Maris had had the benefit of a longer season to squeeze in his sixty-one.***** As a result, Roger Maris was remembered as much for the footnote to his feat as for the feat itself, and it seemed that he'd be doomed for all eternity to swing futilely at the asterisk that beleaguered him like a fastball up and in.****** Then in 1998, Mark McGwire and Sammy Sosa raised the bar again, making Maris and his accompanying punctuation moot. It took only three years more for McGwire to be outstripped in turn by Barry Bonds, at which point it seemed that major league baseball would be rid of the asterisk forever—that is, until the accusation that these recent sluggers benefited from steroids, thereby requiring that a new battery of asterisks be commissioned to accommodate them.******* Grown to adulthood, these worshipful boys would be assaulted by all manner of asterisks, ranging from fine print in contracts to codicils to wills. They would only half-realize that their consternation originated in the disavowals that came to hobble their sports heroes— heroes who should have risen uncontested, winning nothing but the finest print, their wills clearly established and free of encumbrance.

Asterisks are the standby passengers of idea: wishing to edge their way onto the flight just prior to its taking off, they hold close to the departure gate. Or they are the uncles that barge in drunk at the wedding just as the vows are being completed, determining that that is the ideal time to bring up old abuses or to update the gathered on the state of their prostates. ******** Or they are moles that suddenly catch your attention, begging to be looked into or, should an aggressive editor's convictions be heeded, simply excised. To be sure, each of these incremental revisions of metaphor, from standby passenger to drunken uncle to dubious growth, suggests that an asterisk could have been included to show the shift.

I've never inspected any politician's early drafts, but I'd be willing to bet that Congress is prime real estate for the establishment of asterisks, with a protected percentage of the national budget vouchsafed each year for "see further's" R and D.********* The reams of paper dedicated to any bill prove that its author has a sort of perpetual filibuster going on in his head, for which the asterisk is aptly suited. Lawyers, too, in their love of surplus, are particularly given to asterisks, as are those baroque architects who cannot resist the draw of addenda.********** Even the parent who plans to discuss the reasons behind her wrath after she delivers the spanking is guided in part by that dutiful mark of punctuation, which seeks to explain the hand it did not stay.

Emily Dickinson once inferred a "Splinter in the Brain" that can divert the whole flow of thought despite its meager size. In my mind, at least, that splinter tends to twist into an asterisk—a contortion that seems to me in keeping with the intricacy of thought processes typical of Dickinson. But as all readers of poetry know, Dickinson's true addiction was to dashes.*********** To find the mother lode of asterisks, you have to abandon poetry for research papers, which are as notoriously susceptible to them as fair skin to freckles from the sun. Indeed researchers will occasionally season their paragraphs with so many asterisks that the additives overwhelm the intended dish. So devoted are they to their data—they cling to every cell of their findings, holding every hard-earned jot and scribble dear—that they cannot bear to lose the least or least relevant of them. So they asterisk the lot—"It gives us strangely little aid, / But does tell something in the end," noted Frost—and whatever facts won't fit on board their texts are fastened beneath.************ It does not pay to ask who but the author of the document who consigned them there cares that in the anonymous bowels of argument lies a cargo of stars. Should the practice persist unchecked, a given dissertation may compete with space itself for constellations.************

Yes, it's an academic's method, this "there's more where that came from" aesthetic, whereby concepts always come with codicils, directing us to the bottom of the page, the orlop of thought. What's more, especially when an essay of mine is in its infancy, barely able to roll over on its own,

I grow rather attached to attachments myself. If I am in the midst of invention, or purport to be, I keep paper and pen on the nightstand, and when the writing is going well—*well,* mind you—I pop up several times a night to inscribe, annotate, alter, and re-alter something that I trust is taking shape between the snores. The fabled princess who squirmed because she couldn't sleep atop a single pea cannot match me for restlessness when a newborn notion, figure, or phrase infests my bed.************** So as not to bother my beloved more than inspiration requires, I try to light the notepad with the glow mode of my watch, but it's like composing by semaphore or under enemy fire—blink, scribble, blink, scribble. Eventually the morning reveals how many of my asterisks have overlapped, star succumbing to subsequent star, half-obliterating one another, or how they have trickled into oblivion altogether, unsalvageable.

But the excavation will have to wait, because it's a weekday and I'm off to campus, where a few days into each semester I must fend off students hoping to add one of my courses late.************** They barnacle my desk, nibbling at the extra syllabi—the gasping, grasping undergraduates, the asterisks of higher education. And they are brazen about it, shouldering toward me, as is so often the way with us. We are convinced that we must be crucial, for isn't each of us the center of what he wakes up to every morning, with his wonders and hungers the origin and measure of all wonder and hunger? Hasn't the universe worked billions of years to engineer our species?*************** Look at us, the latest upgrade, the newest model on the lot. No one really believes himself to be a postscript. In every diary the writer is the protagonist of whatever happens—not the tailing of Creation but the crux of the tale.

We flatter ourselves to think people are the thesis of things. "What a piece of work is a man!" cried Hamlet, in what conventional wisdom claims to have been one of his saner moments. And, indeed, combining the evidence that, with their respective instruments, science and faith have been able to cull from visible and invisible vicinities, it might well be argued that we are not only the pinnacle of the universe but its purpose, the raison d'etre of reality.*****************

That assumption is one reason why it is so hard to digest catastrophe on a large, and seemingly indiscriminate, scale. Abraham Lincoln famously appealed to the better angels of our nature; is it more presumptuous to expect better nature from our angels?****************** But before we infer either heaven-sent vengeance from the storm or supernal absolution from the clement weather in its wake, consider the possibility that human destiny is nothing more than a late addition to the agenda. Do deities really lobby for every baby and cast ballots before every evolutionary turn? Do they regulate extinctions like the stock exchange? When the volcano erupts, the virus breaks out, or the furnace in the basement blows, what immortal hand or eye frames its awful telemetry? It may be arrogance to ask the question, much less to suppose that we are the audience designated to hear the answer. Perhaps, rather, we are not nature's singular intention so much as its "by the way"—the asterisk, in other words, added late to the Universal Maker's affidavit or, for antitheistic theorists, some collateral damage caused by the Big Bang and not the boffo event it announced at all.

Speaking of arrogance, try offering that logic to the survivors of the tsunami that scoured most of Southeast Asia, in an instant's ambush ripping away so many lives and livelihoods and, in an oxymoron the faithful gamely cling to against the deluge, divinely slaughtering tens of thousands of Sri Lankans more.******************* Tell them that they were just the epicenter of the disaster instead of the cynosure of heavenly intention. I don't know that they would find it more consoling to think that those who were ruined, crippled, or orphaned were not afflicted according to plan, or that the kill ratio obeyed no rationale whatsoever. Still, even for the devout, it is a difficult commitment God exacts from earth; it is a rough grace he imposes. The only situation that might be more strenuous would be that we are victims of negligence. That tens of thousands suddenly dead manage nothing more than a parenthetical note in the census of the next edition of the almanac, a brief distraction from the central destiny, an asterisk imbedded in the figures like a bit of gristle in the teeth, is as unimaginable as the catastrophic instant itself and as inescapable. Mourning reveals how many of them have overlapped, hundreds succumbing to hundreds more, half-obliterating one another, or how they have trickled into oblivion altogether, unsalvageable.*********************

By the way, a baby boy was born prematurely as his mother fled the tidal waves smashing into the Indian coast. That is, unless the birth is the essential news and the ocean's onrush was the "by the way."************* ******** It's ambiguous at best, the way we're given notice.

As the damage is being assessed, the diagnosis of God goes on. One philosopher calls God confounded by the demands of his own Creation;

a second figures he's well meaning but forgetful, which accounts for the disruption of the covenant he purportedly struck with mankind a couple of testaments ago.*********************** A third determines that God's utterly just but inconsistently effective; a fourth agrees with the latter half of that reasoning but thinks that it's not love but malevolence that God can't sustain 100 percent of the time. Or he is mischievous or merciless, diabolical or disorganized. He clearly supervised the wave, or he never intervened. He had a bipolar episode or a conniption fit. God had a grudge. God had a hangover. God suffers from Alzheimer's or from adult-onset ADD*********************** The rumors abound, turning God into one more casualty to grieve for.

At any rate, no single motive behind these fatalities arises from the varied and ambiguous remains. As many women as men, as many children as adults were done in.************************

All over the world, at churches and synagogues and mosques, on religion channels and college campuses and the Internet, they are organizing group prayers. They are harnessing their pleas and taking aim. The reasoning appears to be that, launched God-ward in concert like that, they will not be neglected, the way they worry that asterisks in so extensive and complex a master plan can be. One Taoist, his eulogy by no means confined to the Taoist dead, references the concept of *wabi-sabi,* which urges appreciation of the beauty in what's flawed.************************* There is the blemish in the skin, for instance, as well as the virus in the body. There is the imperfection in the artwork. There is the very fact of mortality, which may seem massive to contemplate or just two cents' worth of afterthought. The glitch in the system. The defect in the text. For all things are impermanent. For all things are imperfect. For all things are incomplete. For all things, expect asterisks.

Now that the weather has relented, bulldozer crews are digging through the wreckage to find bodies. Once they've been identified, they'll be reburied in newly constructed cemeteries certain to brim with tombstones within days of their opening like volumes full of bookmarks, urging us to come back to the site, promising further elucidation down below.**************************

I was mulling this over the other day when I realized that I was driving toward the scene of a recent accident involving a friend of mine. The debris had been cleared away, and the street had been reopened to traffic, but you can still see the scar left by her tires when her brakes bit for the collision. There's a scar on the bumper of the truck that pinned her Caprice to the curb and a scar on the curb itself, not to mention several scars (in the midst of so much worse) on what's left of the Caprice. There's a scar on her left shoulder where the surgeons went in to pick out the chipped bone and reattach the torn muscle; there's another scar outlining her left knee where they cleaned that out, too. Julie won't ever drive past there again, she says, nor will she allow herself to be driven past there.*************************** Too many reminders: the asterisks left on the street and on her body, as if denoting passages to return to. She absolutely will not.

Her injuries continue to heal, but there will always be a ghost showing. The gash in the asphalt is there for good, too. *Wabi-sabi,* one might whisper to her, now that her ears are no longer ringing from the crash.

Instead her doctors told her, "It's a miracle that you're alive at all."**** ************************

"The same goes for all of you," she replied. "God knows." At least, that's what I've heard. After her rehab, when she's up for interruption, I'll have to get back to her on that.

*Conversely, "asterisk" may put one in mind of a prehistoric protobird, one about three incarnations away from full flight.

**And doesn't an asterisk look like nothing so much as a bug that's been accidentally squashed in a pile of papers? If you're lucky, you might be able to pick it out shard by shard with a needle to save having to reprint the page.

***Some contend that the Annunciation was issued in just such a way, as an aside delivered sotto voce. In the phrase of Emily Dickinson, the Lord of scripture had a penchant for telling truth at a "slant" like that.

****Academics is admittedly a pretty nebbishy business to begin with —and probably too cautious by half to deserve so valiant a term as "pursuit."

*****"Sixty-one in '61" is the common mnemonic. If Maris's successors bested that record, they never inspired any saying so memorable.

****** Robert Frost was apostrophizing another star when he proclaimed, "We grant your loftiness the right / To some obscurity of cloud," but the combination of altitude and ambiguity suits Maris's controversial status just as well.

*******As of this writing, Bonds is still playing and in inexorable pursuit of Hank Aaron's career home run record. "Pursuit" rings more convincingly in the case of athletics than it does in the case of academics, regardless of how statisticians ultimately decide to punctuate Bonds's numbers.

********Remember Coleridge's Ancient Mariner, who "stoppeth" the "one of three" he managed to latch a hand on for scores of stanzas that digressed from the wedding? Here was a true captain of the asterisk, more insistent than any above-mentioned uncle could ever be.

*********Research and Development, that is, and should probably go without saying, not to say that in government much of anything ever does.

**********I received a gift of architectural vocabulary cards, a deck rife with ornate astragals, volutes, abaci, fillets, and helices: a veritable entablature of asterisks with which to decorate one's columns and friezes, not to mention pepper one's vocabulary.

***********If you see her dashes as precipices to be peeked apprehensively over, those dashes may be seen as cousins to asterisks. If you see them as diving boards, not so much.

************Note that these are the second references to both Dickinson and Frost. Nor are they the only passages from their poems begging relevance. Nor are they the only poets who could be adduced on the topic. In a sense the whole of lyric poetry could be defined as the intersection of cadence and afterthought. Should a future doctoral candidate wish to address this contention at dissertation-length, I ask only for a brief acknowledgment.

*************Oddly—oddly, at least, to all but astrophysicists—the sky seems chockablock with stars, yet you can barely find your way in the darkness.

**************It probably isn't necessary to mention lice here, but as asterisks breed in my head, they feel like them and, apart from their comparatively regimental appearance, look something like I imagine they do, too.

***************My office hours are at 8:00 and 10:00 Mondays, Wednesdays, and Fridays, 8:00–9:15 Tuesdays and Thursday, and by appointment. I suggest arranging to see me in advance, for although I am available at those hours, I tend to stray from the premises.

***************Somewhere in the neighborhood of thirteen to fifteen billion years, according to the latest estimates, which are, it must be admitted, heavily contested even by those among the hard sciences whose mission it is to do the counting.

****************Having as yet detected no alternative and heard no objection, we continue with something like impunity.

******************This scheme is a form of chiasmus, a term I provide in part because it sounds like apt company for Asterisk and might likewise be indexed in Bulfinch.

*******************Sri Lanka was originally known as Ceylon, which is how you'll find it on an old map. Actually, given the impact of this cataclysm and of cataclysms likely to come, every map is old soon enough. When the weather plays billiards with the world, cartographers and demographers need to rerack their maps after every break.

*********************And did God hear them keening, "Please see below"?

**********************"But then I have to admit that I cringed when I read the words of the baby's father (who had given him the name 'Tsunami'—I'm sure the parents of those who *lost* babies will think this is really cute)." Ron Rosenbaum, "Disaster Ignites Debate: 'Was God in the Tsunami?'" *New York Observer,* 10 January 2005, http://www.observer .com/pages/frontpage3.asp (accessed 10 January 2005).

***********************"I establish my covenant with you, that never again shall all flesh be cut off by the waters of a flood, and never again shall there be a flood to destroy the earth"—a covenant struck without attorneys present, although evidently with a recording secretary on hand. The recent devastation leads one to suspect that there may have been an asterisk or two implicit in the proceedings.

************************Attention deficit disorder, lest I forget. Not to be confused with ADHD, although it inevitably is, even by professionals, who, to their credit, do a conscientious and usually reliable job of diagnosis considering that they are positively drowning in potential new cases nowadays.

*************************The figures change almost daily, as do the relative percentages of losses as organized by age, gender, and nationality, rendering efforts to ascertain or ascribe some sovereign intention to the tsunami problematical and, for the time being, unconvincing.

************************Because of the imprecision inherent in English transliteration, readers interested in the concept may have to seek it out under any one of six or seven "acceptable" alternative spellings. In keeping, perhaps, with *wabi-sabi* (or *waab-saabi,* or *wahb-sahbi,* et al.), that no flawless, incontrovertible form exists not only may not detract from its appeal but might actually demonstrate it.

*************************Is there any religion that places heaven beneath the earth instead of above it? Is the subterranean set aside in every religion for infernal purposes? That I've happened upon both "God is in the details" and "The devil is in the details" as axioms makes me wonder. Similarly, when someone suggests there's a subtext to watch out for, I'm not sure whether I should prepare to be enchanted or entrapped.

***************************"Julie" is not her real name. Like writers of advice columns, I reserve the right to protect the identity of someone who has already had her vulnerability revealed and taken advantage of. Those closest to her will recognize their loved one from the wreck, which should be enough.

***************************The transcript of this exchange represents a compromise among hearsay, projection based on what I know of Julie (or rather, "Julie"), and artistic license. Operating under different assumptions or auspices, others may posit competing versions of this and every other aforementioned event. I invite them to asterisk this testimony accordingly and, if they can, show us the way.

That Subtle Knot

Dogberry: *Are you good men and true?*
Verges: *Yea, or else it were pity but they should suffer salvation,*
body and soul.

William Shakespeare, *Much Ado about Nothing*

When we refer to the "soul" of something, whether it's goodness, discretion, or wit, we pretend to have discovered its fundamental quality. Whatever metaphor we favor, from root to headwaters to core, the point is that in reaching the soul we've hit pith. It is when the subject is the human soul, however, that paradox sets in. For if the soul of a person is that man's ideal promise, propensity, or paraphrase, it is hard to imagine it as having all that much to do with almost any of us at all. This is not only due to our going astray, to any little wickedness or awful trespass we may have committed, which aside from the odd saint goes without saying. It is basically a matter of our material makeup. The fact of the matter is that our matter is our most inevitable, most demonstrable fact. From the highest personage in the church to the fellow who wipes down the pews after services, we are bodies first and foremost, born and bound there.

If it daunts or demeans us to suggest that these bodies, infested with mortality like termites in the foundation, are unfit residences for the soul and should be condemned, that attitude doesn't liberate the soul so much as leave it homeless. Released from that sad sack of self, the soul cannot fend very effectively, much less find its way. Certainly we are flattered to think of the soul as something private and apart from the body that possesses it, as if it lingered indelibly yet lightly as a whisper in a lover's ear.

We imagine that the soul slums for a while in our midst and membranes, then departs for heaven's gated community. That the soul is a transient by nature is key to most of the conventional metaphors that surround it. Thus the soul is a bug in the bottle of the body or a kind of isotope invisibly at large. Or it is somehow wriggling within, unique and indelible as a signature in cursive etched into every living cell, yet separable from the entity it entitles to an afterlife. Or it starts as an annuity, the protected savings we don't cash in until we . . . well, until we cash in. Then death snaps the tether on what's really eternal about us, and the real "we" are free to rise above our earthly circumstances. The soul expiates the body, as it were, much the way a supplicant would expiate his history of sin.

By this reasoning, the body is so much ballast to be cast off for the long flight. Indeed the way religion treats the body as a hostel and the soul as its itinerant boarder, its dividing each man's dross from his gist like this, coincides with the way we daily conceive of ourselves as well. We prefer to believe the body, like any other personal property, is ours but not us. John Donne makes the argument in "The Extasie," when he designated bodies as our contexts and conveyances: "We are / The intelligences, they the spheares," he says, and by that sophistry he tries to respect and restrict the flesh simultaneously. So, too, when we console the rape victim or amputee that she is still intact on a deeper level than any abuser or accident can touch, our counsel corresponds to the faith that when death does come, the soul will swim clear of the sinking ship of what deteriorates. Having descended for the space of a lifetime "T'affections, and to faculties," all men will jettison the inessential for the hereafter. At that point our physical selves, like our fungible assets, may be argued over and parceled out, but some ineradicable, unbequeathable aspect of us will survive the reading of the will to carry on, persisting outside the finagling of the relatives and the intercession of the court. The self's true equity is unaffected, then, by either market fluctuations or the unmaking of physique.

But what if the body is not merely the scaffold of the soul's construction but the edifice of self itself? What if our essence is utterly, if bitterly, physical, with the soul permanently interred in the flesh like a corpse in a crypt? According to this theory, if "the soul selects its own society," as Emily Dickinson famously assumes, it's a fairly claustrophobic gathering of family relations, the most unpalatable of whom (the liver that always acts up, the unappeasable spleen) cannot be spurned. Every event now and all events hereafter must be held inside the body's cramped quarters, no other venue being available for booking. Then, when the body dies, it is not simply a negligible percentage of self that departs with it.

And there is the real rub of being. Incarnation is the soul's first betrayal; it is also its only chance. Sure the soul would rather talk ballistics, but it may be forever in bed with—and in—the body. Maybe we have to tweak the myth a bit, with God bequeathing man's sum and substance, his word becoming our flesh: I give you the body, your exclusive, fatal attachment, and nowhere and nothing else.

Nothing frustrates theologians and other like-minded immaterialists so much as the evidence of just how thoroughly embodied we are. They pull every ligament, strain every muscle, and contend over every bone, all in the name of delivering the spirit from incorporation. It is intriguing to note, however, that for every high-flown sentiment mustered on behalf of the beleaguered soul, the body seems to have a ready counter. Consider, for example, the debate conducted in Andrew Marvell's "A Dialogue between the Soul and Body." "Dialogue" implies a dignified exchange, as befits a literature syllabus, but Marvell's poem sounds more like the predictable bickering of an old married couple, who have been sniping along the same lines for as long as they've lived together. In its opening statement, the soul compares the body to a dungeon, into which it has been cast for crimes beyond its ken. To hear the soul tell it, every joint, organ, and physical accoutrement is a torment and an injustice. Every enabling feature of the body is an aspect of the soul's enslavement: the bones are bolts; the feet, fetters; the hands, manacles. Hence the flesh is an ambiguous confinement, which curtails the elevated urges of its inhabitant. Eyes blind and ears deafen; all senses must be suffered both for what they inflict and for what they constrain, until death do they part. The soul demands to be sprung from loins, prays to be extracted from the grave of muscle and guts it lies awake inside, but to no avail. Blood drowns the soul out. It struggles in veins in vain.

But Marvell does not cheat the body out of its cross. The soul may feel insulted by their association, but it is the body, says the body, which takes the abuse for it. If the body is a barricade for the soul to transgress, the soul is a predicament for the body to solve. As the soul complains, the body, at once jailer and jail, has to put up with its petitions and the shaking of the bars for the same period of time, which is to say that until the soul is expunged, the body is in bondage, too. To be sure, the soul bears

the blame for the body's lusts and hungers, its fears and vexations, its restlessness and recrimination. We tend to think of the soul as subtler and
suppler than the carcass that carries it about, but in Marvell's argument,
the soul inhibits activity more than age or handicap can. It is the soul that
chafes the body with the sorrows of consciousness by imbuing it. The
soul harrows and convulses the flesh, so that it is no better than a fever—
worse, in fact, given the virulence of its assault, not to mention the invari-
ably lethal nature of the cure. The body concludes its outrage and this
poem by blaming its failures and misfortunes entirely on the soul—
"What but a soul could have the wit / To build me up for sin so fit?"—and
adds a final curse for the plague of that awareness. As we might expect,
because the body has a mouthpiece in its employ, it gets the last word in.

William Butler Yeats presides over the appellate court some three centuries after Marvell in "A Dialogue of Self and Soul." Here again we find
the soul yearning to escape the bunker of the body, seeking release from
history, memory, and the mundane: "If but imagination scorn the earth /
And intellect is wandering / To this and that and t'other thing, / Deliver
from the crime of death and birth." Unfortunately the soul's elevated
rhetoric about distinguishing "Is from the Ought" seems flimsy in face of
the self's (the body's) celebration of the here and now, even "if it be life
to pitch / Into the frog-spawn of a blind man's ditch, / A blind man bat-
tering blind men; / Or into that most fecund ditch of all, / The folly that
man does / Or must suffer. . . ." The moment the self evades the soul's
carping, even the impurities of our human portion are suddenly sacro-
sanct: "We are blest by everything, / Everything we look upon is blest." As
in Marvell, so too in Yeats: the mortal body has the final say. Given that
in Yeats's version of the dispute the body is regarded as "My Self," it should
not surprise us that "My Soul" has its suit trumped. As ever in legislative
matters, possession is the lion's share of the law.

By the time the battle passes to Delmore Schwartz, the soul's plea is
almost completely muffled by the body's circumference, constancy, and
bulk. The body may be mute in "The Heavy Bear Who Goes with Me"—
unlike Marvell's and Yeats's poems, Schwartz's is a monologue—but its
silence is a tactic, not a surrender. Having incontrovertibly made the case
for the body's superior presence—there is no denying its status as "the
central ton of every place"—the defense rests. Otherwise it lumbers,
craves, howls, trembles, struts, stumbles, flounders, strives, and in every

way dictates each gross, transitive verb in the poem, leaving the soul to describe the terms of its mortifying subservience:

> That inescapable animal walks with me,
> Has followed me since the black womb held,
> Moves where I move, distorting my gesture,
> A caricature, a swollen shadow,
> A stupid clown of the spirit's motive,
> Perplexes and affronts with his own darkness,
> The secret life of belly and bone . . . .

As the soul inventories its afflictions, denouncing the strict terms of its occupation, the body's dominance preempts alternatives. Despite its assertions to the contrary, it is the soul that emerges as caricature, shadow, and clown.

The best model for a viable détente between body and soul may very well be Walt Whitman's "I Sing the Body Electric." Befitting Whitman, it is no doubt the most expansive effort in the canon. Whitman arbitrates better than Marvell, Yeats, or Schwartz can between the soul's desire for eminence and the body's need to redeem its slandered reputation. He begins the process of "discorruption" with two rhetorical questions that posit the necessary, inevitable, and mutually sustaining relationship between body and soul: "And if the body does not do as much as the Soul? / And if the body were not the Soul, what is the Soul?" For Whitman, who is a notoriously formidable campaigner for the splendor of the human form, detaching the soul from its humble digs would deprive the soul of its noblest revelation.

But "humble" is hardly the case, what with Whitman doing the describing. The poet takes great pains to worship at the mass of man, laying paean upon paean in honor of his every contour, undulation, and ache. To do less would be impiety. When it comes to Whitman, to do less would be impossible.

After fifty lines the soul takes the hint: "There is something in staying close to men and women, and looking on them, and in the contact and odor of them, that pleases the soul well; / All things please the soul—but these please the soul well." The tangible man shows the "measured and beautiful motion" of the universal procession as well as anything else in nature might. To abjure even one of its details detracts from the soul's holdings: "O my Body! I dare not desert the like of you in other men and women, nor the likes of the parts of you; / I believe the likes of you are to stand or fall with the likes of the Soul, (and that they are the Soul)." This triggers a catalog of body parts and capacities spread over thirty more sprawling lines, including everything from "neck-slue" to "finger-balls," from "breast-front" to "back-bone," from "knee-pan" to "man-root," from the freckles and flex of the mouth without to the "thin red jellies" within. "O I say, these are not the parts and poems of the Body only, but of the Soul," he concludes. "O I say now these are the Soul!" And that is Whitman's best finesse: the soul's proximity becomes the soul's property, then the soul's most sublime expression and chief appeal.

We might want to break Whitman's good news to the soul, if only we could track it down. For even assuming that the soul exists to be extricated from the body or to be reconciled with it, where it's been closeted remains an open question. The body is still philosophy's odds-on bet, but so far it's provided one dry hole after another. Many ancients conjectured that the soul was enthroned in the pituitary like a tiny prince biding its time until it could effectively assert its reign. Science has since scuttled that belief, having found other, less exalted functions for the pituitary, but when it comes to prospecting for essences, no more convincing location for the soul has yet been suggested. Maybe it lurks in some as yet unpenetrated neighborhood of the brain or in an anatomical back alley behind the vitals. Perhaps it's been tucked beneath an unmapped membrane, hidden under one of our knuckles, injected into our gristle, or planted in an anonymous gland. A dowser might strike its source in the kidneys or the corpuscles—we already know that the body is not above such oddness and delinquency. Who can say for sure that the soul isn't perpetually being renewed like the cells themselves—kindled, for instance, where ribs rub together.

"I have come to believe that it is the flesh alone that counts," confesses Richard Selzer, a surgeon turned essayist, who in neither capacity repudiates the search for something to outlast corruption. As he explains in "The Exact Location of the Soul," both enterprises compel him to witness affliction without flinching, to plunge into suffering when most men would cower or content themselves to leave our sometimes remarkable, sometimes vile chemistry to the professionals. "Man is albuminoid,

proteinaceous, laked pearl; woman is yolky, ovoid rich. Both are exuber-
ant bloody growths." The descriptions alone are enough to turn weaker
stomachs; the sticky, squinchy actualities must repel all but the most
hardened doctors, and even they don masks and gloves before descending into a splayed patient's oily rubble. Yet in the midst of our churning
mass, this physician seeks evidence of the grace that explains us better
than a dispirited body can by itself. Like the poet, he hopes to encounter
the soul.

Selzer cannot say whether or not the soul jostles in bondage when the
surgeon intrudes upon the body, much less if, as old wives might have it,
a sneeze threatens to evict it or a heavy sweat to expel it at the gym. But
his solid grounding in science does not prevent Selzer from suspecting
that the night he tried to drain an abscess from a young man's arm he
roused the soul from its lair. The patient had returned from an excavation
of Mayan ruins in Guatemala; now his own body has become the site of
a dig the likes of which would amaze any shaman and overwhelm the
most seasoned archaeologist.

> No explorer ever stared in wilder surmise than I into that crater
> from which there now emerged a narrow gray head whose sole
> distinguishing feature is a pair of black pincers. The head sits atop
> a longish flexible neck arching now this way, now that, testing the
> air. Alternately it folds back upon itself, then advances in new bold-
> ness. And all the while, with dreadful rhythmicity, the unspeakable
> pincers open and close.

Selzer manages to clamp the creature and wrestle it, writhing, out of the
infected arm and into a jar. The thing is dark, vile, "hung everywhere with
tiny black hooklets." In all honesty, the doctor's initial reflex is to think
he's gotten hold of a devil or the concentrate of some vile nightmare, not
that he's snared anything so ethereal as a soul. Nevertheless he can't help
but wonder whether it might not after all be, if not the soul itself, some
netherworld harbinger of the soul that's come sopping and dully awake
in his grasp.

The next day a pathologist identifies the captive as the larva of a bot-
fly, which had evidently bitten into the man's arm and deposited its egg
there, where it hatched and began to mature. In this way the thing is exposed as a fraud, as is the unwitting physician who imagined he'd won

something that at once united faith and biology and exceeded the limits of both. So the doctor applies medication and the poet metaphor; each can ease pain but not guarantee salvation. So the body heals, if only for the time being, while the soul still tasks and eludes our disciplines.

Who is to say, though, that had Dr. Selzer done a little more rummaging inside his patient he might not have cornered his ghostly quarry up against a lung or found it twisted in the sinews like a netted fish? Maybe the soul automatically pulls a quick transmigration the instant we approach it, whether we do so with a scalpel, a psychoanalytic theory, a sermon, or a figure of speech.

In "The Soul inside the Sentence," William Gass puts forward the last of those strategies as the most promising. A soul can reside prominently and lastingly in words artfully arranged, he claims, so that certain sentences constitute memorials as befitting the soul's eminence as any cathedral ever could be. Such sentences, Gass says, "persist past all utility" and live as deeply within us as any substance the body generates on its own; "uttered under the heart as beneath the breath, they act like anxious tics; repressed, they return: and we protect and repeat them as though they were charms against our insecurities." To join Gass in deeming Shakespeare, Browne, Donne, Jonson, Tennyson, Rilke, Proust, James (and I'd add Gass himself, which Gass is too modest to do) geniuses of style is nothing new. But Gass goes on to grant them the capacity to animate in a way that Doctor Frankenstein could never completely emulate (his best effort ending up mottled and botched, dreadful as sentences by Gass's ideal team of craftsmen almost never are), anchoring us unexpectedly in the body, in consciousness, and in the world. Such sentences, composed according to our innermost rhythms and "the hidden internality of things," lie "as deep inside us as our bones." Surgery and poetic introspection are in this sense complementary examinations of the self, which is the central province upon which they stake their respective claims. It comes to small distinction in the end: the one makes a text of the body; the other makes a body of the text.

What is the soul if not the aspect of each of us that is most worth enduring? So let us love and honor sentences that most faithfully serve and sanctify the soul. "If we think it odd the gods should always choose a voice so full and gloriously throated, when they could presumably toot though any instrument," Gass argues, "we should remember that it is their choice of such a golden throat, each time, that makes them gods."

If the soul is the profoundest part of speech, then perhaps speech can be the profoundest part of the soul. As for the "subtle knot" between body and soul, which John Donne pretends to slip in ecstatic interludes and which he depends on death to undo once and for all, it proves too intricate for any poetry to negotiate. Neither fancy nor faith saves us from being laid up for the foreseeable future in the bodies we're brought forth in. The books and bloodlines descending from them, their bones and their poems, will constitute our most solid achievements, our richest manifestations, and our remains.

In Praise of Pointlessness

"But I tell you you don't get the point."
"Blame de pint! I reck'n I knows what I knows. En mine you,
de real pint is down furder—it's down deeper."

Mark Twain, *Adventures of Huckleberry Finn*

I could begin with the fins on a 1958 Chevy, going on to include the chrome gills along its front panels and the overdone grillwork gleaming at the front like a Vegas greeter. Or with the nailed-up icons and memorabilia of bygone phenomena—baseball games, world's fairs, small-scale agriculture—that serve as wall decor in family restaurants all over the Midwest. Equally meretricious, however more exalted, is any architecture that isn't absolutely angular, including every flute, volute, filigree, helix, and whorl of which the Renaissance boasted or on which the Age of Pericles built its reputation. And six or seven smallish glands of obscure purpose, packed away in the Balkans of the body like foil-wrapped leftovers forgotten at the back of the fridge. All of them pointless—blatantly pointless, irredeemably so.

By some standards, any AM music produced since 1972 is pointless; by most standards, so is every variation of solitaire described by Hoyle. I could add pretty much every floor vote at both the Democratic and Republican National Conventions, and while I'm at it, the conventions themselves, which commend the attendants but don't convert. Also pointless is any discussion, however courteous or brief, about how although it's still raining it's bound to let up soon, about the relative merits or misguidedness of competing religions, or about what your team needs to do to make the playoffs. Any casual conversation, actually, that does little harm and less good is just as prevalent and just as pointless, too.

In terms of cities, there are thousands, but different ones fill each man's inventory. In my case, take Cincinnati, which is but one of countless locales where I'm as secure in my anonymity as a son-in-law in his sinecure or a post in its hole. There I can overeat or underdress, frequent a bar or a brothel, run up a tab or afoul of the law, because it's Cincinnati, isn't it, home of the do-over, the inherently undercover, and the undetectable. It's a city that does not take offense. It's a city that does not take notice. I don't even have to visit the place, much less move there. There where I am pointless I feel that I am freer than the significant, the practical, and the mandatory ever can be.

On the home front, there's all the attic crap we cannot find the opportunity or the gall to display or dispose of. Plastic fruit, for example, which we've accrued as mysteriously and inexorably as acne, as well as plastic vegetables, plastic flowers, leaves, and stems—in fact, everything kitsch that tells on us. I mean all the gauche adornments, from garden gnomes to bobble-headed dogs, whose ubiquity belies our better judgment. If you ever get the last kitchen drawer to the right of the sink unclogged, it will fairly burst with cancelled checks, expired coupons, dried-out markers, torn recipes, and packets of substitute buttons to garments long ago discharged from the wardrobe—nothing indispensable, certainly, and certainly nothing that wouldn't have been better left interred. How mortifying to discover under the bills on your desk the birthday card you'd meant to mail to your nephew for his eighth birthday. (You hold the mail in place with a lock whose combination you've lost. The job of paperweight represents a sort of WPA consolation and last resort for any item that's been outplaced. Just so, the key to the door of your old apartment is at best a bookmark now.) The birthday card's gigantic eight, rough with green glitter, makes it worthless for any future remembrance, and you are out of relatives seven and under anyway for whom it could one day be conducive. But back it goes. Upwards of half of all you've hoarded, quite frankly, fits into the category of pointless, even when—especially when— it doesn't appear to fit in anywhere else. (And that goes for most parenthetical comments, too, stuck into punctuation's version of a drawer because, in spite of its status as an afterthought, it still retains just enough potential, like a half-finished packet of soy sauce or a single chopstick, to protect it from the trash.)

What about all the laden spaces that somehow resist spring cleaning? In terms of legitimate content, each area has more fleas than marketability about it, yet their owners get testy as museum curators if anyone so much as touches their junk. Bulging hutches, cabinets, and closets truly constitute the foul rag and bone shop of the hearth. In my own bedroom closet hang one jacket with missing, unmatchable buttons and another whose zipper is irremediably seized, plus at least a couple of pairs of pants I can't convince myself to get rid of, although the chances that I'll fit into them eventually are slimmer than I'll ever be again. Men like me who keep keeping them must all come from mothers who scrubbed behind the stove and vacuumed corners that no line of sight, much less any guest, would ever penetrate. Instead of scolding us for obsessive behavior, I prefer to relate us to those medieval artisans who took pains to decorate the undersides of church pews, their own pointlessness serving as prayer on another level.

That same justification goes for the otherwise inexplicably enduring businesses out there devoted to the manufacture of novelty items. Their workers come home after a hard day of sticking plastic bugs inside plastic ice cubes, pressing wax lips out of their molds, or sculpting artificial clods of vomit; their sons and daughters still hug their daddies when they come through the door, but even at home, the uselessness of all they do all day is an open secret. Their salaries spend as well as anyone else's, to be sure, but while that argument justifies their jobs, it doesn't change their essence.

That goes for the vestiges of all the obsolescent industries that once buttressed a way of life but that our children will have to go to history books or visit their invalid elders in nursing homes to hear about. Metal telephone dialers designed to spare blistered index fingers. Carbon paper layered in flat boxes like dried flowers and just as friable. Adapter inserts shaped like little mandalas to fit 45 r.p.m. records onto turntable spindles, not to mention the turntables and the 45s themselves. Eight-tracks and Beta-format videotapes, long ago orphaned from any machine that might be able to play them. Floppy disks large and flexible enough to flop as promised. Every year the ratio of people who can identify a slide rule or a darning egg to those who can't gets smaller. At the heart of all the accelerations that every generation perfects is the acceleration of obsolescence, the result being that pointlessness is the fastest growing industry on the planet.

Do not be too quick to pity the pointless, however. Unnecessary though they may be, their proprietors are nevertheless not necessarily desolate about it. Do not underestimate the pleasure of reprieve from consequence. Think about the employee's paid vacation and the soldier's leave. You have seen the kite flyer's delight, whose pointlessness you couldn't prove from the pleasure on hand. As much as the updraft does, being unencumbered by appointment or occasion is what gives the thing its lift.

So when will they commission an anthem to confetti or dedicate a statue in the park to Silly Putty? Why doesn't anyone plan on naming her next child Nerf?

To this pointless list I could add the sexual efforts of couples too old for procreation, but here I hesitate. That might lead to the cynic's long view on the subject of love, which is that, based on the few decades at most that we get to do the loving or the viewing, it all comes to naught in the end no matter if there's a pregnancy or not. That is too arch an outlook for the purposes of the purposelessness I can appreciate. Suffice to say that nature is positively roiling with pointlessness. From the rabble of algae in a hidden lake and the witless rigor of insects dismantling a fragment of hamburger at the bottom of a garbage bin, to probably a lot of what jostles invisibly in any drop of water, to the many miles of untenanted space being heated by unwitnessed stars, nature regularly, perversely combines urgency and purposelessness. In his poem "Conserving the Magnitude of Uselessness," A. R. Ammons encourages us to celebrate "all things not worth the work / of having," in part because, once he totes up the examples of what's "crusty or billowy with indifference" in the world, there isn't much that misses his inventory. The deep sea vents are made darker still by all the anonymous populations down there that, frankly, no one would ever miss; every fissure, pock, fault, vug, and cranny in nature crawls with negligible creatures hard at some labor whose significance escapes us. And when we widen the lens to cover all the squandered quanta in the Out There that we don't address; when we consider how everything keeps fleeing the center of an expanding universe, hollowing it out like a downtown whose businesses have abandoned it for fringes that lie ever farther and farther away, then we begin to realize that irrelevance is not only rife in the cosmos but always on the move.

Detractors rail against extravagance as if they had some permanent alternative to show us. But what, including their complaints, doesn't fit the definition?

Nor, obviously, are our own bodies exempt in the long run, which, in the context of the escaping cosmos, isn't much of a measure at that. Athletes who look as though they did their first wind sprints down the aisles of Toys "R" Us, who have always policed their calories like convicts on parole, manage to back themselves away from the precipice by a margin of error too slight to make a difference. A personal hydrologist may monitor their water and a sommelier of atmosphere discreetly mete out every breath they take, but they cannot step around their dooms any better than the rest of us. Maybe they began as babies to do crunches in their cribs, but behind that perfect curtain of abs it turns out that biology has bugged their cells, too, from the instant of conception. (And if the genetically favored cannot deceive themselves forever, what hope is there for the majority of us who wrinkle and sag our way toward the same destiny?) One peek at a posthumous body must send a quiver through even the most ideally sculpted flesh. Mortality is the most disqualifying context of all. ("Are you afraid," writes Mark Doty in "Murano," "now you're salts and essences, / the flung and gathered / elements from which any art / is fused and blown?") Thus the workout warrior crashes his diet and gives up the gym because he knows he will give up the ghost. Or he would, that is, if pointlessness were a deterrent. Since people continue to practice with their jump ropes and paddleballs, to condemn neighborhood dogs for what they've left on their lawns, to fire off editorials to their local papers, and to hold their breath hopefully during the latest round of Middle East peace talks, the evidence is against it.

I've heard it said that nothing matters because all matters come to nothing, as, indeed, all matter will. Rearranging deck chairs on the *Titanic* —the saying could be applied to any effort whatsoever, I suppose, whether man's or nature's. ("Are the roses not also—even as the owl is—excessive?" asks Mary Oliver in "Owls," testing that perspective.) But I prefer to appreciate those musicians aboard ship who persisted in playing regardless, in their own small way buoying the doomed in their sinking.

"What difference does it make? In a hundred years we'll all be dead anyway." It's a motto broad enough to consecrate any surrender. But that we don't live forever doesn't disqualify chocolate. On the contrary, if our tenure is limited and our universe is absurd, we need all the confection we can get. And that includes the waste of lilies and of poetic language, the distraction of infatuation and the dissipation of song, as well as amateur sports, ballet, table settings, grade school pageants, decommissioned silos strangled by vines, sidewalk chalk drawings, bingo, seashells, and every other blessed silliness under the stupidly dutiful sun.

Albert Goldbarth respectfully remembers how there was a time when people believed that all matter was sentient, every particle conscious. The concept helps to validate his appreciation of crafted appetizers, salt and pepper shakers shaped like lobsters, fondue accoutrements—of *stuff*, in short. The jettison of essences is essential nonetheless. "And if they *are* a denatured version of such primacy? Still, they're a version," Goldbarth concludes in "Parade March from *That Creaturely World*." Who knew it was all so crucial? Surprisingly, unaccountably, it all counts.

It is no accident that I quote poets to help to make the case of pointlessness. For its refusal to be done with stuff, to leave well enough alone, poetry is another oddly tenacious occupation, an elaborate game of hope against hope. What is a poetry anthology, after all, but a compendium of backward glances? For that matter, what are all of those stylish excesses we honor Shakespeare for if not sublimely pointless? Ben Jonson famously conjectured that Shakespeare might well have blotted a thousand lines at least without staining a single significant incident, but centuries after his diagnosis, it's the unabridged Bard that survives. Utility is an undeniable virtue, but so is pushing a broom. Ultimately it is not the burden but the embroidery that his readers crave and take away with them.

As far as metaphor in general goes, which is probably not ever going to be far enough to bridge the whole hereafter, it, too, says Robert Frost, cannot outlast its warranty. It pays to appreciate "how far you may expect to ride it and when it may break down with you." In other words—and for the foreseeable future at least, there will be other words—we should make the most of the ride.

And if we admit metaphor, let us not neglect bottle cap collections, balloons, parsley, jigsaw puzzles, checkers, pennies, cathedrals, and tree limbs that died too high for the saw to reach, on which nothing lights but the random eye and nothing nests but snow. If the Pledge of Allegiance is pointless, let us stand for it nevertheless, hands over dumbly fluttering hearts. Let our gratitude extend to the frivolous and the tentative, omitting not a single empty yard of large intestine nor vast tracts of uninhabited Canada. Grant us the vanity of most of television and all jewelry and the end-zone dance, for as long as we are able to caper. Give us this day our daily gossip columns, our wainscoting, wallpaper borders, and tattoos. Toss in fireworks, while we're at it, for their bright and evanescent curriculum. And lest we forget, allow pinball and bric-a-brac on mantelpieces and coffee tables, flags and the front lawns over which they preside, snow globes and ornamental iron and bowling and needlepoint and playground equipment and gum. All aboard to all gay abundance and plussage, to shaggy dog stories and sports talk radio, to impresarios of whistling and yo-yo virtuosos, to mustaches and wrapping paper and cartoons. For the time being, this dubious interlude between void and void is what we have to fill.

I am no aficionado of science fiction. I'm seldom able to keep the characters' odd names and odder endowments straight, and I tend to find the formulaic machinations of orotund evildoers from distant galaxies numbing. But there is one particular short story that has stayed with me. The special-effects-free premise is that everyone on Earth has awakened from the same prescient dream that the new day will be the planet's last. There is no consensus as to how the extinction will happen, only that we have all been alerted and unanimously acknowledge it. From here, the most ordinary story proceeds. People eat their breakfasts, go to work, spend their usual day as they usually would. No one contradicts our destiny or rails against it; no one mentions it at all. Maybe a dog that's been put out for the night trots back and forth in front of the screen door the way it does every night, unable to stop hoping that he'll be let back in. Quite likely, in fact, although the story doesn't say. The final scene—*the Final Scene, that is*—features a young man and his wife tucking their infant son into his crib for sleep. Then they put out the last light, get into bed, and kiss each other good night.

And that's the end. If it strikes you as arbitrary or unconvincing that people don't gorge themselves on ice cream and pizza, rush to get in that one skydiving experience, burn down their office buildings, sin vigorously, or simply run raving into traffic since there is no point in going on as they have, I submit that you have missed the meaning. There is just as much reason for them to live their lives as there always had been, or just as little, depending on how one chooses to look at it. We are invited to imagine people everywhere gathering their photographs and souvenirs about them, treasuring their remembrances so long as they remain capable of remembering, clutching every scrap of themselves to themselves, which they cherish for letting them cherish them, for suffering their love. If their crises and delights are trivial, they are what they have to chance and to treasure.

"We didn't leave anything in the pockets by any chance?" Samuel Beckett's Mercier asks of his companion. "Punched tickets of all sorts," Camier replies, "spent matches, scraps of newspaper bearing in their margins the obliterated traces of irrevocable rendezvous, the classic last tenth of pointless pencil, crumples of soiled bumf, a few porous condoms, dust. Life in short." Their last gestures, their last embraces, their last words, all futile, relinquish nothing of the world, where life is a punched ticket, as if they didn't know any better. As if there were a point to it all. But the point never has been the point.

About the Author

ARTHUR SALTZMAN is a professor of English at Missouri Southern State University. His work has appeared in *Gettysburg Review, Iowa Review, Black Warrior Review, Gulf Coast, Modern Fiction Studies, Review of Contemporary Fiction, Contemporary Literature, Baltimore Review,* and numerous other journals. He is the author of ten books, including the essay collections *Objects and Empathy, Nearer,* and *The Obligations of the Harp* as well as the critical works *The Novel in Balance* and *This Mad "Instead": Governing Metaphors in Contemporary American Fiction,* both available from the University of South Carolina Press.